The Norton Introduction to

LITERATURE

SIXTH EDITION

Instructor's Guide
for the Complete and Shorter Editions,
The Norton Introduction to Fiction,
and
The Norton Introduction to Poetry

The Norton Introduction to

LITERATURE

SIXTH EDITION

Instructor's Guide for the
Complete and Shorter Editions,
The Norton Introduction to Fiction,
and
The Norton Introduction to Poetry

Gayla McGlamery

Bryan Crockett

Loyola College in Maryland

W • W • NORTON & COMPANY • NEW YORK • LONDON

CONTENTS

* denotes selections not included in the Shorter Edition.

Exploring Contexts   66

Evaluating Fiction 100

POETRY

TEACHING
POETRY 114

Poetry: Reading, Responding, Writing   119

Understanding the Text   125

Exploring Contexts   175

Evaluating Poetry   208

DRAMA

Exploring Contexts   253

Evaluating Drama   281

Using the *Instructor's Guide*

The materials in this Guide offer informal, nonprescriptive assistance to teachers using *The Norton Introduction to Literature*, Sixth Edition Regular or Shorter. Three new features expand the range of suggestions offered in each chapter; almost every chapter in the *Guide* has five sections, as follows:

- An introductory headnote treats the chapter topic, often including teaching strategies and suggestions.
- A new section, *Planning Ideas*, is designed to be helpful for teachers as they prepare for class. Among the *Planning Ideas* are suggestions for constructing a syllabus, assignments to be given before class, and possible in-class activities.
- Discussions of individual texts take up the bulk of each chapter. All of the stories and plays included in the chapters of *The Norton Introduction to Literature*, Sixth Edition, are discussed; approximately 30% of the poems in the book are either discussed in depth or addressed through as series of questions.
- *Questions for Discussion* follow each story, play, and many of the poems.
- Additional writing assignments, different from those in the text, are provided.

▽ ▽ ▽

Teaching Fiction

T he materials that follow offer suggestions for teaching the stories in the fiction portion of *The Norton Introduction to Literature*. Almost invariably some information reinforces or extends the guidance offered in the text itself, but this is not done systematically, nor is it the primary function of the Guide. Instead, I have aimed to share my thoughts on and experience in teaching the stories.

Thus, sometimes the commentary offers a reading or interpretation of the story, or alternative interpretations. When I have a firm opinion about the reading of a controversial story I will say so—not in order to close the issue but in order to avoid the false permissiveness that all of us fall into from time to time and that is the worst sort of intellectual bullying ("What am I holding in my hand?"). At other times I will discuss what worked best for me in opening and directing discussion about a particular story. Occasionally I warn against pitfalls that I have found in teaching a story or in teaching fiction in general.

I have not tried consciously to impose any fixed system of pedagogy, and I have tried to make the comments such that anyone teaching any selection of these stories in any order would find them helpful (if only by provoking argument). Methods of teaching fiction are as various as the personalities and preferences of the teachers of fiction. I have tried to touch on various methods, reader-response, aesthetic, historical, sociopolitical, among others, without emphasizing any one unduly. The first section, *Fiction: Reading, Responding, Writing,* is designed to be discussed as it stands, and I have not offered alternative approaches there. *Reading More Fiction,* on the other hand, belongs entirely to you, and I offer only minimal guidance.

∨ ∨ ∨

Fiction: Reading, Responding, Writing

Planning Ideas

- Instead of assigning **"The Zebra Storyteller"** to be read outside class, read it aloud the first day, pausing at key moments to ask students what sense they make of the story and what they anticipate will happen next. This exercise can provide a good introduction to a discussion of literary conventions and reader expectations. (See commentary on **"The Zebra Storyteller"** below.)
- If you include **"No One's a Mystery"** on your syllabus, ask the class to imagine what will happen to the narrator, to Jack, and to Jack's wife in the future and to write diary entries for each. This assignment usually works well whether you have students prepare the entries before class or write in class. (For more detailed suggestions, see comments on **"No One's a Mystery"** below.)
- When I assign Maupassant's **"The Jewelry,"** I sometimes ask students to prepare for class discussion by marking the specific points in the story at which their feelings toward M. Lantin begin to change. I ask them to be ready to provide the class with reasons for their shift(s) in perspective.
- If you teach Tallent's **"No One's a Mystery"** and Maupassant's **"The Jewelry,"** you might find it worthwhile to spend some time comparing the treatment of marriage in each. (See also Writing Assignment 1 at the end of this chapter.)

SPENCER HOLST

The Zebra Storyteller

Discussing this short, whimsical story is a good way to begin talking with students about what short stories do and why it is worthwhile to read them. I think the selection works well both as an introduction to the genre and as an object lesson in how to engage a text. Rather than assigning it to be read outside class, I like to read "The Zebra Storyteller" aloud the first day, pausing after each paragraph to ask students what they're thinking. I ask students to note which aspects of the story seem familiar and conventional. Someone almost always mentions the fairy-tale opening "Once upon a time" and the one-sentence "moral" at the end. Sometimes a student observes that the story is structured as a fable.

As I read, I prompt the class to tell me when the story has startled them or upset their expectations in some way. I do this in a very forthright manner by pausing after each paragraph and asking, "Any surprises? Is this what you thought would happen? Why or why not?" It can be useful to record these responses on the blackboard to provide a visual record of how reactions are shaping up.

Once we've finished reading through the story, I turn to the lists on the board. The list we've compiled of "Conventional Aspects" gives me an opening to talk about the relationship between reader and author. For example, when an author begins a story with the opening "Once upon a time," I ask, what expectations about the kind of story we are reading has he or she created? In talking about the conventions the students have listed, I ask them to name types of narrative that depend heavily on conventions, on the implicit agreement between author and reader that the story will take a certain form—in effect, that there will be a limited number of surprises, or only (if I may be forgiven the phrase) "expected" surprises. Most classes are able to come up with several examples from their own reading—the stories of Agatha Christie, Stephen King, John Grisham, Barbara Cartland, Sidney Sheldon, etc. (I try, by the way, to avoid making critical judgments on the relative merits of the formula fiction the students mention, however tempting it may be. If students are reading at all on their own, they should be encouraged.)

Discussing conventions usually makes it easy to move on to talking about the points in the story at which the author ignores or subverts them. A good example is the phrase "Here now" at the beginning of the third paragraph. You may want to ask the students why this phrase sounds wrong or, to use Holst's word, "inappropriate." Under the heading of "Unexpected Elements," someone will probably mention the cliché about the zebra's reaction to the cat—"he's just fit to be tied"—and the author's literal use of the phrase in the action of the story. If you have a bright group, someone may notice that the cat is guilty of using trite, cliché-ridden language in his greetings to the zebras.

Eventually, of course, the class will want to tackle the "moral" of the tale. As mentioned in the text headnote, the story suggests that one function of the story-teller is to prepare us for the unexpected. I sometimes ask the class if the story implies that the storyteller has other functions as well. A good way to explore this question is to ask about the cat's "inappropriate language"—his use of clichés. If the cat uses language poorly, then the storyteller might be said to be one who must stamp out poor usage (storyteller as teacher?). Because the storyteller knows a lot about language, he or she is not easily manipulated by it.

Clearly the story also emphasizes the power of the imagination. By imagining himself to be a lion, the cat accomplishes lion's feats. By imagining a story, the zebra storyteller arms himself against attack. If you are feeling particularly brave—or if student comments open the door—you may want to discuss the notion that the storyteller's function may have an ethical component as well.

ELIZABETH TALLENT

No One's a Mystery

Perhaps because this story is at least partially about an eighteen-year-old and sex, I find many students have very definite opinions about it. After all, most of them are about the same age as the narrator, and they usually have given some thought to the questions the story raises about sex, love, marriage, loyalty, deception, self-knowledge, etc. I sometimes take a few minutes at the beginning of class to have students imagine, as Jack does, what the narrator will write in her five-year diary one year hence, two years hence, and five years hence—and to jot down these entries. It can be entertaining and revealing to ask a third of the class to write as if they were the narrator, a third to imagine and record what Jack would write in a diary at these intervals, and a third to write diary entries they imagine Jack's wife writing. (You might ask whether students would expect each of these characters to keep a diary—and why or why not.)

In discussing what the class has come up with, some of you may want to encourage individuals to talk about their own experiences and expectations, but I have trouble handling such exchanges, especially so early in the course, so I steer clear. I do sometimes ask how many identify with the first-person narrator and how many identify with Jack. Expect surprises here. You will probably find, as I have, that both gender and age influence the degree of identification—but some students may refuse to identify with either character, perceiving both as immoral and utterly unlike themselves. If stereotypes emerge, as I have found they sometimes do, you may want to probe them a little: are young women unrealistic Pollyannas? Are men, on the whole, more cynical about relationships? Do "good" people ever do things that hurt others?

According to Jack, the narrator is a "kid" who still believes the two will live happily-ever-after and can't "imagine" another scenario. You might want to ask the class why Jack's own scenario for the relationship is so bleak. After all, men do leave unsatisfying marriages and marry younger women, so why can't Jack? Or why won't Jack?

Tallent's story seems to me a miracle of compression and suggestion in this regard. Jack flirts with danger—he drives too fast and carries on an affair with a girl who is legally underage—yet he minimizes his risks, keeping the girl hidden. What do you, what do your students make of Jack's projections? Is he merely cynical? Or does he have no intention of divorcing his wife? What do details such as Jack's letting the truck get so dirty also suggest? There is surprisingly little agreement among my students about this, so I find it advisable, at least at first, to give them their say.

And what about Jack's wife? How much of Jack's judgment of her can we accept? What about the narrator's behavior? Do either of these characters express any sense of guilt? Should they? What obligations do students believe marriage entails? love? fidelity? working to make a relationship stimulating?

The narrator's "voice" is very flat and realistic, except when she is imagining a future for Jack and herself. For me, much of the story's comic effect is generated by the narrator's matter-of-fact descriptions issued from a truck-floor perspective (her description of Jack's pants and observations about the trash, for example). If your students find this story funny—sometimes they do not—you might get them to talk about the particular flavor of its comedy. Is it light and whimsical, like the comedy of "The Zebra Storyteller"? or is there a darker tone? Do we (or should we) also feel a little guilty about laughing with Jack and the girl about his wife?

If it hasn't come up earlier, I also ask students to address the title. When Roseanne Cash sings, "Nobody's into me, no one's a mystery," what does she mean? The lines might imply that the singer has everyone all figured out—or they could suggest that at the moment, no one has a hold on her, the kind of hold one who seems mysterious can have on another. I'm not sure myself.

Discussion of the title's meaning can provide a good transition to treating the end of the story. There Jack's closing lines express the tension between his desire to believe in the narrator's optimistic view of the world and his own experience.

Questions for Discussion

1. Is no one a mystery to Jack? to the eighteen-year-old narrator? to experienced people?

2. Should we read the title straightforwardly or as an example of irony? If the title is ironic, what does it tell us about the future of this couple? about Jack's future relationships?

GUY DE MAUPASSANT

The Jewelry

Part of the pleasure of reading "The Jewelry" comes from the significance the details of the story assume when we think back over the story or reread it. When assigning this selection, I encourage students to read very slowly and carefully (as suggested in the introduction); then I ask them to go over the text again, noting the new or additional shades of meaning that play about certain phrases ("the slight smile . . . seemed a reflection of her heart," "finally she yielded, just to please him," "You would swear it was real jewelry"). A second reading (or third, or fourth) will also help students chart their shifting sympathies in regard to M. Lantin. When his wife suddenly dies, we pity him. When do his feelings toward his wife begin to change? What are the stages of Lantin's emotional reactions, and why do his grief and shame disappear so quickly? How are our feelings about him related to these changes? Had he known how much money was at stake, would he have prevented her from going "out on the town"?

Sometimes just to shake things up a bit, I pause in the midst of discussion and ask the class if infidelity is the only explanation for Mme. Lantin's possession of the jewelry. After all, the author never spells this out. If the class agrees that Mme. Loisel probably was in some sense a "kept" woman (who thereby managed to keep her husband in comfort), I might ask why the author doesn't come right out and state this. What, if anything, is gained by leaving Mme. Loisel's activities a mystery? I'm not sure I can answer all these questions with certainty—and I let the class know this (but not too soon). Does our being led on by the narrator—we suspect something is wrong, but don't know just what—make the story more effective? more pleasurable? more meaningful? If so, in what ways?

You might ask students whether they believe the story considers adultery a sin, and if so, how serious a sin—and whether it is better for the victim of infidelity to know or not to know. In the story itself, are we given any hint as to why Mme. Loisel might cheat on her husband? If so, are we offered any justification for the wife's behavior—or does she need justification?

No discussion of "The Jewelry" can come to a satisfactory close without addressing the last paragraph, one of Maupassant's "surprise endings." Some students will want to interpret M. Loisel's ill-fated second marriage as a case of the sinner receiving his just deserts. Others may note that, after having his fling, M. Loisel tried to settle down to a decent life with an "upright" spouse and was repaid with a life of misery.

Questions for Discussion

1. Does the narrator seem to suggest that virtue and conventional morality are overrated?

2. Does the ending simply supply a neat twist, or does it suggest that this is the way the world really works?

3. Does anything about Mme. Lantin's supposed infidelity and her husband's reaction to it seem strange or foreign? What, on the other hand, is recognizable and familiar about the characters' reactions?

Writing Assignments for Fiction: Reading, Responding, Writing

1. One way to approach the Maupassant and Tallent stories together is to discuss them in the context of differing societal norms. "No One's a Mystery" is a fairly recent story, written by an American and published in 1985. "The Jewelry" was written by a Frenchman almost exactly a century earlier. Do some library research on mores governing fin de siècle French society, and write an essay discussing how late-nineteenth-century French conventions about marriage differ from those that governed marriage in America in 1985.

2. Write an analysis of "The Jewelry" discussing which events in the story fulfilled your expectations and which plot developments surprised you. Did the surprises seem to have a purpose in the story—other than providing entertainment? Explain.

∇ ∇ ∇

Understanding the Text

1 PLOT

As the text suggests, a good way to stress the difference between plot structure and mere chronology is to compare a story's plot to a criminal plot—the criminal's plan for committing a crime. I tell students to assume the author has a plan for each story (just as a jewel thief makes specific plans to pull off a particular heist) and that the author has some purpose in arranging the elements of the story in a particular order. In a traditional short story, if the author has plotted well, the casual reader won't be aware of the way the author manipulates plot to create emphases or build suspense; the reader won't "catch" the author plotting but will simply enjoy the result. (This is where my analogy of criminal and crime breaks down!) Of course, careful, analytical readers will pay special attention to the way authors arrange the materials of their stories and will thereby gain a better understanding of the craft of fiction. In less-traditional stories, like Margaret Atwood's "Happy Endings," the author may raise questions about the nature of fiction by handling plot(s) in ways that are contrary to our expectations. In such stories, getting "caught" in these manipulations is part of the point.

Planning Ideas

- If you have a fairly sophisticated group of readers, you may want to dive right into Atwood's **"Happy Endings"** and discuss the issues it raises concerning the nature of plots in particular and fiction in general. If you believe your students would benefit from a more gradual introduction to plot, you might begin this section by studying a story with a more straightforward suspense structure—Connell's **"The Most Dangerous Game"** or Poe's **"The Cask of Amontillado"**—using the simpler plot as a basis for comparison with the more complex plot structures of the stories offered here.

- Assign a nineteenth-century novel published serially: *Great Expectations*, perhaps, or *David Copperfield*. This will provide an opportunity to examine how plot can be structured to meet the demands of the readership, the marketplace, and a particular mode of production. (For example, *Great Expectations* was issued in weekly installments, and the ending changed to make it more audience-pleasing. If you assign this novel, be sure to order an edition that provides both endings.)

- Before class, ask students to imagine that they are writing several versions of their life-stories: one in which they emphasize their educational history, one in which they emphasize the importance of their relationship with a family member, and one in which they construct their story as a comedy, a tragedy, or a romance. With what event, description, and details would each begin? How would each story end? Have students bring to class a brief sketch or outline of each story, and ask several volunteers to share their plot outlines with the class.

- If you assign **"Sonny's Blues,"** bring in recordings of Louis Armstrong and Charlie Parker to play during class so that students can hear the difference between Armstrong's fairly close adherence to the melodic line and Bird's freer interpretations.

MARGARET ATWOOD

Happy Endings

Some students will recognize that Atwood's story is a *metafiction*—a story that comments on the nature of fiction itself. Others will be completely puzzled by it. One way to approach this work is to begin with a discussion of short story conventions and reader expectations, drawing on Atwood's "stories" A through F. (If you have spent some time discussing these issues in regard to Holst's "The Zebra Storyteller," you may want to refer back to that discussion as well.)

Students likely will find stories A–F lacking in a number of ways. It may prove fruitful to discuss what seems to be missing in *all* of the stories—then to draw some distinctions between them. Atwood suggests at the conclusion of "Happy Endings" that the "how" and "why" are missing from these plots—but I try to nudge student to see that Atwood hasn't really supplied plots at all. If you revisit the definition of plot provided in the text, students should quickly recognize that in "Happy Endings" Atwood has simply provided several histories or chronologies—merely the raw material of plot structure.

Once we reach this stage in the discussion, I ask students to imagine why

Atwood might write such a story: what does "Happy Endings" suggest about the nature of fiction? the nature of life? Several possible answers occur to me, although my list is certainly not exhaustive:

A. The story suggests that fictions lie about life if they don't end in death—as all lives do (see first three paragraphs after F)—or at least it wants to provoke thought about the relationship between fiction and "real life."

B. Atwood is poking fun at the notion that writing fiction is just a matter of putting together so many plot elements (see especially the endings to stories E and F). Perhaps this is the response of a writer who's been handed too many such elements by strangers, with the comment: "I've got a great story you should write."

C. The grab-bag structure of the work—and particularly the cafeteria menu ending of E—is purposely unsatisfying, implying that readers welcome, and even need, the direction of the author—that readers *want* to experience someone else's world-view. By implication, this structure devalues so-called interactive fictions, which ask the reader to choose among alternative paths and alternative endings to create a story free (or relatively free) of *authority*.

D. A and D seem to ask whether virtuous people make interesting subjects for fiction and perhaps even whether happy, conflict-free stories are worth writing. (Students often complain that the short stories they read are depressing and too few have happy endings. This story provides an opportunity to discuss that perception and evaluate it.)

You may want to lead the class in reexamining the endings of other short stories they have read, using the implied criteria provided at the end of "Happy Endings": (1) Are the endings "fake"? (In terms of the narrator's standards, do they end with the deaths of the characters or not?) (2) Do they seem "deliberately fake"? (3) Do they appear "motivated by excessive optimism"? Ask the class to defend the stories against the charges they imagine the narrator would level against them.

Questions for Discussion

1. Analyze the language of the last sentence of story F. What type of fiction might Atwood be satirizing?

2. In what sense are all endings the "same"? Is this true in life? In art? What is the relationship between life and art with regard to endings?

3. Has the narrator of "Happy Endings" indeed said "about all that can be said for plots" by the end of the story? Are plots *just* "a what and a what and a what"? If not, then what else are they?

4. Is Atwood the narrator of "Happy Endings"?

JOHN CHEEVER

The Country Husband

The problem I find with "The Country Husband" is not that my college-age students don't understand the neighborhood. If you add a few divorces and lots of working mothers, many of them come to school from suburbs like Shady Hill. Even among students from very different neighborhoods, I find the problem is the character, not the place. Perhaps Francis Weed is in some sense too close to their experience or their dreams—a man near their fathers' age, someone they might someday marry, or become. Despite his goofiness, Francis is desperately unhappy, and it is always disconcerting—but particularly so in our success-oriented, money-driven society—to confront the notion that we may find a mate, establish a family, buy a nice house, accomplish all our career goals, and suddenly find ourselves, as Francis does, trapped and woefully dissatisfied.

Some students, particularly those who are social activists, may be uncomfortable with the story for a different reason—because they find it hard to sympathize with Francis's plight. Why should we care about this whiner, this aging Lothario, this wife-abuser, they sometimes ask. The guy lives in a relative paradise within commuting distance of people who don't have enough to eat. What is his problem, and why should it make any difference to us? I have the feeling that Cheever would chuckle ruefully to hear such questions. Clearly he doesn't expect us to take Francis entirely seriously, and this is where I generally start. I ask the class whether "The Country Husband" is a serious story, and I try to get them to characterize the tone in which it is written. If your students don't pick up on the comedy of the narrative—and sometimes they don't—you might try asking them about the many literary, historical, mythological, and military allusions peppered throughout the work. Do they find anything incongruous about Mr. Nixon using the language of Shakespeare to chase off a dog? About Francis comparing his retreat from his children's squabble to returning to "headquarters company"? What about Francis thinking to himself that he was "meant to be the father of thousands"? Once we've established that Francis is a comic figure—an ordinary middle-class American male who is suddenly engulfed by longing for youth, for a life without constraint, for a more heroic time, which he and the narrator express through excessive, elevated language—we can move on to taking Francis's plight seriously, or at least semiseriously.

One way to talk about Francis's crisis is to talk about the events that brought it on. Cheever's plotting is a good place to start, and he provides the perfect hook, since he opens the story with the sentence, "To begin at the beginning, the airplane from Minneapolis in which Francis Weed was traveling East ran into heavy weather." I like to ask students to explain in what sense the plane crash is the "beginning" of Francis's story. Why does Cheever start here? These questions often lead to some discussion of near-death experiences and the ways that such adventures can affect the actions and perceptions of those who survive them.

As we focus on plot structure, someone will mention that a seemingly random series of events appears to throw Francis off his stride and to feed his dissatisfaction with his life in Shady Hill: the plane crash, the unexpected appearance of the woman Francis had seen punished at the crossroads in France during the war, Francis' sudden attraction to Anne Murchison (hard to say whether this a cause or effect of the crisis), his glimpse of the golden "Venus" on a passing train. As these events occur, Francis begins to feel less and less comfortable with his life in the present. In effect, each event takes Francis, either actually or imaginatively, backward in time. Both the plane crash and recognizing the Farquarson's maid recall France during World War II. Meeting Anne Murchison and visiting her neighborhood, Francis also has the sense of visiting an earlier time. (When Anne holds his hand as he walks her to the door, he's a young man again on a date.) Seeing the beautiful, naked woman on the train from the station platform affirms Francis' awakening sense of youthful romance, but she travels past him, and he is left standing alone, savoring his secret vision.

You might want to ask your students why Cheever describes these scenes in such detail. Or, to get at the same issues another way, what do these scenes have in common? If all goes well, someone will observe that all share the quality of being exciting and / or forbidden, all are associated in some way with an earlier, more youthful part of Francis's life and that Francis, for one reason or the other, cannot share them with anyone he knows. (No one understands or even seems to care about the plane crash, for example.) In effect, all these experiences set up barriers between Francis and the world he inhabits. They make him long for a world of adventure and romance—half-glimpsed, half-remembered, half-imagined.

At some point in class discussion, I like to ask students whether they approve of Francis's actions in the story before he seeks the help of a psychiatrist. This is really a throw-away question because their disapproval is usually fairly strong, although Francis always has defenders who sympathize with his feelings of frustration and entrapment. I ask the question to get us on to the next topic, which is to find out what students disapprove of most. Usually hitting Julia wins out by a few votes over sabotaging Clayton Thomas's job opportunity or grabbing Anne Murchison for a kiss, but not always. Then I like to ask students whether they are satisfied with the final picture of Francis in the basement of his Shady Hill home doing woodworking for therapy.

If the class has trouble articulating a response to the story's ending, you might call their attention to final, panoramic vision of Shady Hill and the lyrical language the narrator uses to describe it. I'm not entirely sure I know what to do with the tone of the ending myself. Certainly there's a difference between the boisterous, boastful (too-boastful?) tone of the proud host who says his wife makes him feel like Hannibal crossing the Alps and the narrator's magical evocation of kings in golden suits in the last line of the story. What I can't say for certain is exactly how we are to read the latter statement. It could be the concluding line of the artist / alchemist, who creates a comic world, then waves a wand and wishes it away like Oberon clearing the magical mist in A *Midsummer Night's Dream*. The words seem other-worldly, enchanted. The narrator could be trying to tell us that anything is possible—even in Shady Hill—that on a night like this, anything can happen. On the other hand, these words, like several other examples of elevated language in the story, could be used satirically in humorous contrast to the insignificant or ho-hum doings in the neighborhood (see the footnote tracing this allusion to Sinclair Lewis's *Main Street*).

Note: According to Cheever, when he was growing up in Boston, E. E. Cummings befriended him and gave him some advice. Cummings said, "Boston is a city without springboards for people who can't dive. Get out! Get out!" Cheever claimed that the poet's words influenced him to leave home and move to New York at seventeen to try his chances as a writer (*Southwest Review*, Autumn 1980, 344). I like to save this anecdote for the end of class because it seems to me that students are all too prone to read stories through the author's lives, as veiled biography. Nevertheless, I find it too appropriate not to mention. To keep students from drawing too-facile parallels between Cheever's experience and Francis's, I like to remind them that Cheever's purpose in leaving Boston was to become a writer, and ask them, if Francis left home, what his purpose in leaving would be.

Questions for Discussion

1. Why, if Shady Hill is still the same old peaceful suburban neighborhood he's lived in for years, does Francis begin to see it as a trap? What has changed Francis's perspective about Shady Hill?

2. Why does the narrator describe Francis's comfortable, polished living room in the words Julius Caesar uses to describe Gaul in *The Gallic Wars*? (At some point along the way, you may need to stop and talk briefly about point of view. Are there times when the narrator seems to be seeing through Francis's eyes and speaking for him? times when the narrator's perspective diverges from Francis's?)

3. Students who don't think the rest of the story is funny almost always find Francis's rudeness to Mrs. Wrightson (notice the name) more amusing than reprehensible. Why?

4. Do you believe the narrator when he says Francis is happy? Does Francis seem at home in his shop in the basement? Why or why not?

5. What does Cheever's ending reveal about his world-view? What are we to make of the frolicking Babcocks? of the cat trussed up in doll's clothes? Why does the story close with the vision of Jupiter holding a lady's slipper in his mouth?

6. If Francis is happy in the fictive present of the story, do you believe he will remain so? why or why not?

7. How would you describe the tone of the last line? Is it different from the

tone of the line alluding to Hannibal earlier in the story—when the Weeds' host declares that his wife makes him feel like "Hannibal crossing the Alps"? (See the footnote regarding Sinclair Lewis's *Main Street*.)

JAMES BALDWIN

Sonny's Blues

Students from Harlem will know; African-American students, especially those from the inner city, will pretty well know; other students from wherever will recognize and will usually at least try to empathize with this story of black experience. Many African Americans in college or university as well as some second- or third-generation Americans will understand the narrator's uneasiness, aloofness, and guilt about having made it and being proud of it as well as his guilt about those he left behind. A great many in each generation and in every ethnic group ought to be able to empathize with the narrator's plight. That the death of his child has sensitized him to his brother is a kind of wound that makes us recognize our common humanity, perhaps. The story is a relatively recent one; the setting is familiar indirectly to all of us and directly to a fair number; the emotions are accessible.

"Sonny's Blues" is a story with an intricate and significant time structure, and could be profitably studied alongside "Blow-Up" or "A Rose for Emily." I like to begin discussion by asking students how the story would be different if Baldwin had begun with the scene in which the narrator's mother tells about the death of the narrator's uncle at the hands of drunken, careless white men. If need be, I try to jostle the students' thinking by asking them why the narrator's mother has waited all these years to tell him the story. What would be the effect if the story began here? What would it suggest the story will be about? I sometimes use this to discuss the relevance and importance of how the story begins.

The way Baldwin crafts the opening of the story can also be a useful topic for discussion. As suggested in the text headnote, his repeated use of the pronoun "it" without antecedent draws us into the narrative. We want to find out what "it" is. Students pick up on this fairly quickly. I like to ask them what other purposes the use of "it" serves. Someone usually comes up with the notion that the narrator won't give a name to what Sonny has done because he wants to distance himself from Sonny's involvement with drugs. He finds the mere thought of Sonny's trouble disturbing, hateful, even frightening. From here we can go on to talk about the differences between Sonny and his brother and how these differences create distance and eventually estrangement.

To launch into this topic you may want to ask how the first-person narrator is identified or characterized in the first sentence of the story, in the first paragraph, in the first couple of pages, and in the story as a whole. We learn about Sonny through the narrator. What effect does this form of presentation have on our view of Sonny? How does the narrator let us see more than his own judgment? When does our judgment of Sonny vary from the narrator's? At what point are his judgment, the story's judgment, and our judgment of Sonny identical or nearly identical?

While some of your students may be jazz aficionados, I find that many of mine don't understand the musical references. A quick explanation of the differences between Louis Armstrong's style of jazz and Charlie Parker's will suffice, but if you have the resources, you might bring in brief recordings from each to play for the class. (See Planning Ideas at the beginning of this chapter.) At the close of the story, Sonny invites his brother to hear him play. When the brothers arrive at the nightclub, the older musician Creole welcomes the two, and it becomes clear to us—and to Sonny's brother—why Sonny had once acted as if his friends in the Village were more his family than was his brother. The musicians act like a family. They understand what Sonny cares about; they applaud his faltering return to the music; they know what he's been through; they welcome him home. You may want to ask your students how Baldwin's writing style changes in the nightclub section of the story. As Creole, Sonny, and the others play, something happens to the words the narrator uses to express himself. How are they different? why this change? What does the change tell us about the narrator's state of mind?

Toward the end of the discussion, I often ask the class to tie the musical references of the story together—for example, to tell me whether the woman singing gospel songs on the sidewalk earlier in the story has anything to do with the men making music at the nightclub. I find that the narrator's thoughts about his family and his heritage don't always make sense to students until they stop to think about the history of African-American music—that behind jazz lies the blues, behind the blues lies the spiritual, and behind the spiritual lie the songs of slaves. You may want to use the last four paragraphs of the story to open up the question of the transmutation of life or emotion into art, as a theme of this story and an explanation of its title.

The ending of "Sonny's Blues" is so intricately tied up with African-American experience and African-American music that it may be useful to ask, if the issue hasn't already come up, whether white readers can really understand the story (can men really understand stories by and for women). It is difficult to avoid having the discussion get to the point of "Can," "Can't," "Can," "Can't," either in an obvious or subtle way. One way I've found to break the magic circle is to ask to whom the story is addressed. Is it aimed at whites, either as a plea or demand for understanding and sympathy or as an indictment? Is it aimed at blacks, giving a voice to their long silent experience and, if so, for what kind of response? Is it directed to educated, more or less successful, upwardly mobile blacks, both to show understanding and sympathy for their plight and to remind them not to abandon their brothers and sisters?

I rather think the last, but not with real confidence. There is little about white persecution in the story, and that incident is narrated about the somewhat distant past and is placed in the South. I must admit I was a bit more confident of my reading before I looked up the cup of trembling passage in Isaiah. "Sonny's Blues" is a fine story about relationships, but it also raises questions about sociohistorical context and its importance in understanding as fully as possible the meaning, the methods, the tone, and other aspects of fiction— even conjectural questions about what students think readers a hundred years from now will get and what they will miss, or how this story might be read in India or Australia, or what the relevance of the date of publication is and how things or our perceptions have changed. Such questions might be especially effective if the story is taught with other stories that raise questions about cultural contexts: "A Souvenir of Japan," "The Water People," "Sánchez," "The Last of the Menu Girls," "The Loons," "A Rose for Emily," "A Pair of Tickets," "The Management of Grief," "Young Goodman Brown," "Love Medicine."

Questions for Discussion

1. How do you react to Baldwin's change of prose style in describing the scene at the nightclub? How does the change of style contribute to his message? In what ways does it make his message harder to decipher?

2. How should we read the reference to the "cup of trembling" in the last paragraph of the story? Should we read it to mean that trembling and fury will be visited on whites ("them that afflict thee")? or pushers? Or is the full bibilical passage not relevant? Would whites or blacks be more likely to recognize Baldwin's allusion?

Writing Assignments for Chapter 1

1. Write an essay defending or at least explaining Francis Weed's actions and providing evidence from the story.

2. Rearrange the scenes of "Sonny's Blues" into chronological order, and explain how this rearrangement would alter the meaning and effect of the story. Supplement your analysis by describing how other orders might effect the story.

3. Evaluate the endings of "The Country Husband" and "Sonny's Blues" using the implied criteria for endings supplied in "Happy Endings."

2 POINT OF VIEW

Just as perspective and focus influence the way a play in a basketball game is viewed (did the player shoot from outside the three-point line? was the player fouled in the act of shooting? Coach, player, and referee may have different answers), perspective and focus influence the way we view the events of our lives and the way we tell stories. Sometimes we distort (consciously or unconsciously) in reporting our triumphs and failures. Sometimes we simply don't know all the facts—or don't remember them clearly. Sometimes we are distracted or confused. The author's choice of focus, of point of view, imitates this reality; the decision to tell a story from one perspective or another puts a "spin" on the action—creates a perspective from which the truth is revealed and concealed to greater and lesser degrees. The purpose of raising to consciousness the way narration distorts experience is not to belittle narration; on the contrary, it suggests to students that learning to read stories, learning how people tell stories, and what's involved, can make them aware of how they make stories out of their own experiences, and how they try, through narrative, to make sense of their own lives.

Planning Ideas

- Along with **"The Cask of Amontillado,"** assign Robert Browning's **"My Last Duchess,"** a poem published just four years before Poe's story was first published, and discuss first-person murdering narrators, character types, literary tradition.
- When assigning Cortázar's **"Blow-Up,"*** hand out a list of leading questions to guide students in their reading—such questions as: To what sorts of necessary, writerly choices does the narrator call attention in the first paragraph? What other choices or problems involved in telling a story does the narrator address in the first five paragraphs? How is it that in the photograph that Michel takes and blows up to poster-size the characters move (if this indeed is what he does)?
- If you assign Cortázar's **"Blow-Up,"** and you have a fairly sophisticated class, you might want to pair the story with a viewing of one of the films influenced by it: Michelangelo Antonioni's *Blow Up* (1966), Brian DePalma's *Blow Out* (1981), or Francis Ford Coppola's *The Conversation* (1974).
- Ask students to rewrite a page of a story in this chapter from a point of view different from the original (for example, retelling part of **"Sonny's Blues"** from Sonny's perspective or retelling part of **"The Cask of Amontillado"** from the third person omniscient point of view). Use these exercises as the

bases for talking about the effects of point of view when you take up the stories for discussion.

- If you assign **"An Occurence at Owl Creek Bridge,"** ask students, in advance, to keep a brief record of their expectations as they move from paragraph to paragraph through the story.

EDGAR ALLAN POE

The Cask of Amontillado

I like to discuss a story like "The Cask of Amontillado" fairly early in the course because it is familiar—many students will have read it in high school and almost all will have heard of Edgar Allan Poe; it is brief—instructor and students, after a couple of readings, can hold the story in mind almost in its entirety and virtually isolate details with a mental pointer—and its devices and structure are rather obvious (one might say that Poe lays it on with a trowel, but of course one wouldn't). The story is useful in talking about point of view because it is told entirely in first person by an at least partially unreliable narrator who reveals only at the end of his tale that the events he describes happened a half a century ago. Many of Poe's plot devices hinge on Montresor's first-person narration—upon Montresor's early revelation that he hates Fortunato and is determined to get revenge. Most of the suspense is founded on the reader's expectation that Montresor will gain revenge and curiosity (even anxiety?) about how he will attempt to do so.

The plot structure seems fairly obvious here, with the exposition largely in (but not wholly confined to) the first three paragraphs; the rising action continuing until the climactic chaining of Fortunato to the wall (his recognition scene corresponding to that of many readers' recognition of precisely what Montresor has in mind); the action falling to the last paragraph's conclusion, and the leap of fifty years to the time of the narration (a gap we previously did not know existed, but which might allow us to conjecture just why Montresor is narrating—or confessing).

There are only two characters here, and Fortunato will be able to tell no tales, so only Montresor or an omniscient narrator can tell the story. It might be profitable to ask some or all of the students to try rewriting this story in the third person to see what's lost. [See Planning Ideas.] Early on, I like to ask students what effect(s) an author might expect to create when choosing to tell a story in first-person. You might point out to them that it is our tendency in reading fiction to take high moral ground and to damn all characters who are imperfect (for not being like ourselves). The first-person pulls us closer to the narrating character, makes us cheer for him or her, as it were. When that narrator is a murderer, as here (and in Graham Greene's *Brighton Rock* or in Burgess's *A Clockwork Orange*), or even just a snob, like Pip in *Great Expectations*, our emotions are more complicated. Is it that we understand or sympathize with the "sinner" more? Or is it that we say, "There but for the grace of God go I" and so think about our own fallibility (not yours, of course)? or both?

This might be a good story to introduce the notion of character types or stereotypes. Why Italy? What period is the story set in? What do the students know or feel about the kinds of people and kinds of actions that took place then and there? You might want to bring up Machiavelli; or pair this story with Browning's "My Last Duchess" and get at the issues raised by setting through discussion of Browning's dramatic monologue.

The macabre story is almost a fable for readers, a paradigm of the relation between writer and reader, with Montresor as author and Fortunato as the unfortunate reader. So, you can tell your students, if they don't want to get pinned to the wall, they'd better pay attention. Montresor as author of the plot begins by announcing that there is a plot—as authors implicitly do by writing a story—and he announces too that he considers a good plot one in which the perpetrator-author doesn't get caught. This challenges the reader to try to catch him, to try to guess what will happen next. The author challenges the reader's pride just as Montresor's dubious amontillado challenges Fortunato's pride in his knowledge of wine; the cask as wine and the cask of amontillado as title are thus central to both plots. (You might not want to call attention to the fact that Fortunato is dressed as a fool.)

The first thing a story must do, then, is to arouse a certain amount of expectation or anticipation, to get the reader to follow the story—to read on—and to try to guess with the story what is going to happen next or how it is going to happen. In order for there to be suspense or anticipation, there must be some doubt or alternative possibilities, and in order for there to be more than one possibility, at least one possibility must turn out to be wrong. Using a first-person narrator contributes to this effect because a narrator can purposely (or unconsciously, as in the case, for example, of someone who is self-deceived) mislead us about the action. False leads are inherent in plotting, and being aware of them (but not necessarily aware that they are false) is essential to participating in the story.

I like to ask students if they believe Montresor is a dependable narrator. We usually discuss whether Montresor really has a legitimate complaint against Fortunato and then talk about whether Montresor as a narrator is unreliable in a way that confuses readers and / or interferes with the story's building suspense. Usually students observe that, whether or not Montresor has a legitimate beef with Fortunato (the vagueness of his charges raises the possibility that Fortunato is entirely innocent), Montresor does appear single-minded in his pursuit of revenge. We feel we can count on him to carry out his plot—whatever it is—and this certainty is the basis for the suspense about what he will do and when.

Because I think such alertness important, I often ask students to stop at certain points in reading a story and to write down what they think might be going to happen next. Perhaps the first reasonable stopping place would be as Montresor and Fortunato are about to enter the vaults. A later one might be just after Fortunato's first coughing fit. You might even want to have the students stop reading as late as Montresor's stapling Fortunato to the wall, to see if they picked up the significance of the trowel (not too well buried in the mason joke). After discussing these scenes, we might ask what would be lost if the story were told from a third-person omniscient perpective.

If there are false leads, there must also be true leads, and you might want to suggest that even Montresor "plays fair" with Fortunato by ironic indications of his intentions, such as his agreeing that Fortunato will not die of a cough, his drinking to his victim's long life, his producing the trowel. These spots might make good stopping points too, or you might want to ask, once the story has been read, just when it becomes clear just what Montresor is up to.

I like to call attention at this point, or at least early in the discussion of point of view, to how much of the reader's guesswork is based on cause-effect, on the reader's assumption that there is logic in the sequence of events and in the characters' motivations. We assume Montresor is leading Fortunato into the catacombs for a reason; in searching the story and our minds for the reason we notice the cough; when Montresor agrees that Fortunato will not die of a cough, we either discard that possibility or believe the narrator to be a liar, or keep both possibilities in mind; if we notice the trowel and take it seriously, we have an answer. In one sense, plot and suspense seem to depend on logic—how could you guess what's to happen next in a wholly irrational universe? In what we can call the non-Western tradition, however, there is the suspense of expectation of sheer wonder, as in *The Arabian Nights* (The Thousand Nights and a Night) or tales of magic.

There's another way of guessing with an author, of course, and that is by the conventions of the kind. Though you may want to hold off any lengthy discussion of this until you get to the chapter on literary tradition, there's no reason not to acknowledge that some of our guesses come from what we are used to in the way of stories on the page, screen, or tube.

Questions for Discussion

1. Who (if anyone) is the narrator talking to at the end of the story?

2. Why do you think the narrator has waited fifty years to tell what he has done? Under what circumstances is he reporting his deed?

3. How would you assess the mental stability of the narrator?

4. Why does the narrator call for Fortunato after he has walled him in? Why does he report that his "heart grew sick"?

AMBROSE BIERCE

An Occurrence at Owl Creek Bridge

As suggested in the text headnote, this story scarcely could exist were it not for the focus shifting in section three to Peyton Farquhar's consciousness for much of the rest of the story. Indeed, between the sergeant's stepping aside at the end of the first section and the final paragraph nothing much happens: Farquhar merely hangs.

You might want to ask students about the second section and what would happen to their expectations if it were removed. This is not exactly a false lead, but like a false lead it distracts the reader from anticipating correctly or certainly. Of course it does something else: by characterizing Farquhar as patriotic, dedicated, and daring, and by revealing that his crime was an entrapment, the reader's sympathies are entirely enlisted on his side. You might ask how many students basically side with the Union and whether any of them wanted Farquhar to be "caught." If not, you may ask, why not? Getting us on Farquhar's side, to cheer him on and to hope for his escape is, of course, an important element in the strategy of the story.

There are a number of clues in the story pointing to what is actually happening. You might ask the students to identify them. You might also ask them in advance to keep a brief record of their expectations as they read through the story.

I often call attention to some of the minute, realistic details in the first section, and then have the students identify others and ask them why there are so many and what they do. One of the functions seems to be to slow down, almost stop the fictional clock—there's so much description that we seem to be looking at a tableau or still picture. Why? Where's the focus? What's going on?

There is a fairly common feeling among many of us and many of our students that this is essentially a story with a gimmick and, therefore, not "serious" fiction. Though it may seem contrived to us, it is very likely that when first published, like the stories of Guy de Maupassant, this story was considered "realistic." For adventure stories and romances, the popular fiction of the time, usually ended happily, and heroes did miraculously escape. That Farquhar did not, that he was misled by the fiction his mind made up, may, in context, appear bitterly realistic. The story, then, may ask us to contrast wishes, wish-fulfilling fantasies—including the kind of heroism suggested in section two—with the cold external realities. Just as Poe makes us for a time identify with a villain, here we emotionally identify with a hero who doesn't make it.

Questions for Discussion

1. Both "The Cask of Amontillado" and "An Occurence at Owl Creek Bridge" are stories that rely on gimmicks. Should these stories be considered serious works of literature? Why or why not? Do you rank one story above the other? If so, why?

2. How would you film "An Occurence at Owl Creek Bridge?" What technique might you use to convey the experiences Farquhar imagines?

JULIO CORTÁZAR

Blow-Up

If your students have read Margaret Atwood's "Happy Endings" and grasped some of the purposes and techniques of metafiction, they may be able to make some sense of "Blow-Up" on their own. I find, however, that most need considerable help to get a handle on this work, and that is why I give out a list of very specific questions ahead of time to guide their reading. (See Planning Ideas.) I also suggest, in one way or another, that the first five paragraphs of the story are, in part, about something probably all of them have experienced—the need to write something, the dread of doing it, and confusion about how to begin and proceed.

Sometimes I do this in a roundabout and fairly personal way by asking members of the class to talk about their worst experiences in trying to write a paper. This approach can spiral out of control, but generally I find that sharing a few paper-writing war stories helps to orient the class toward the writer's perspective and enables students to grasp some of the issues raised early in Cortázar's story concerning point of view, subjectivity, temporality, the ordering of events, realism, and the workings of the imagination.

In my reading of the story, the photographer (who may be Roberto Michel or perhaps our narrator himself) wanders about Paris, eventually fixing his attention and his camera's eye on a scene between a woman and a teenager. The narrator has made it clear that Michel's aim in taking pictures is not to document as a journalist might—"I'm not talking about waylaying the lie like any old reporter, snapping the stupid silhouette of the VIP leaving number 10 Downing Street"—but to record his personal vision: "The photographer always worked as a permutation of his personal way of seeing the world." This description of the photographer's art provides one of myriad opportunities in the story to talk about subjectivity and the way writers as well as photographers unconsciously as well as consciously "frame" the events they record.

In the first report of the encounter between the teenage boy and the older woman, the photographer immediately identifies with the boy and takes an equally immediate dislike to the woman, imagining that she is trying to make an unwilling young man her sexual prey. When, to the displeasure of the woman, the photographer takes a picture of the pair, he believes that he has foiled her seduction attempt.

A later report of the encounter occurs after the photographer has gone home, developed the film, and blown up the picture of teenager and woman to near poster size. As he looks at the photograph, works at his translation in fits and starts, and recalls what he has seen in the square, he begins to revise his ideas about what he witnessed. His imagination once again takes over, but this time he focuses in his memory on the man waiting in a car in the background, even though the car has been cropped out of the enlarged photograph—"carefully eliminated." While staring at the photograph with an obsessive intensity, he devises a new, darker interpretation of the scene involving this shadowy figure, imagining that this mysterious man—not the woman—is in charge and that the woman is simply someone he uses in order to trap and recruit young, male prostitutes. Caught up in his new vision of events, the photographer / narrator "watches" helplessly, imagining that he has missed his opportunity to intervene. The photographer's nightmare vision ends when a bird flies by the window of his room, bringing him out of his imaginative reverie and allowing him to revise once more his version of the scene he photographed so that the boy, once again, escapes.

Questions for Discussion

1. What do you make of the ending? If the narrator has been looking at a poster-size blowup of the photograph in the previous paragraphs, what is the narrator looking at in the last paragraph?

2. How would you identify the narrator? Can you identify the narrator definitively?

3. When is the "Now" of the last paragraph? How does the narrator call attention to the problem of conveying temporality in a story elsewhere in this story?

4. In what sense(s) is the photographer sitting before the picture similar to an author sitting before the words he or she has placed on the page?

Writing Assignments for Chapter 2

1. Write a comparison / contrast essay discussing the function of point of view in "The Cask of Amontillado" and "An Occurence at Owl Creek Bridge."

2. In the style of Cortázar, write a meditation on a photograph picturing two or more people that stimulates your imagination. Explore at least two possible scenarios for the persons pictured. Attach a copy or photocopy of the picture. (This can be a personal photo or a picture from some other source—a magazine or newspaper, perhaps.)

3. In the library, find two "opinion pieces" (op-ed articles) about the same topic but written by people who have opposing views. Investigate the backgrounds of both writers, and then write an essay suggesting why they approach the same topic from such different perspectives.

3 CHARACTERIZATION

In some sense we judge characters in fiction much the way we judge the real characters in our lives, the people we meet day to day. Our responses are based on what the characters say and do, how they say and do it, and what others say about them. Our job in analyzing fiction is to read characters carefully—to try to understand who, in all their individualities, they really are. "Fenstad's Mother" and "My Friend Judith" provide opportunities to talk about the influence of cultural stereotyping in fiction and in life. Both stories suggest that human character doesn't lend itself very readily to pigeon-holing; Fenstad's mother and Judith are complex personalities, reacting according to type one moment and the next, confounding all expectation.

How close we get to a character in a story is, at least in part, a function of point of view. First-person narration—the perspective of three of the four stories in this section—provides a close encounter, a kind of intimacy and proximity to one character's thoughts and experience that may cause us to respond more sympathetically than we otherwise might to the character's situation—or to feel a greater sense of outrage or betrayal if the character lets us down.

Planning Ideas

- If you have not assigned Maupassant's **"The Jewelry"** and Chekhov's **"The Lady with the Dog"** earlier in the semester, assign these stories as background reading for Grace Paley's **"A Conversation with My Father."**
- Have each student bring to class an analysis of a single paragraph from one of the stories that reveals something important about the main character. Ask volunteers to share these at the appropriate time, and encourage students who have written about the same character, but with different results, to confront the conflicts between their perceptions.
- Assign a student who is a good actor to practice and then read a key section of **"Why I Live at the P.O."** *—perhaps the first page or so—during class. This is often a useful way to prompt thinking about Sister's character and to help students appreciate the story's humor.
- If your students are keeping journals as part of their classwork, ask each to write a paragraph characterizing themselves as honestly as they can, mentioning at least four major character traits—both positive and negative. Then have them write characterizations of themselves as they imagine might be written by (1) a parent, (2) a sibling, (3) an instructor with whom they get along, (4) an instructor with whom they do not get along, (5) a good friend, or (6) a rival.

EUDORA WELTY

Why I Live at the P.O.

Surely Welty's Sister is one of the great comic characters in American short fiction, although Sister's is not a voice students always appreciate at first exposure. (In my experience, many students have difficulty "hearing" the comedy in fiction unless it comes directly from puns or overt jokes.) To help the class tune into Sister—some are ready to dismiss her as "stupid" and the story as equally so—I like to have a student with some acting ability read aloud the first dozen paragraphs. (If I don't have a talented student reader, I do the reading myself, striving for the rapid-fire, sharp southern twang of a Holly Hunter—or a female Ross Perot—as opposed to the slow drawl so often assumed by non-Southern actors playing Southerners without regard to character or background.) The reading, if it goes well, will prompt some chuckles and provide an opening for talking about Sister's character and her role as narrator of recent events in China Grove.

Discussion might start with a close analysis of the first paragraph and what it reveals about Sister as a character and as a filter for the story. Students immediately will note that Sister's resentment over losing Mr. Whitaker to her younger sister Stella Rondo taints her testimony and causes us to question Sister's reliability almost from the first sentence. Fairly detailed analysis of Sister's vocabulary, sentence structure, tone, and emphasis in the opening paragraph helps the class to sketch out some notions of her character. The melodrama of such phrases as "a deliberate, calculated falsehood," Sister's willingness to recount Stella Rondo's crudely intimate lie—she "Told him I was one-sided"—to whomever will listen, the tawdriness of her meeting with Mr. Whitaker when he came to town to take "Pose Yourself" photos, the non sequiturs, and her fragmented style of delivery all help to flesh out her portrait.

Since the story is Sister's explanation of why she's living at the post office instead of at home (why, by the way, the P.O. instead of the post office?), I sometimes ask students to give *their* analyses of why she lives at the post office—that is, to explain what we reader / listeners understand about Sister that she seems not to understand about herself.

Questions for Discussion

1. How much of what Sister reports can we believe? Does she appear to have good reasons to resent Stella Rondo?

2. Why does Sister insist that Stella Rondo's daughter is not adopted? What point is she trying to make? Why? Why does Mama accept Stella Rondo's story that Shirley T. is adopted?

3. How would you characterize the other members of Sister's family? Stella Rondo? Mama? Papa-Daddy? Uncle Rondo? Which characters in the story are most fully fleshed out?

4. Is there a realistic way to account for the melodrama of Sister's family life, or is Welty merely exaggerating for comic effect?

5. What do you make of Sister's revelation at the end of the story that she has been living at the P.O. "for five solid days and nights"? What does her choice of words convey about the way she views this self-imposed exile?

6. What do you make of the bigotry the characters display? Is this a racist story?

CHARLES BAXTER

Fenstad's Mother

One of the delightful things about the experience of reading this story is the way that Baxter flirts with stereotypes. Repeatedly he tempts us to press Fenstad and his mother into neat little boxes marked "milk-toast son" and "domineering mother," or "well-meaning Christian" and "lefty activist," and then he makes it impossible for us to do so. An action occurs, a gesture is made, a phrase is uttered, a thought is revealed, and the characters overflow their boxes — gradually revealing themselves to be too complicated, too unpredictable, and too humanly perplexing for such neat and dismissive packaging.

Such an approach to characterization can make students uncomfortable. Those who typically read stories hoping at the end to distill a hard, gold nugget of wisdom — or at least an unambiguous theme or two — may not know what to do with "Fenstad's Mother." This type of student may simply "resolve" the characters' inconsistencies by ignoring evidence that doesn't conform to stereotype. To counter this tendency, I like to call the class's attention to several passages in the first twenty paragraphs of the story in which at first we are tempted to embrace a stereotypical view of Fenstad or his mother, and then find the stereotype overturned.

Baxter creates the first temptation at the beginning of the very first paragraph:

> On Sunday morning after communion Fenstad drove across town to visit his mother. Behind the wheel, he exhaled with his hand flat in front of his mouth to determine if the wine on his breath could be detected. He didn't think so.

I ask the class what sorts of expectations these three sentences create. One normally imagines that a mother would be proud of an adult son who gets up on Sunday morning to attend church and take communion, but Fenstad doesn't want his mother to detect that he's been drinking wine — even communion wine. Could Fenstad be an alcoholic, covering up his weakness for morning drinking with an early visit to church? Is his mother an old-fashioned teetotaler who disapproves of the use of wine even in the communion service? Is Fenstad a Jew who has provoked his mother by converting to Christianity? As it turns out, the third guess is the closest to the truth—and yet still far off the mark; the truth is both less expected and more complicated. Fenstad's mother appears to think of Fenstad's church going as a mild form of rebellion against her life-long socialism. But, as the story unfolds, we realize that she is also amused at her son's attempts to be "good" in some vague Christian sense and dismayed at how ineffectual he is at it, how often he fails to make the essential human connections that goodness requires.

Later, in paragraph eight, Clara Fenstad questions the necessity of Fenstad's divorce, now a decade past, and wonders aloud why he and his former wife Eleanor couldn't live together. This exchange seems a reprisal of many such conversations between elderly, conservative parents and their grownup children, but Clara is politically more liberal than her son, and so her seemingly stereotypical reaction is the one that is unexpected here. Of course, things are never quite so simple as they seem. In the next several paragraphs, Clara reveals a rather tough-minded, unromantic view of marriage, one that values companionship as a stay against loneliness over romantic attachment. It is a response that reveals her own situation as well as her concern for her son's happiness. She doesn't want him to end up, as she has, alone and lonely.

Clara Fenstad's desire to get out of her apartment leads to her son's invitation to attend the night class he teaches in English composition and sets us up for other surprises. When Fenstad's mother responds to his invitation with the statements, "They'll notice me. . . . I'm too old," we scarcely expect that she will virtually take over Fenstad's class and demonstrate a talent for teaching that her son cannot begin to approach. When we are told that Fenstad teaches the course, not because he needs the money, but "because he liked teaching strangers and because he enjoyed the sense of hope the classrooms held for him," we imagine that he will be a far better teacher than he turns out to be.

Only later do we reexamine this notion that Fenstad likes to teach strangers and realize that it is, sadly, literally true. He doesn't connect with his students. He doesn't become friends with any of them by the end of the semester. He lacks the personal touch that his mother so abundantly exhibits, and that is why his well-meaning Christianity gets him nowhere. Fenstad embraces a religion based on the idea that the divine entered human history to show love for mankind by becoming intimately human, but Fenstad gives so little personal attention to his fellow human beings that his Christianity becomes a joke. From this perspective, his mother's gentle mockery of his beliefs seems almost too generous.

Questions for Discussion

1. Why does Clara Fenstad hate "niceness"? What does this attitude suggest about the way she prefers to interact with people?

2. What kind of architecture would you expect a socialist to approve? What is Clara Fenstad's reaction to the architecture of the school where her son teaches? Does she like what you would expect her to like?

3. What is wrong with Fenstad's approach to teaching? Why is his mother a more effective teacher than he is? Is her approach more political or personal?

4. Why is Fenstad so upset by the encounter with the homeless woman in the all-night restaurant? Why does his mother excuse herself and go to the restroom after the encounter? What is her reaction to the scene? To her son?

5. Why does Fenstad's mother risk her health to go out and watch Fenstad skating with his girlfriend? What reason does she give? What reason(s) would you add?

6. What draws Clara Fenstad to York Follette and him to her? Why does York Follette visit Mrs. Fenstad when she is ill and bring jazz recordings for her to hear?

7. What are these "glimpses" Fenstad's mother keeps referring to? Glimpses of what?

DORIS LESSING

Our Friend Judith

This is one of those stories about which some students are likely to say, "Nothing happens," so it might be a good idea from the beginning to ask them to list all the things that do happen in the story. In a sense the students are right—many of the things that happen do not happen in the story but are told about by the narrator or Betty or Judith herself. It's probably important for students both to know that a good deal happens and to understand why it doesn't seem that anything happens. It might be useful, then, to have them show how the interesting things in the story—Judith's affair with Luigi, the young cat's labor and delivery—are distanced by having to be reported. This is an aspect of focus—a kind of mediated mediation—not directly treated in Chapter 3, that might be useful to discuss at this point: its effect, its relation to the play-within-the-play or "embedded" narration, perhaps its relation to dialogue. (A return to Baldwin's "Sonny's Blues" might prove enlightening in regard to the narrative filter.) There is little sense of suspense; the major question we ask while reading the story is not "What's going to happen next?" And that's probably what the students mean by "Nothing happens."

If it is going to take so much of the anticipation away, why, then, have the friend narrate and why have so many things told to her? What's gained? To what questions, what other centers of interest, is the reader's attention shifted?

Of course if you ask the questions that way and if you are following the chapters in the text, the brighter students will put two and two together and come up with Judith's character as the center of interest, following with the question, "What's Judith like?" Good enough, but you will have to look out for—or hope for?—the reductive readings: she's this cool-seeming, intellectual, respectable type who's really all fire and like that underneath; she lives one kind of life in the open and another in secret. With any luck, you'll get a more contemporary and subtle but perhaps equally reductive reading—Judith is her own woman, who does not need a man to lean on or depend on, but lives in the world, has her profession, and does her own thing in a liberated way that used to be thought of as only the province and right of men. If both those readings come up—or if you can provoke the other once one comes up—your problem will not be to arouse discussion but to keep things in hand.

To pursue another direction, it may be useful to suggest that this is a detective story in which the detection seeks not the solution of a crime but the understanding of a character. You might want to start with the narrator's rejection of the two smug assumptions in the first two paragraphs—that Judith is a typical English spinster and that she has given up. The narrator's experience of other spinsters, her aunts, suggests first that Judith does resemble them but that they are not fossilized, conventional old maids; and suggests then that the narrator may have to change her "pitying" attitude toward women without men. The narrator then sadly confesses that through her own stupidity she lost her chance to find out what Judith and her life are really like. We need to get on the table what the lost opportunity was and whether the narrator really blundered. But suppose we can read through the story, beyond the stupid blunder in a way the narrator cannot? Imagine a detective story in which Holmes or Ellery Queen is stumped, but the reader is left with what seems to be a sufficient number of clues to solve the crime.

The narrator sets forth some clues in the three revelatory incidents: the dress that Judith refuses to wear (Judith says, "One surely ought to stay in character, wouldn't you say?"); the refusal to castrate the tomcat ("It's the nature of a male cat to rampage lustfully about, and therefore it would be morally wrong for Judith to have the cat fixed"); Judith's ultimate "apology" to the young man who damaged her flat (". . . having chosen that you should have it, it was clearly an unwarrantable infringement of your liberty to make any conditions at all.") "The facts about Judith, then, are all in the open," the narrator says, "unconcealed, and plain to anyone who cares to study them"; or, as it becomes clear she feels, to anyone with the intelligence to interpret them. The challenge is thrown in the reader's face: Are we intelligent enough to interpret the facts with any certainty? (I'm not sure I am, by the way.) Perhaps students should be asked to stop reading the story at this point, as they have been asked to stop reading suspenseful stories at certain points, and to use their intelligence to "interpret" Judith's character as they were earlier asked to predict plot developments. Then they might compare their conclusions here with what they think of Judith at the end of the story. Regardless of how successful the predictions are, this should show students that as readers they collect, recollect, and project as they read in areas other than plot.

When I teach Lessing's story, much of the discussion is shaped by the questions for discussion listed below. I use these not as a pedagogical device—though I do think these and similar questions ought to stimulate discussion—but because I feel they are real questions—that is, they are without single, simple answers. Or, to put it another way, I'm not sure I understand exactly what we are to make of Judith, or whether what we are to make of the story is the difficulty of making anything about people's characters. One of the reasons I like Lessing so much is that she, like Lawrence, gets the reader to make human judgments about human actions and character, and that there is no one "literary" answer planted symbolically or structurally in the story. This is not to say that Lessing and Lawrence have not made judgments, but that the judgments are complex, variable, individual; your judgments of the human issues in the story define your character, not your moral or intellectual worth necessarily, but what you are "like." Since our egos make us to some extent want to "like" the creator of the fiction we are reading, we try to understand and intuit that vision. In inviting us into their worlds such writers "teach" us, not judgments or maxims, but how to judge.

As I have earlier suggested, students are often uneasy with this kind of openness—not just a paradox or literary irony or structural ambivalence but an openness that tests the readers' characters rather than their intelligence alone. They're especially uneasy when you can't or won't give them some answers to write in their notebooks. So it might be best in some classes to hold off on this story until you're well into the course. On the other hand, if you have a sharp, articulate, aggressive group, it would be well to throw this at them early—and not let them off the hook with modish, ready-made answers.

Questions for Discussion

1. This story, as the narrator suggests, should modify our notions of the typical English spinsters, largely through our knowledge of Judith. How is our stereotype modified? Is it wholly reversed? drastically changed? changed in all superficial aspects (celibacy, prudery) but retaining some of its inner nature?

2. What sort of image do the students have of the narrator? She calls herself stupid yet sees and interprets much evidence convincingly (the two rows of books from Judith's former lovers, for example), but at the same time she seems to fall into such banalitites as saying oh, yes, Judith would have a cat, and she must be lonely sometimes. Is the narrator "interfering" when she asks Judith about her leaving Italy?

3. Do we agree with Judith that the narrator is "stupid" for using the word "interfere"? What do the students make of Judith's failure to understand why the narrator, Betty, and the Rinieris "care"?

4. Who is right about why the cats gather to watch the painful labor of

Judith's pregnant kitten? What do your students make of Judith's reaction to Luigi's killing the kitten?

5. Why, you might ask, are the other women friends involved in the story at all? Why is it our rather than my friend Judith? Why is Betty involved? (How much do we learn about her?)

GRACE PALEY

A Conversation with my Father

Paley's brief but richly nuanced story offers a number of perspectives from which to talk about characterization. Since the story focuses on two versions of the framed tale the narrator writes for her father—and since students usually pay close attention to these when they read—it may be helpful to begin discussion with the differences in the ways the two characters judge a story's merit, focusing on the two tales the narrator constructs. As the footnote points out, one of the father's favorite writers, Turgenev, is best known for his novel *Fathers and Sons*, a work treating conflicts between generations. Mentioning this detail can provide an introduction to discussing the differences between the kinds of stories the narrator likes—and prefers to write—and the stories of which her father approves.

The father says he wants a "simple" story with "recognizable people," but those familiar with the literary models he cites will realize that this is an oversimplification of his requirements. Maupassant and Chekhov (both writers represented in this anthology) wrote stories that are straightforward, but also sophisticated and characterized by somewhat bleak realism. (If you have assigned Maupassant's "The Jewelry" and Chekhov's "The Lady with the Dog" earlier in the semester, you may want to refer back to discussions of those works as a means of identifying the type of story to which the father is attracted.) Both writers are capable of great humor and remarkable insight, but they are associated with a vision of reality more dark, fate-ridden, and cynical than optimistic. The daughter has always despised the kind of plot to which her father is attracted "because it takes all hope away." "Everyone, real or invented," she says, "deserves the open destiny of life." Still, she wants to please her father—and he is dying—so she makes an effort to write the kind of story he has requested.

Probably no one in the class will approve of the story the narrator first constructs, an "unadorned and miserable tale," as she describes it. I like to ask students what they make of this first story and of the narrator's aims in writing it. Someone, quoting the father, will observe that the narrator has "left everything out." If the class has read Atwood's "Happy Endings," someone may note that the narrator's first story is similar to the stark plots Atwood constructs. The narrator doesn't describe the characters or create a real background for them, and we have no sense of their lives unfolding over time. She appears to have left out almost "everything" that provides interest in a story—or, to put it another way—meaning in life. The brevity of the first story also suggests the narrator's lack of enthusiasm for writing it. Her description of the tale she has produced appears to be a judgment on the kind of story her father likes, perhaps even an (unconscious? semi-conscious?) form of retaliation against the parent who doesn't approve of the stories she normally creates.

When we take up discussion of the second version of the narrator's story, I ask students to explain how this tale is an improvement over the last. I also ask why it doesn't fulfill the father's request. At the heart of the matter, of course, are the differences in the two characters' perspectives. The father is old; he has a damaged heart and is dying. Both a former doctor and a former artist, he unflinchingly confronts the reality of his situation—"Despite my metaphors, this muscle failure is not due to his old heart, he says, but to a potassium shortage"— and he yearns for stories that imbue human life—and the end of life—with resonance and meaning. His daughter, differently situated, believes she has "a different responsibility"—a responsibility to maintain hope. Rejecting the father's characterization of her second story as a "tragedy," she imagines a scenario in which the drug-addicted woman reclaims her life and lives on. Her father recognizes in his daughter's rejection of fictional closure her attempt to deny his approaching death and the inevitability of her own, and his final question implies that some day—perhaps some day soon, when he dies—she will have to "look it in the face."

Questions for Discussion

1. What do you make of the jokes in Paley's story? Of the jokes in the narrator's second story? Are jokes out of place in a story about someone facing death?

2. Why is the father impatient with the daughter's statement that sometimes "you have to let the story lie around till some agreement can be reached between you and the stubborn hero"? What is the difference between her conception of characterization and his?

3. In the second, comic version of the narrator's story, the young man at first sees life through the perspective of drugs. Drugs create the meaning in his life. Eventually he meets a woman who sees life through the perspective of health food and is converted to her perspective. Through what perspective does the father see the world?

4. What characteristics do you value in a short story? Why? Do the stories you like reflect your interests? your age? your experiences? your attitudes toward life?

Writing Assignments for Chapter 3

1. According to the stereotype, spinsters like and keep cats. Write an essay about Judith and the cats. What role(s) do the cats play in "My Friend Judith"? How does Judith's treatment of and interaction with the cats help to characterize her?

2. Compare and contrast the relationships between parent and child in "Fenstad's Mother" and "A Conversation with my Father"—or in another parent / child story—for example, "Everything That Rises Must Converge."

3. Do some library research on Eudora Welty and discover what she has said about "Why I Live at the P.O." Write an essay evaluating the contribution of her comments to your understanding of the story.

4. Write a personal essay about a time when you felt that someone was viewing you stereotypically instead of seeing you as you really are or were. What stereotypes did the other person impose on you? Did you challenge his or her perception of you in any way? If so, did you get a reaction? What sort?

4 SETTING

Each of the stories in this chapter takes us to unfamiliar places—whether the South of fifty years ago, war-torn China during the Japanese invasion of World War II, or Moscow in the late nineteenth century. The chapter focuses attention on three questions: (1) When does the story take place—at what hours of the day, what seasons, over what period of time? (2) Where does the story take place—in what rooms, buildings, places, regions, countries? and (3) What part does the setting play in the experience and meaning of the story? It may be well to set out these questions very simply before beginning your study and to ask that students underline the answers they discover as they read. I find that, while students have little problem grasping the significance of setting in abstract terms, they have a tendency to skip over descriptions of setting when reading, and they often lack the geographical and historical knowledge to make settings foreign to them come alive. For the latter reason, it may also be helpful to bring maps into class and supply abbreviated historical backgrounds when appropriate.

Planning Ideas

- Ask students to write and bring to class a description of the scene they would show during the opening credits of their film version of **"A Rose for Emily," "A Pair of Tickets,"** or **"The Lady with the Dog."** Use the descriptions as a jumping off point for talking about the importance of setting.
- Before class, have students write a paper or draw up a chart for class discussion of the time scheme in **"A Rose for Emily."**
- Assign *The Joy Luck Club*, the novel from which the Tan story is taken, or assign another Faulkner story, **"Barn Burning,"** that is set, as is **"A Rose for Emily,"** in Faulkner's South.
- Film versions of **"A Rose for Emily," "Barn Burning,"** and *The Joy Luck Club* are all available on video. Discussing the way the directors choose to convey settings can be a good way to begin talking about the function of setting in both film and original work.

WILLIAM FAULKNER

A Rose for Emily

The most striking and memorable thing about "A Rose for Emily" is its shocking revelation at the end, and that, naturally, is what most students—even those who have read the story before—will want to talk about. You might want to talk time and place, but it is probably advisable to give students their heads. For one thing, it is rather easy to turn such a discussion to the recuperative aspect of reading—that is, how later elements in a story make us selectively recall and reconsider earlier ones. I often ask students to compare Faulkner's surprise ending with Maupassant's; I then point out how the typical structure of detective stories—a kind most students are familiar with—forces you by the revelation at the end to go back over the story recalling "clues." In "Emily," of course, you don't know that you are working toward a revelation—or do you? Isn't there a kind of expectation based on the very lack of an obvious "plot," an obvious sense of suspense or curiosity? Doesn't the fact that you are reading a story mean that you have to expect something—or otherwise it would not be a story?

When you are talking about later events in the story recalling earlier ones, you are really talking about sequence, not necessarily chronology—for one of the more obvious characteristics of this story is its elaborate and complex treatment of historical time. (This manipulation of the history of Emily, you may want to point out, is a dramatic example of structure.) It may be useful to have the students write a paper or draw up a chart for class discussion of the time scheme in the story. (See Planning Ideas.) Such an exercise highlights the structuring, draws attention to how many time signals and specific dates there are in the story, ensures careful reading, and results in enough differences (I know every time I try to work it out I get a few more specific dates and a few different answers) to ensure a lively class discussion.

Why so unorthodox a time scheme? (If one of your students does not, with more or less exasperation, bring this up, you just may have to do so yourself.) I always have at least one student who believes authors are deliberately, even perversely, obscure, and another who thinks "obscurity" is a sign of "art" or "modernity" or both. I'm afraid I usually put such students off and say, "Well, let's talk about this story for a while, and I'll come back to that question." If I don't do that, I find myself forced into giving my "reading" of the story to "justify" its structure. It is possible, however, to deal with the issue of plot manipulation, which often arises at this point. Isn't the purpose of the complicated time scheme to delay the revelation or to put the reader off the scent? Probably so. We cannot know whether manipulation is good or bad unless we explore what the relationship is between the structure and the meaning of the story. If some students attack the story hard enough, others are sure to leap to its defense, and one fairly obvious defense is more than likely to come up: the time shifts are mimetic; this is the way people tell stories, and this is the way memory and gossip and oral narrative generally work. Now you're forced to be the devil's advocate. That reasoning may explain shifting time in general but it does not help with these shifts, these particularities.

If the world, or the world of the classroom, were an orderly place, you would always reach exactly this point and turn to the second paragraph of the story. I want to talk about structure and time scheme and all that I've mentioned, but I also really want to get to that second paragraph and a discussion of setting, so I get there one way or the other, even if it means saying, at some irrelevant point, "Speaking of the second paragraph, . . ." What is there in this paragraph that suggests that the narrator, the voice, is not just spinning a yarn, happening to tell the story in this seemingly casual way?

It usually does not take too long for someone to point out that the description of Emily's house "lifting its stubborn and coquettish decay" is not entirely innocent or accidental, that the noun and both adjectives relate to more than just Emily's house. And, if the class has brought up the time element, it should not be too long before someone mentions that there are the three specific times suggested in the paragraph: the 1870s, when the house was built; the more-or-less present with garages and gasoline pumps, probably the 1920s; and the 1860s, the time of the battle of Jefferson in the Civil War. Emily is joining the Civil War dead in the cemetery. It is at this point that I like to look forward to the next paragraph—"Miss Emily had been a tradition, a duty, and a care"—and back to the first—"the men [went to her funeral] through a sort of respectful affection for a fallen monument"—and ask what the title means.

The narrator offers only glimpses of Miss Emily, standing behind her father at the house door, riding next to Homer Barron in his carriage, waiting at the druggist's counter to purchase poison, presiding over a class of young would-be china painters, sitting upright in the window. We are limited to what the townspeople can see of Miss Emily's life and guess about her thoughts. From mere glimpses of her over the years, they construct a life for her and envy, pity, marvel, or disapprove largely according to what they imagine. What we and the narrator find out at last is that their imaginations are too small to take in Miss Emily as she really is. In her imagination—unbalanced as it may be—she creates and holds a world in stasis.

The standards and beliefs of this world are implied in the story, but it may be useful to make the implications explicit by listing some of them on the blackboard.

With the list as backdrop, we can then discuss not only the focus of the story but the voice. Who is speaking? What is he like? To what extent are we supposed to share his values? The answer to the first question is easy—he's a (self appointed) white male representative of the townspeople. The answer to the second question is just a bit more complicated. The narrator tells us that men go to the funeral out of affection and respect, the women out of curiosity, wanting a peek inside the house; only a woman would believe Colonel Sartoris's gallant lie; the very title suggests a male tribute to a "lady." Sexism in "A Rose for Emily" should generate good papers or a good discussion; nor is this to merely suggest a fashionable subject for the 1990s, for the question of the narrator's attitude toward Emily and ours toward the narrator is central in our reading of the story.

The question does not involve only gender roles, of course, but the values of the whole town or society (and the attitude of the story toward the attitude of the town). To what degree are these values a function of setting: of time and place? How are we supposed to feel about Colonel Sartoris? He gallantly remits Emily's taxes and protects her pride by telling her that the town owed Emily's father money. Yet it was Colonel Sartoris's edict that decreed that "negro" women should not appear on the streets without an apron. How are we supposed to feel about Emily's proud refusal both to lie and to obey the law when she purchases arsenic? Matters of sex and race and class permeate the story, bringing a whole bygone society back to life. Good or bad, it's gone, and not even Emily can pretend that it is not dead.

Questions for Discussion

1. Can this story really be a tribute to someone whose gray hair is on the pillow next to a skeleton? What are we supposed to think of Miss Emily Grierson? Who is Emily? What is she a monument to, and why does she deserve a rose?

2. Is the narrator's opinion of Miss Emily at all influenced by the place and time in which he lives? If so, how?

3. Does Miss Emily's status as a town monument suggest a reason for the manipulation of time sequence, a spatializing of the fifty or sixty years following the Civil War?

4. Can your students imagine this story told any other way, perhaps as a Poe story, "The Casket of Homer Barron," beginning, "The dozens of insults of that low-born Yankee I had borne as best I could, but when he ventured to injure my good name before all the town I vowed revenge"?

AMY TAN

A Pair of Tickets

The first five paragraphs of "A Pair of Tickets" provide the seeds of the story. I like to start discussion by asking the class to notice the clues the opening offers about what will be important as the narrative unfolds. The first paragraph situates the narrator in the fictive present, crossing from Hong Kong—symbolic gateway between East and West into China. The second paragraph reaches back through memory to a time twenty-one years before when the narrator, a high school sophomore in San Francisco, told her mother that she didn't feel Chinese and made it clear she didn't particularly want to feel Chinese. Paragraphs three through five project foward into the future—first the humorously awful future the narrator imagined when she was young (her transformation into a "mutant" with all her mother's Chinese behaviors), then the unknown future of the journey to China, which the narrator makes carrying the dreams (the hoped-for future) of her dead mother. Students will probably mention that the opening paragraphs suggest the story will concern itself with the relationship between the narrator and her mother, the narrator's perspective on her heritage, and the interrelations of past, present and future.

If the class has read "A Rose for Emily," you might want to ask how the style of narration and the temporal arrangement of Faulkner's story compares and contrasts with Tan's. In both stories the narrative reflects the movement of memory. In "A Rose for Emily," the narrator manipulates the shifts in time so as to delay revelation and create a surprise or shock ending. He already knows what the outcome will be. Jing-Mei, the narrator of "A Pair of Tickets," reports from the narrative "present." Her journey becomes our journey. We piece together the facts of her mother's past and discover the narrator's heritage as she does. What is the difference in effect?

One good way to talk about setting is to start with the many names and references to names in the story. Jing-Mei's sense of dislocation from her ethnic origins and her parents' physical dislocation from their homeland find expression in places and place names, and of course in the narrator's two names: Jing-Mei and June May. (Someone may note that neither name is "purely" of one nationality. Jing-Mei is a Chinese name written in Roman—"American"—letters, and June May seems a Chinese notion of an American name.) The name of Jing-Mei's San Francisco school is Galileo High. An Italian name, of course, is perfect to suggest cosmopolitian, melting-pot America.

When Jing-Mei visits 1980s China, the old, westernized city names have been replaced by more authentically Chinese names approved by the postrevolutionary leadership. This China both is and is not the country her mother knew. With its luxury hotels stocked with Western products, it is certainly not the China Jing-Mei expected. (Only the hotel shampoo, "the consistency and color of hoisin sauce," seems to her sufficiently, authentically Chinese.) The landscape she has read and heard about has changed, just as the landscape had changed when her mother returned with her new husband to look for her twin daughters and the rest of her family in 1945, after the Japanese invasion.

Mr. Woo's description of her mother's trek from Kweilin during the invasion is vivid, and with it we move to yet another landscape. Little topographical detail is given, but the description of the roads filled with people, the trucks passing by, the mother's agony, and the children make it easy to visualize the scene. The landscape particular to China is unimportant because we are really in "War Land," that zone where separation and tragedy occur despite all best intentions.

At some point in class discussion, I like to ask why Jing-Mei goes to China. The obvious answer is that she goes to meet her newly discovered sisters, but I think, perhaps, that she also goes out of a sense of guilt—feeling that she didn't appreciate her mother sufficiently (are there children who do?), that she somehow should have shared her mother's secret pain and compensated for the loss of her sisters. She goes to China thinking that the least she can do is accomplish her mother's dream of recovering her children, however inadequately, by proxy. In some sense, perhaps inadvertently, she also goes to China to meet the mother she never knew—the woman who hid her hopes and deepest grief from her husband as well as her daughter.

If you are lucky, someone will mention that this is a story of self-realization—

if not, you may want to bring it up. An aspect of Jing-Mei's character or soul has been obscured, and this odyssey enables her to uncover it, she discovers her Chinese self. But there are other people, other discoveries about the nature of family and identity. (It is significant, I think, that Jing-Mei's mother is certain all the people in the family house are dead because she knows how they as a family behave—that they would all be together.) You might ask the students what they make of all the activity with the Polaroid and the narrator's observations about physical resemblances.

The miracle of this story is, for me, the "rightness" of its resolution. I like to ask my students to tell me what Jing-Mei needs in order for her story to have a happy ending. What are the shapes of her fears? the sources of her grief? One possibility is that Jing-Mei fears she will be insufficient for her sisters, as she was insufficient for her mother (through no real fault of her own). She fears her mother never loved her as much as she loved her lost children. She grieves over the loss of the mother she knew and over the loss of the mother she has come to know during her journey. Like all of us who lose loved ones, she has regrets. She wishes her mother had lived to see her hopes rewarded, and she feels unworthy to meet her sisters in her mother's place.

Near the end of class, I like to ask how the meeting at the airport satisfies Jing-Mei's longings. Her mother will never come back to say, "You're wrong; I always loved you," but in her sister's expression—"the back of her hand pressed hard against her mouth"—her mother is returned to her with evidence of her love. Recalling her mother's gesture of tearful relief when she discovered the five-year-old Jing-Mei was safe and not dead as she had feared provides the necessary affirmation. In the faces of her sisters, Jing-Mei recognizes her lost mother and her lost self. The important part of her that is Chinese is her family. In finding her sisters, she finds not only what her mother wanted for herself, but what she also wanted for her three lost daughters.

Questions for Discussion

1. What does it mean to be a member of a family, even when you've grown up without ever seeing them?

2. What are "blood ties" and what is their power? Does being Chinese by blood and family expand or modify what we mean by "self"?

3. Why is Jing Mei reluctant to go to China? What are her fears? How are these fears resolved?

4. What is the meaning of the Polaroid photo at the end of the story? Why does Tan describe it coming into focus?

ANTON CHEKHOV

The Lady with the Dog

For the average student this story does not seem to have immediate appeal, perhaps because the setting seems so unfamiliar, perhaps because it doesn't seem much like a "story." If this objection comes up, you might be able to use it. In what ways do stories perform that this one does not? I try to lead the discussion toward the point that in most stories emotions such as love are explained, defined, understandable, whereas here the love seems simply to happen for no good or obvious reason at all. At this point I try to lead them to move away from fiction and "stories" to their own experience. Can they explain how or why they fell in love with the person they love or loved? Is he or she the most beautiful or handsomest? the most intelligent or kind? the "best" person they have ever met? in real terms, not just in romantic hyperbole? Did the circumstances of their meeting have anything to do with why they fell in love?

If the class is made nervous by the intimacy of such questions, I shift ground and ask if they've ever found themselves in a setting—at the beach, for instance, or in a foreign city—where they felt free to behave in an uncharacteristic manner. (I find if I probe a bit that some students will admit going off to college has offered this kind of liberation.) From this discussion, it is easy to turn back to Gurov and Anna in Yalta and the circumstances of their meeting. Before they meet, what has Gurov been doing with his time? How has Anna spent hers? What are the circumstances of their everyday lives? Both Gurov and Anna seem genuinely, not fashionably bored, both are in Yalta alone, and both have unhappy marriages. You may want to ask your class at what point in their reading did they discovered Yalta was a beautiful place. The descriptions that make the resort sound appealing begin only after the two meet and stroll by the sea. It is as if meeting Anna opens Gurov's eyes to the beauty around him, even though he believes that his relationship with her is nothing special.

To Anna the relationship is from the first something "very special, very serious," a reaction Gurov finds "disconcerting." There are two widely separated scenes in which Gurov sits beside Anna while she suffers. I like to ask students to compare his reactions in the two scenes and account for the differences. How are the connections between the scenes related to the structure of the story? At some point I like to call attention to the four divisions of the story and ask the class to outline briefly what happens in each.

Gurov thinks of Yalta and vacation time as unreal and Moscow and snow as real, yet somehow the unreal becomes his real reality. You might ask your students to speculate about what causes this change in perception—whether Chekhov offers us any clues ahead of time that Gurov's affair with Anna will surprise him.

I have to watch myself in teaching this story because it is one of my two or three favorite stories in the volume, and I cannot let my enthusiasm show too soon. (When I have done so it has the effect of dictating responses, or appearing to do so.) I like this story in part because it surprises convincingly: Gurov begins a routine and even somewhat sordid vacation affair and surprisingly falls in love with Anna. The story does not say why or how, does not show Anna to be in any way remarkable, yet I am convinced that Gurov is in love with her, that love can happen this way and that human actions are often inexplicable, not in any final way to be analyzed or explained.

It does more, too, because it is about more than love. It shows the depths beneath even ordinary experience: it suggests something about the relationship between inner and outer reality (or appearance and reality) and, both in some expository sentences describing the beauty of the world Gurov begins to notice and in the way that Gurov and Anna act and express their feelings toward each other, it suggests that life retains meaning, even in the face of what seems like an indifferent universe.

When Gurov seeks out Anna in S., they stand together in a theater staircase under a sign inscribed "To the upper circle." The allusion to Dante's Inferno seems obvious, if not entirely clear in its implications. Does their meeting present a last chance to avoid the hell of a clandestine relationship, or are they offered no more than a choice between one circle of hell and another (the pain of separation vs. the misery of an affair)? If Gurov and Anna are already imprisoned in one of the lower circles of Hell, what kind of hell might it be? Dante consigned the lustful to the second circle of the inferno, but Chekhov is writing in a different time and culture. His lovers forgive one another instead of seeking absolution from a priest.

Questions for Discussion

1. How does the weather and season described in each section relate to the action? If Gurov's and Anna's affair heats up under the hot sun in Yalta, why doesn't it cool down, as we would expect, in the snow of a Moscow winter?

2. Compare and constrast Gurov's reaction to the pomeranian in Yalta and later in the town of S. where he travels to see Anna. Why are his reactions different?

3. What do you make of the house in S. where Anna lives? What does Gurov make of it?

4. What hope does Gurov hold out for Anna and himself as the story closes? How would you describe the tone of the last two lines?

Writing Assignments for Chapter 4

1. Analyze the photographs in Amy Tan's "A Pair of Tickets." What do they represent? Do photographs represent the same things each time they are men-

tioned in the story? How is the significance of the photographs influenced by setting?

2. Write a personal essay about a) visiting a place in which the prevailing standards and values seemed very different from your own, **or** b) visiting a place that holds significance for an older family member—parent, aunt, uncle, grandparent.

3. Read Flannery O'Connor's "Everything That Rises Must Converge," and write an essay comparing and contrasting the use of the Southern setting in "A Rose for Emily" and "Everything That Rises." What impression of the South do you receive from each story?

4. Write an essay analyzing the treatment of societal values in "A Rose for Emily." Does "A Rose for Emily" affirm the values of Jefferson society? describe them objectively and noncommittally? treat them ironically, critically? nostalgically? Do we need to distinguish between "the story" (that is, Faulkner, or even the reader) and the voice? Is the story obliged to evaluate the narrator's values and those of the society he represents?

5 SYMBOLS

Among the stories in this chapter, "Young Goodman Brown" seems to offer the most straightforward approach to symbolism. The semi-allegorical form employed by Hawthorne tempts the reader to draw simple equations between names or objects and ideas, which is one reason I like to assign this story first. Discussing the allegorical aspects of "Young Goodman Brown" helps to lay the groundwork for exploring the more complicated symbolism of "Janus" and "The Loons." Yet a close analysis of Hawthorne's conditional phrasing can also explode easy assumptions about matching symbol and meaning. After first guiding the class through a fairly narrow allegorical reading of the story (assuming that student comments stay within those bounds), you might want to go on to the other stories in this chapter and then revisit "Young Goodman Brown" afterward, urging the class to look more closely the second time around at the way Hawthorne plays with the allegorical form.

Planning Ideas

- Bring in an American flag, and ask students to imagine what the flag might symbolize to different people in different contexts: a World War I veteran on Veterans Day, a grandmother on the Fourth of July, a teenager at a ball game, a French student protesting NATO exercises, a Russian politician up for reelection, an Iraqui soldier on guard duty at one of his country's borders.
- Assign a straightforward allegory—part of *Everyman* or *Pilgrim's Progress*—along with Hawthorne's **"Young Goodman Brown"** so that students can see more clearly how Hawthorne manipulates the allegorical form for his own purposes.
- Before coming to class, have students . . .
    a. Underline the ambiguous words and phrases in **"Young Goodman Brown"** as a prelude to talking in class about the differences between traditional allegory and the symbolism in Hawthorne's story.
    b. Write a paragraph explaining the symbolic meaning of the bowl in **"Janus*."**
- Before discussing **"Janus"** in class, photocopy and hand out a description of the god Janus (see commentary) or ask students to find out who or what Janus is for themselves and bring a description to class.

NATHANIEL HAWTHORNE

Young Goodman Brown

This deceptively simple story works well in class, I find, and is particularly useful fairly early in an introductory course. There may be a few students who will see none of the allegorical implications and little if any of even the more conventional aspects of the initiation theme. Most, however, will see some of the "clues," and classes often come to life as they pile on detail after detail; even those students who saw nothing at first will get into the act before the discussion is turned to the less obvious elements in the story. There will be an initial sense of accomplishment and contribution, then a deep breath, further discussion, and, one hopes, greater illumination.

The initial stage of the class discussion, if you are lucky, may wind up with something like this: The innocent hero learns that there is evil even in the best of us, that all men are sinners, that we all partake of original sin. This participation in sin is represented in the story by the townspeople's participating at night and in the woods in a satanic version of their daytime religious services and rituals. Salem, the scene of the notorious witch trials, is thus an appropriate setting. Though "goodman" is a title merely meaning "husband," the allegorical weight of "good man" is clearly appropriate; "young" clearly suggests "innocent"; "Brown" is so common a name that, like Tom Jones, perhaps, it can suggest "Everyman." Other events, phrases, objects point to the struggle with evil: when Brown says, "What if the devil himself should be at my very elbow!" the traveler suddenly appears; Goodman says, "Faith kept me back awhile"; the stranger's walking stick has a snake carved on it and looks alive.

The story seems to work best in class when the allegorical reading comes out piecemeal but rather fully and without nagging doubts. If it goes on long enough someone in the class is bound to react, relieving you of the responsibility. There are bothersome details. Why does Faith wear pink ribbons? What's the innocent Brown doing going into the woods at night in the first place? Clearly, he's up to no good, and he even feels guilty about it. So maybe he's not quite so innocent, at least about himself. Why does he undertake the meeting soon, but not immediately, after he's married? Why is it that Faith's participation in the rites is more crushing to him than his father's or even the preacher's?

Students are used to discussions in English class turning to the subject of sex, and clearly that's where this one is leading. It could also lead to the subject of sexism, however, and this might be a good point to distinguish between what a story shows and its attitude toward what it is showing.

Questions for Discussion

1. How can we take seriously, and treat as meaningful for our own problems and experience, a story about Satan and witches and people who

lived a couple hundred years ago and had problems other than our own?

2. Is the story acceptable simply as "allegory," as "message-bearing," or are we more concerned with the questions it raises about human actions and attitudes than with precepts or adages that it might offer?

3. Should this story be read as a straight allegory? What do you make of the conditional language in which the action is sometimes described?

4. If the "sin" has to do with sex and sexuality, and if the hero accepts his own share of sin, no matter how guilty he feels, but is traumatized by seeing his bride's complicity, does all that add up to a sexist attitude? Is the story sexist for showing it or antisexist for doing so?

5. Does it make any difference in your understanding of the story to know that one of Hawthorne's ancestors was a judge involved in the Salem witch trials?

MARGARET LAURENCE

The Loons

While I rarely begin class discussion by focusing on the end of a story, that is where I like to start in talking about "The Loons." I begin with the conclusion because it is only at the end of the narrator's reminiscence about her childhood encounter with Piquette Tonnerre that she explicitly links Piquette with the loons that have vanished from Diamond Lake—"It seemed to me now that in some unconscious and totally unrecognized way, Piquette might have been the only one, after all, who had heard the crying of the loons." The narrator's belated epiphany is expressed in language more poetic than purely logical, thereby forcing us to reach our own conclusions about the kinship she now sees between the lost birds and the lost girl. If, after rereading this passage, students seem ready to speculate about what the narrator means, I let them run with their ideas, pausing only to jot abbreviated versions of what they say on the board and to press for supporting evidence from the text.

However, if the class seems less than surefooted, I ask students to turn back to the passages where the narrator describes the loons, and we construct together a list of characteristics associated with them. The narrator's father has taught her to treasure the loons and to think of them as living vestiges of an ancient and uncivilized past. They are wild and shy and emit a mocking but plaintive cry that seems almost elemental. The narrator's father tells her that when civilization encroaches, loons disappear, and indeed when the narrator returns as an adult to the now heavily developed lake she knew as a child, she is met with a too-quiet silence that tells her the loons have gone.

Usually by the time our list for the loons is complete, several students have begun to talk about the parallels between Piquette and the loons, and I have begun another list on the blackboard for her. Students will note that the narrator's father has taught her to value the loons and that he tries to teach her how to value Piquette, a lesson that she later realizes she could never get right. Like the loons, Piquette is both wild and shy. Like the loons, she seems vulnerable and endangered. In some sense, too, Piquette's characteristic voice is both mocking and plaintive.

Yet in the final line quoted above the narrator refuses to draw a neat parallel between Piquette's situation and that of the loons, and at some point, someone will probably note this. Perhaps this is because Piquette never really has a place in the world of Manawaka, even a precarious one. A child of mixed race, she is neither at home in the wilds, as her native ancestors would have been, nor in the town, where her mixed ancestry makes her an outcast from respectable society. Piquette's struggle to make a place for herself, "a place of belonging" where there is no place, appears doomed from the outset.

Questions for Discussion

1. Why does the narrator feel guilty about Piquette? What do you think she feels guilty about? Do you believe the narrator could have helped Piquette? If so, how?

2. After the narrator hears about the circumstances of Piquette's death, she observes, "I wished I could put from my memory the look that I had seen once in Piquette's eyes." What look was this? What haunts the narrator about this look?

3. Why was Diamond Lake renamed? Why do you think the narrator notes this detail?

4. What would Piquette think of the narrator's final statement?

5. Margaret Laurence had a life-long concern for native peoples who are oppressed. How is her concern conveyed in this story? Is Laurence's portrait of the Tonnerre clan helpful or hurtful to Canadian people of mixed race? Why?

ANN BEATTIE

Janus

Like "My Friend Judith," this is a story that resists simple answers and tidy interpretation. It is also a story without a plot. Before you tackle the one hundred-million-dollar question—"what on earth does that bowl represent?"—you might want to ask the class the same question that sometimes comes up with "My Friend Judith" —whether "Janus" really qualifies as a short story. Does something actually have to happen in a short story, or can something else substitute for action?

Some students are uncomfortable with the story because it lacks a traditional plot, but I find many more who are disturbed by what we might call its symbolic latitude. We are never able to state with finality, "The bowl represents X," nor are we able to say with any real assurance what we are to think of the Andrea, the protagonist. Students sense that the bowl symbolizes something about Andrea and the life she has chosen, but many will be frustrated in their attempts to move beyond that basic observation. Those who have managed some comparisons may be hard pressed to pull them together coherently. If the class has discussed "Young Goodman Brown," you might get things rolling by asking students to compare the way symbols operate in each story.

Clearly Beattie's story is more oblique. While the bowl is described, it remains essentially mysterious to its owner and to us. (I like to suggest at some point in the discussion that with a different ending Janus could have been turned into "The Story of the Magic Bowl: A Modern Fairy Tale.") The impersonal third-person narration tells us something about the bowl, what it looks like, how people react to it. We also learn something about Andrea and the way she feels about the bowl, but when we try to set up parallels between the two, we flounder. While the narrative offers information of apparent significance (the bowl is cream-colored, like some flesh; Andrea believes it "was meant to be empty"; she has "never talked to her husband about the bowl"; she has had an affair), it is remarkably free of indicators about which pieces of information are important. We need a reference point or some voice of authority to tell us what to pay attention to.

After we establish that Janus lacks the reference points and relatively clear parallels Hawthorne offers in "Young Goodman Brown," I like to ask the class if Janus offers reference points of another sort. Are there elements in the story that seem more significant than others, elements that might be used at least as guides to reading, if not keys? I think there are at least two—the title of the story and our delayed discovery that the bowl is the present of Andrea's former lover— and with a little probing, a bright class will come up with them.

It seems to me noteworthy that Beattie never mentions Janus in the story itself. (Andrea's lover calls her "two-faced," but he doesn't use the term in the way that it's commonly used: to label one who is deceptive.) The title remains "outside" the narrative, and it is up to us to establish its connection with the tale. We've got to fill in the blanks. For this, a little background may be in order, and you may want to give your students something like the following description on a handout so they can consider possible applications:

> Janus was the Roman door god, and each ancient Roman household had its own Janus. The Romans thought there were gods everywhere and in everything and that the most important feature of successful living was getting along with these myriad gods. Good relations with the gods was known as the pax decorum, and the Roman politician / literatus / philosopher Cicero could claim, quite seriously, that the Romans owed their success in conquering the world to their exceptional care in religious matters.

The Roman state also had a temple in the forum dedicated to the god Janus that was open when they were at war (most of the time) and closed (rarely) when they were at peace. It was the "religious door" of the Roman people and the Roman state. As the door god, Janus was also, appropriately, a god of beginnings, transitions, and even of exclusion. Hence, the month January, the first month, the month of transition, is named after Janus. Janus was conventionally depicted with two faces pointed in opposite directions (going in the door and going out). By extension, someone who was perceived to be "two-faced," duplicitous, or deceptive came to be called a Janus.

The second element students will want to consider—the narrator's revelation that the bowl is a gift from a lover—is significant not only because it provides an emotional background, if you will, for the bowl, but also because the narrator so clearly saves this piece of information for last. We feel, whether it is true or not, that this is the piece of the puzzle we've been waiting for.

At some point you might want to get students talking about how Andrea uses the bowl in the first part of the story to manipulate potential real estate buyers. It is one of the "tricks" she uses to "convince a buyer that the house is quite special." It is a deceptive practice, but one we may not think too much about until the word "trick" pops up again near the end of the story (and until we ponder the title). I like to ask the class what is different about the way the word "trick" is used the second time. In the first instance, the real estate tricks are cited simply as common practice, and Andrea is portrayed as one who uses them with exceptional success. In the second instance, such practices appear to have convinced Andrea that she lives in a world where you can't trust anything to be the way it seems—"a world where people set plants where they did not belong, so that visitors touring a house would be fooled into thinking that dark corners got sunlight—a world of tricks." Ironically, her own deceptions have made her profoundly mistrustful of the rest of the world.

In the paragraph immediately following, we discover that Andrea has participated in another kind of deception. Several years earlier she has had an affair—judging from the details, a fairly extended one that must have required her to deceive her husband repeatedly. In leaving Andrea, her lover hopes to "shatter her intransigent ideas about honoring previous commitments." I like to ask students whether they think Andrea has a real commitment left to honor. How close does Andrea seem to her husband? Has she already broken her commitment to him by having the affair? How completely should we trust the lover's assumptions about Andrea? Is she "always too slow to know what she really loved," as he has told her, or does she simply find it hard to love? Is she "two-faced" in the sense of being pulled in two directions, as he seems to think, or is she simply deceptive?

At this point, I like to go back to Andrea's relationship with the bowl and ask the students to characterize it. They usually mention that she says she loves the bowl, that she is obsessed with keeping it safe, that she even compares the experience of leaving it behind for a few minutes to a parent forgetting a child. In the second paragraph after the section break in the middle of the story Andrea tries to analyze her feelings toward the bowl and becomes confused. I like to ask students what else she expresses confusion about in that paragraph. Someone will always note that she's at least as confused about her marriage ("people who lived together and loved each other . . . But was that always so clear, always a relationship?") as she is about the bowl. The bowl is always kept empty, and Andrea doesn't let her husband put his keys in it. (If you want to go Freudian at this juncture, I think the story invites it. Empty bowl = empty womb / woman = empty heart / life, and so forth.) If Andrea believes she loves this bowl, then what is her definition of love? (As we've already noted, Andrea is disturbed about this question herself.) What is the difference between loving a person and loving an object?

It may be, as I have suggested in the introduction, that the bowl symbolizes the empty half-life Andrea has without her lover, that she has somehow transfered her love for him to the bowl he gave her, that she cannot talk to her husband about the bowl, not only because her feelings about it are tied up with her former lover but because her response to the bowl is so complex and mysterious. Andrea, we are told, is attracted to ironies, but her husband grows "more impatient and dismissive when matters [become] many sided or unclear." On the other hand, a less romantic interpretation might be that Andrea is a deceiver—perhaps even a self-deceived deceiver. Incapable of real love, loyalty or commitment, she attracts people (a husband, a lover) as the bowl attracts admirers, but she remains essentially untouched, "smoothly empty," safe and alone.

Questions for Discussion

1. If the bowl is a symbol, what does it symbolize? How many possibilities can you come up with?

2. What is your view of Andrea's marriage? Does the fact the she has had an affair mean that she doesn't value her husband? Why do you think she refuses to choose her lover over her husband?

3. What symbolic significance would you attach to each of the gifts Andrea receives from her lover?

4. How should we interpret the ending of "Janus"?

Writing Assignments for Chapter 5

1. Read *Pilgrim's Progress* and explain the differences between Bunyan's use of allegory and Hawthorne's.

2. Analyze the symbolism of the sweatshirt Andrea receives from her lover.

3. After reading "The Loons," write a personal essay about someone you avoid because his or her appearance or behavior embarrasses you.

6 THEME

Somewhere along the way, many students have gotten the impression that reading literature is a bit like panning for gold. You sift through the work looking for bright glints of meaning. When you find the meaning, the gold at the bottom of the pan, you extract it and tuck it safely away—maybe in a quiz or exam; then you dump the rest of the story or poem out like so much sand into a riverbed and move on. To disabuse students of this notion, it is sometimes helpful to return to a work taken up earlier in the course for a brief discussion of themes. If your class has read "Sonny's Blues," for example, constructing a list of even a half-dozen themes will not be difficult, but the list will probably fail to satisfy everyone as an appropriate distillation of the story's meaning. It shouldn't take much prompting from you—"What important things about 'Sonny's Blues' are missing from this list?" I sometimes ask—for someone to complain that none of the elements that make Baldwin's story so profoundly moving and absorbing are on the list. Other stories that work well for this exercise include "The Country Husband," "Fenstad's Mother," "My Friend Judith," and "A Pair of Tickets." This approach works best with a stories that students like and have responded to on multiple levels.

Planning Ideas

- Assign **"A Souvenir of Japan*"** to be read along with Atwood's **"Happy Endings"** and Cortázar's **"Blow-Up*"**—other stories that call attention to the process of writing fiction and imagining stories.
- Divide the class into four groups. Ask one group of students to bring to class a one-sentence statement of the theme(s) of **"Her First Ball."** Ask one group to bring in a two-sentence statement, another to bring a three-sentence statement, and the other to bring in a four-sentence statement of theme. Work through the statements, using elements from student contributions, to gradually create a complex statement of the themes of the story. Then discuss what important aspects of the story are left out. This exercise—like the one suggested in the headnote—can help to combat the misconception that a story's theme is simply a one-line moral or message that one extracts from the interaction of characters and events.
- Have students bring to class a one-page description of the souvenirs they imagine the narrator of **"A Souvenir of Japan*"** taking away with her after she leaves the country. Encourage them to think in both concrete and abstract terms.

LEO TOLSTOY

How Much Land Does a Man Need?

What do you mean, Leo, that all a man (or person) needs is six feet of land (or seven—another title for the story is "Three Arshins of Land" and an arshin or archine is twenty-eight inches)? I guess that's true if all you're concerned about is dying and being buried (though come to think of it, you don't even need that—you could be cremated). But suppose you're interested in living. Then how much land does a person need? Probably more than forty acres and a mule, wouldn't you say? Probably less than the hundred square miles or so that Pahom seemed after—if by need you mean enough farmland to supply a family with food, shelter, and a modest income. So it comes down to what you mean by need. This is the way a discussion might begin. Then again, it might not. But the point is that, although I made Tolstoy's theme and parable sound pretty simple, it is not quite so simple.

You might want to take off from this point on the difference between need and greed. The desire to have enough income to support a family in modest comfort is, no doubt, admirable; the desire to want more and more, to work yourself to death for material possessions is foolish, life-denying or -destroying, sinful. The last term is the most appropriate to the details of the story, for here the instigator of greed is the devil himself. You may want to ask whether there is a secular equivalent to the devil here, whether property or income or material-ism itself engenders the desire for more . . . and more. You may also want to ask your students if they have ever been guilty of avarice. They may even be able to describe their own bedevilment.

Material wealth as land and need as burial plot work very well to define the distinction between material and spiritual need. Is there some way we can incar-nate this distinction in terms appropriate to our materialist consumerism? How Many Ferraris Does a Person Need? somehow does not seem to make it. Perhaps an exercise or contest seeking such a term would bring home to difficulties and triumphs of finding precisely the right symbol to carry the meaning, suggestion, tone, and effect we want.

I asked in the text about the country-mouse / city-mouse discussion that begins this tale. You may want to use it to compare to the Rainsford / Whitney dialogue at the beginning of "The Most Dangerous Game": both seem to set up the theme, and the women, like Whitney, disappear from the story. (Is the Con-nell story, then, also a parable?) You may want to point out, however, that the initial scene here actually causes the events that follow when Pahom, overhear-ing the conversation, tempts the devil. On the other hand, you may want to use it to show how Tolstoy universalizes the theme: the urban, commercial life is often compared unfavorably with agrarian life, the former being competitive and materialistic, the latter hard but serene and more "moral." This is not the comparison that is made in the opening scene of the story, the tradesman's life being described as temporarily—but only temporarily—more affluent, but riskier. The story locates competition, greed, and risk in the agrarian world and incarnates materialism in the most stable of material values—land (always, grandparents say, the safest investment). Tolstoy makes materialism part of the human condition, not that of a particular kind or aspect of society, justifying the presence of cosmic evil, the devil, rather than "merely" social evil, as its agent.

Questions for Discussion

1. What does Pahóm mean when he says, "If I had plenty of land, I shouldn't fear the Devil himself"? What does land represent to him?

2. At the end of section II, Pahóm is happy. Why does he become unhappy in section III? Can you imagine an analogous situation occurring in modern life? (For example, what additional worries do you have if you purchase a new car instead of driving an old car? What is the "down side" to living in a mansion?)

3. How many different kinds of temptation does Pahóm succumb to in the course of the story?

KATHERINE MANSFIELD

Her First Ball

Like "Young Goodman Brown," this is a rather subtle story that at first appears to be quite simple and obvious. The apparent initiation is rather conventional: time flies, youth is fleeting, or, as Leila wonders to herself, "Was this first ball only the beginning of her last ball after all?" Even eighteen-year-old students may respond to the passage of time—remember how long summers were when you were nine?

Neither the story nor Leila stops there, of course. The music starts again, a young man asks her to dance, and she is once more enthralled. Youth may respond to thoughts of the ephemeral nature of our lives, but it is swept up again by living in the moment as if that moment will go on forever.

What seems to be the attitude of the story toward Leila's shaking off serious thoughts? Are we to see her as blithely vacant, incapable of taking the older man's warning to heart? Is she merely young and vibrant—after all, what can be gained by sitting around lamenting that time is passing by? These questions may be interesting in themselves, but they are also interesting in terms of the focus and voice. We see in the story only what Leila sees, and hers are the only inner thoughts we're privy to. Clearly some of the language that is not in quotation marks is nonetheless hers ("Oh, how marvelous to have a brother!" for example). Are there words and expressions that seem not to be hers? What is the effect of keeping the story entirely or almost entirely within her mind, eyes, and range of knowledge and emotions? Does it help us to judge her responses? Does it shift emphasis and attention to some aspect other than the questions about youth and seriousness raised earlier? This might be one of those stories in which all or part may be rewritten from another point of view—say, that of the elderly partner, or a more "omniscient" view.

You might want to use this story also to discuss the possibility of distinguishing the attitudes of the characters and the society from those of the author.

Questions for Discussion

1. Why—some students, particularly some women students, may ask—are male initiations in terms of hunting or sailing or journeys or incidents in the "real" or "outside" world, while female initiations are most often presented in terms of such trivialities as dances and other social occasions?

2. Is it the writer, male or female, who is to blame, or is this the material his or her (sexist) society gives the writer to work with?

ANGELA CARTER

A Souvenir of Japan

Since students are sometimes unsure what to make of this story—another of those about which someone is likely to complain "nothing happens"—I like to open discussion by mentioning the narrator's confidence that she can read her lover's thoughts and that she understands his motivations. Sometimes I introduce the topic directly, asking if students take the narrator's word for what is going on in her lover's mind. Sometimes I simply read paragraph five aloud and ask for reactions. Students who have had romantic relationships, as well as those who haven't, will recognize in the narrator the not uncommon tendency to interpret a loved one's unspoken thoughts. And while sensitivity to another's wishes is laudable, she seems to go overboard. I ask students to consider what circumstances might drive the narrator so thoroughly to supply desires, motivations, and excuses for her lover. Is he uncommunicative? Is she trying to create a story to justify her involvement with him? Is she supplying reasons for his behavior that, while disturbing, are not as disturbing as other possibilities? (For me, these are real questions.)

The narrator of the story is a Caucasian woman who has been involved for at least a year with a Japanese man several years her junior. On the face of it, the relationship seems to offer her very little, so I like to ask students what they think of the relationship as she reports it and why they think she has stayed in it. What is the attraction of her Japanese lover for the narrator?

The lover, as the narrator portrays him, appears to use her only for sex—and that in an apartment she pays for. She says he fancies they have a unique and sublime passion, but he spends much of his time at night away from her, never lets her know if or when he's coming home, and seems to take her out only from a sense of duty. He emerges from her description seeming like a sullen, bored adolescent. The narrator provides no evidence of shared interests or experience, no suggestion that their interactions—sexual or conversational—are especially passionate. In fact, strong undertones of resentment at the beginning of the story become overtones by the end. And yet there is something almost magically obsessive about her attraction to this young man and—again, as she describes it—about his for her.

What *is* the attraction here? If comments are not forthcoming, I like to call attention to the paragraph beginning "Sometimes he seemed to possess a curiously unearthly quality . . ." If part of the attraction of one gender for the other is an attraction to "difference," then perhaps there can be a particular *frisson* of pleasure to be derived from extreme difference—from the exotic, the "other" who is very much of another world. Students may note that the narrator describes her lover as appearing "almost goblin," seeming like "a weird visitor." And this alien quality is clearly desirable to her, for at the end of her extended physical description of him she says she would like to "have had him embalmed and been able to keep him . . . in a glass coffin." (You may want to pause over this statement and ask students to do a little psychological analysis!)

A friend of mine who has long been married to a man from a culture very different from her own believes that people who are attracted to such unions don't want to get too close to their mates. They are people who value their privacy and who find cultural and linguistic barriers to intimacy reassuring. I tell students what my friend has observed and ask them whether the story provides any support for her theory. Certainly the Japanese lover appears to have little interest in knowing the narrator or being known by her. What about the narrator's desire to know and be known?

As I suggested earlier, the narrator's undertones of dissatisfaction early in the story seem to come to the fore as the story progresses. What complaints are mentioned? Students will notice that the narrator's benign descriptions of Japanese life give way to more critical comments as the story nears its conclusion. I ask them to what degree they believe these dissatisfactions with the country are primarily dissatisfactions with her lover. Can the two be separated? Are the narrator's criticisms of Japanese life fair? (Is it possible to find neutral ground from which a culture can be criticized?)

Depending on the way you are using this story, you may want to wait until late—as I have—to talk about the "writerly" issues that emerge near the end, or you may want to discuss these issues much earlier. Near the conclusion of her narrative the speaker reveals that she has fabricated the name Taro for her lover and made up the story about Momotaro, the peach baby. She also says that she doesn't want to provide "enough well-rounded, spuriously detailed actuality that you are forced to believe in [the story's characters]." She means to offer only "glimpses of outlines." I ask students whether they believe these observations constitute a statement on the way the narrator thinks fiction should operate—or just the way she wants this particular story to operate. If students believe the statements are general ones about the way the narrator thinks fiction should work, I ask them to restate the narrator's view of her role as writer in their own words. Then I ask whether the same statements might also tell us something about the narrator's interactions with others—whether these statements might not also suggest an unwillingness to be known—or to be known only in outline. Or perhaps the narrator means to suggest that—however we wish to write, or however well we wish to be known—the reality is that we can only be known in "glimpses of our outlines"—whether we share with our readers and lovers the same gender and culture and language or not.

Questions for Discussion

1. Does it make any difference that the narrator is a woman instead of a man? Is it only a stereotype, or does it seem true that women pay more attention to nonverbal signals and are more likely to seek clues from these signals about the thoughts and motives of those close to them? Is the attempt to read another's thoughts a positive or a negative thing?

2. If the narrator is attracted to her lover partially because he is exotic to her, is there also some pleasure for her in being exotic to him? of being an exotic in the culture? Are there elements of pain involved as well?

3. In talking about gender bias in Japan, the narrator observes, "At least they do not disguise the situation. At least one knows where one is." What do you make of this observation? Does it provide another possible reason for the narrator's attraction to Japan and to her lover?

4. How much of what the narrator says about her lover and his wishes and motivations might also be applied to her?

5. What do you make of the story of the peach baby? of the narrator's description of the old, senile woman placed outside the shop in her neighborhood each day?

6. What does the title suggest about the future of the narrator's love affair? Does the narrator suggest a reason or reasons she might leave her lover and leave the country?

Writing Assignments for Chapter 6

1. Compare Tolstoy's treatment of the craving for wealth in "How Much Land Does a Man Need?" and Lawrence's in "The Rocking-Horse Winner."

2. Write a personal essay describing three items that you don't really need to survive but that you feel you need in order to (1) keep up with your friends, (2) maintain your sense of self-respect, and / or (3) be happy. Evaluate your "need" for these objects. In what sense(s) do you need them?

3. Write a personal essay about the first time that you realized that the pleasures of growing up come inextricably packaged with the pains of growing up.

4. Compare Carter's handling of the conflicts between people of different cultures in "A Souvenir of Japan" with Mukherjee's in "The Management of Grief."

7 THE WHOLE TEXT

The focus of this chapter is on the whole text—the way the elements of fiction we've been talking about in isolation fit together and make up a whole that is somehow more than the sum of its parts. Each story—"The Secret Sharer," Love Medicine," and "The Watcher"—is sufficiently complex to reward more than one class period's worth of study, and I generally allow a longer period of discussion than usual for at least one of them. As a departure from my procedure with earlier stories, sometimes I begin discussion by talking about the interplay between certain words or images in a given work—about the network of associations that establish a story's meanings and effects: the references to watching or snooping in "The Watcher" that tie into scenes involving sexuality and / or violence, for example; or the series of anecdotes involving the nexus of love, death, magic, and a "higher power" in "Love Medicine."

Planning Ideas

- "The Secret Sharer," "Love Medicine," and "The Watcher*" are placed in the text where they are because any of the three stories would work beautifully as part of a number of different chapters. For example, each would fit nicely into the chapter on initiation that follows. "Love Medicine" would of course work equally well in Chapter 2 on point of view, Chapter 5 on symbols, or Chapter 9, on cultural contexts.
- Since Guy Vanderhaeghe's "The Watcher" has certain affinities with Flannery O'Connor's fiction, pair "The Watcher" with the O'Connor stories for a week-long comparative study, paying particular attention to dramatic irony and the characters' use of key phrases that attain heightened meaning as the stories unfold.
- "Love Medicine" is in one guise a short story, in another part of a novel. All the characters in the story have histories in the novel. You might want to assign the novel and open up a can of worms called "When Is a Story a Story?" How independent are stories? *Love Medicine* forms one kind of whole of which "Love Medicine" is a part; "The Country Husband" appears in an interrelated volume of stories—not a novel—entitled *The Housebreaker of Shady Hill.* All stories are part of an author's canon. What are the boundaries? This discussion might lead neatly into Chapter 8.
- Before class discussion of "The Secret Sharer," "Love Medicine," or "The Watcher," ask students to locate and then diagram (in whatever way each finds most appropriate) a pattern of images or a series of related statements that they believe are vital to the meaning of the whole text. Have

two or three students reproduce their diagrams on the blackboard and explain them. Use these presentations as a starting point for talking about how issues of character, theme, symbol, point of view, etc., interrelate.

JOSEPH CONRAD

The Secret Sharer

Depending on the personality of the class and how closely I believe they've been reading, I sometimes open discussion of "The Secret Sharer" by calling three or four people up to the blackboard to draw the layout of the captain's cabin, his bath, and the saloon. (If, following the arrangement of the text, the class has been reading a number of fairly heavy, serious selections, this can be a way to lighten the mood—even though "The Secret Sharer" itself is not an especially light story. If your class is anything like mine, you will get some amusing blueprints. Once the drawings are complete, you can ask members of the class to critique them, using their texts as guides.) The exercise is not meant to suggest, by the way, that one has to "know" the captain's cabin to understand the story, although certainly knowledge of the cabin arrangement contributes to the narrative suspense. I use it to call attention to Conrad's careful handling of detail and to remind the class how attentively they must read if they are make sense of this rather long and somewhat difficult story.

In some ways "The Secret Sharer" is an old-fashioned, straightforward narrative, a simple chronology of events told by a veteran ship's captain, who recounts the story of his first voyage in command. His description of setting and character, his recreations of dialogue and thought seem clear, vivid, and meticulous. I sometimes ask my students if they find anything surprising about this. Why might the captain remember this particular journey so explicitly? I also like to ask them if they are surprised that the voice and focus of the story (the seasoned veteran looking back on the adventures of his younger self) impinges upon the narrative as little as it does. Don't we expect the older narrator to reveal more about how we should judge the story he's telling us than he does? Why does the narrator do so little of this?

Despite its apparent simplicity and clarity of presentation, "The Secret Sharer" is a complex and morally ambiguous work. Students usually come to class eager, not to draw the layout of the captain's cabin, but to grapple with the moral and psychological issues the story offers. Since I want to channel this eagerness, I start discussion pretty near square one. (I find that the length of the story and the seeming simplicity of the "double" motif sometimes encourages students to read skimmingly and to jump to interpretive conclusions without basing them firmly in evidence.) I like to ask them, harking back to a question posed in the text headnote, if the opening section of the story provides any clues to the nature of the problems that lie ahead for the protagonist. Because I want the class to piece together in some fairly systematic way the details that inform their interpretations, I often write these "clues" on the blackboard as the class comes up with them.

Frequently the first comment they offer is that the setting evokes a sense of stillness, isolation, and profound loneliness. Someone will mention the fact that the narrator is a stranger to the ship—and that he has confessed to being "somewhat of a stranger" to himself. Someone else—often a student familiar with other Conrad works—will remark that the words "mysterious" and "crazy" create anticipatory caution. Generally we also discuss the last sentence of the opening section in which the narrator makes clear that he viewed the voyage as a personal challenge and a test of character. (I sometimes mention the opening of *David Copperfield* and use the stated focus of David's narrative—"Whether I shall turn out to be the hero of my own life, or whether that station will be held by anybody else . . . "—as a point of comparison.) If it doesn't come up in discussion, I also call attention to the fact that the narrator seems to feel that everyone is watching and judging him: his new officers, even the stars in the sky. (After we've completed our list, I ask students to check their assumptions against the rest of the narrative to confirm that the intimations of the opening are borne out in the rest of the story.) Then, keeping in mind the aspects of the narrator's situation listed before us, we're ready to tackle the secret sharer and his mysterious influence over the narrator.

I find that using the list on the blackboard, we can move pretty swiftly through the more obvious aspects of the story, outlining the similarities between the captain and his secret guest (size, age, training, sense of etiquette, position as strangers aboard their respective ships . . .); the nature of the captain's situation that prompts him to identify with Leggatt and hide him (his loneliness, his lack of self-confidence, his lack of leadership experience . . .); and the consequences of the captain's "decision" to hide Leggatt (profound uneasiness, the sense of having a divided self, questioning his own sanity . . .). Then I ask the class what effect Leggatt's visit has on the captain. Does the experience leave him a better or worse captain? a better or worse man?

In terms of the action of the story, the narrator is successful, a hero. He pulls off the trick of hiding Leggatt until he gets the fugitive close enough to shore to swim safely away from the ship (no mean feat), and he executes a dangerous maneuver the crew did not believe he could complete without wrecking the ship, thereby proving his skill. In terms of pure narrative, the story reaches a satisfying closure. Leggatt is not recaptured by the captain of the Sephora or discovered by the crew of the ship where he hides. He escapes to the life he has chosen, and the captain sails on with his ship, having gained confidence in his ability to command it. I like to ask the class if the ending answers all their questions about the action of the story. Then I ask if the ending answers all their questions about the meaning of the story and the story's moral perspective. In some sense the captain has passed his test, but we are still left wondering whether he has lived up to the "ideal conception" of himself mentioned in the opening section. In fact, we are also left wondering what his ideal conception was. The narrator never tells us, so that the story resists moral closure, even if in some ways it reaches a satisfactory conclusion on other levels.

You may want to ask your students how Conrad injects this element of moral ambiguity into the story. A number of answers may surface. The nature of Leggatt's crime is one area of ambiguity. You might ask students to prepare a defense for him, imagining him brought before, as he says, "an old fellow in a wig and twelve respectable tradesmen." While it is clear Leggatt strangled a man on board the *Sephora*, one could argue that the circumstances mitigated the crime. After all, if what Leggatt reported was true, his rapid, instinctive action saved the *Sephora* when her captain was too frightened to give orders. The man he killed ignored naval discipline during a horrific storm, and when Leggatt (his superior officer) struck him down, out of the way, the man jumped up and made it a fight. (You may want to call attention to how often Leggatt is associated with instinctive, almost animal action. For example, he says if the *Sephora*'s crew had tried to haul him back "Somebody would have got killed for certain" and he "did not want any of that," but his comment makes clear he'd have killed again, however much he might have regretted it. He is, figuratively, the body; the young captain the head.)

Another troubling aspect of the story is the young captain's almost immediate willingness to side with Leggatt—not only to see the crime his way, but to act as if he understands and sympathizes with Leggatt's action before he's spent even an hour with the man or heard his version of the story (" 'Fit of temper,' I suggested confidently"). We can understand from a psychological perspective why the young captain allies himself with the stranger. You may want to ask your students whether it is appropriate or right that he does so.

Closely linked with this question is the issue of the captain's responsibility as the leader of a ship. Once the captain of the *Sephora* comes aboard and is allowed to leave without Leggatt, the narrator commits himself to keeping Leggatt hidden and helping him to escape. Clearly the strain of this commitment drives him nearly crazy. I like to suggest to the class that he is torn between his duty to his crew and his impulse to help Leggatt. I like to suggest this and then hope that someone will argue with me because it seems that another disturbing thing about the captain's story is that he's not consciously torn between two loyalties. He simply identifies with and sides with Leggatt as a matter of course. Just before he helps Leggatt to escape, he realizes helping him may end his own career. Just after he maneuvers the ship near land, he realizes he doesn't know the ship well enough to insure they can avoid shipwreck. But these are not issues he ponders. He seems willing to sacrifice himself and his crew to get Leggatt, not just within swimming distance of land, but as close as possible.

Questions for Discussion

1. To what do you attribute the narrator's successes at the end of the story? Skill? Luck? The "righteousness" of his cause? To what does the narrator attribute his success?

2. Does Conrad point to a moral in this story? If so, what is it?

LOUISE ERDRICH

Love Medicine

It is virtually impossible to talk about this story without discussing its narrator, Lipsha Morrissey, so I like to start by asking the class to characterize him. To the traits mentioned in the text—his kind heart, lack of education, thoughtfulness, naiveté, unintentional wisdom, etc.—which will come up immediately, you might ask students to add what they know of Lipsha's biography. According to Grandma Kashpaw, Lipsha's mother didn't want him, and so he's an orphan of sorts, a "took-in" like some of the other children Grandma and Grandpa Kashpaw have reared. Lipsha is at least part Chippewa, in his mid-to-late teens (having flunked out of school previous to the time of the narrative), and up until the time of the story, he appears to have spent many of his days playing video machines, killing time ("the thing I been training for all my life . . . is to wait"), and occasionally putting "the touch" on people.

"Love Medicine" sometimes confuses students because it seems to mix serious topics and comic topics indiscriminately and because Lipsha's voice assures that no somber subject will come across to us entirely "straight." In talking about Lipsha's "voice," you might want to ask students how many malapropisms, solecisms, and colorful colloquialisms they can come up with. At what points in the story does Lipsha's unintentionally humorous language undercut the seriousness of a scene he's trying to convey soberly? (My favorite example is when he mournfully commands his grandfather's ghost to "Go back" beyond the "wall of death," then whispers, "Look up Aunt June.") Does Lipsha's comic narrative prevent us from taking the story seriously? If not, why not?

Lipsha says that his grandfather told him he'd been "chosen" for his second childhood and "couldn't say no." I like to ask my students to respond to this statement. Does Grandpa really have any control over his increasing senility? Why might he say such a thing to Lipsha? You may want to ask what kind of world we have entered when a statement like Grandpa's is reported uncritically. (Lipsha believes Grandpa made the choice. He only questions briefly whether Grandpa knew what he was doing by saying yes to the "call.") It may be well to take a few minutes to discuss the cultural and social milieau of Lipsha, Grandma, Grandpa, Lulu Lamartine, and the others: their mixture of tribal belief, Catholicism, and superstition, their poverty, their history of hardship, and their lack of education.

And yet "Love Medicine" isn't really a story about oppression or failure, though both topics surface. Despite poverty, alcoholism, exploitation by whites, and the decimation of their tribe through white disease ("outfight germ warfare"), some of Chippewa blood have endured and succeeded. Many of the children the Kashpaws have reared—blood kin and "took-ins"—return from the funeral to jobs that are "numerous and impressive."

"Love Medicine" is a story about love and grief and death and magic and searching for "Higher Power." Many of the anecdotes of the story (Lulu's experience with the parakeet, Grandma's prediction about the car wreck, the story of Wristwatch) and the central story of Lipsha's efforts to create a love medicine are narratives about love (or sex) and death. I like to call students' attention to the many spiritual references that accrete in the course of the story—the anecdote about Grandpa yelling his prayers because he believes God is going deaf, Lipsha's references to reading the Bible, his attempt to have the turkey hearts blessed, his inadvertent reference to the "paraclete" instead of the parakeet. I ask them why these stories are part of the narrative, what they contribute to the theme. All suggest the human need for some sort of help and the search for some sort of consolation with which to confront the hardships of life and the mysteries of death.

Lipsha tries to cure Grandma's grief by concocting a "love medicine" that will bring her straying husband back to her side. This may be the time to ask your students to talk about the other ways the title can be interpreted. Whether or not tribal magic is effective, whether or not God listens, in this story of the Higher Power, the one thing one can count on is love. Love embodied in the Kashpaws rears a family of children, all of whom are "wanted," whoever or wherever some of their parents may be. Love draws these grown children back from their numerous and impressive careers to mourn the passing of Grandpa. (As Lipsha suggests, their common grief—an expression of their common love— gives them a "rock" or anchor in time of trouble.) Love in the shape of Lipsha tries, however ineptly, to cure Grandpa's waywardness. And love, through Lipsha, comforts Grandma when Grandpa dies.

Near the end of the story, Lipsha observes that "Your life feels different on you, once you greet death and understand your heart's position." You might want to ask your students what Lipsha means—and what love and death have to do with one another in this story. You might also want to ask what they think Lipsha is suggesting when he says of his life, "you have the feeling someone wore it before you and someone will after."

Whether or not we're supposed to believe in the magical / mystical things that Lipsha believes in (and I think Erdrich leaves this issue open), what are we to make of the conclusion to the story? After Grandma listens to Lipsha's confession, she puts her rosary beads inside his hand and clasps her hands tightly around his. It is clearly a gesture of love; it may also be a gesture of blessing. When she releases his hand, he goes outside to do what his grandfather used to do—weed dandelions. There, feeling the sun on his back like a "hand," the "touch" seems to come back to him, and instead of healing others, it seems to heal him. (If the "touch" is magical, it is also the touch of love and concern. No wonder those Lipsha treats feel better.) As he pulls up the weeds he observes, "with every root I prized up there was return." What does he mean by this? One answer is that he realizes the seeds of the dandelions will assure their "return" in a season—that the life of even the uprooted dandelions will go on. Another answer might be that in some sense his grandpa's life / love continues through him because all loving life is, like the globe of seeds, "frail," but "indestructible." These suggestions by no means exhaust the possibilities of the conclusion. I find that students are eager to discuss other parallels between Lipsha's life and the way he describes the dandelions.

Questions for Discussion

1. What does Lipsha mean when he observes at the funeral "how strong and reliable grief was, and death." What does he mean when he says "death would be our rock?"

2. How do you think we are to respond to the magical / mystical aspects of Erdrich's story? What are they part of the story? Does Erdrich expect us to believe that Lipsha has a healing touch? that Grandma can predict the future?

3. Is this a comic story or a tragic one? Explain your answer.

4. Why do you think Erdrich chooses to tell this story through Lipsha? How might it be different if it were told from another perspective? through another character?

GUY VANDERHAEGHE

The Watcher

"The Watcher" is, among other things, an initiation story. As is true of most initiations, the one Charlie goes through the summer he is eleven reveals the world to be a nastier and harsher place than it had been for him theretofore. A good place to start discussion is with Charlie's voice. I might ask students to what degree the language and attitude of the narrator are a re-creation of the language and attitudes of the eleven-year-old Charlie—and to what degree they are a reflection of the older and wiser Charlie of years later. Charlie is a character with whom many students are reluctant to sympathize. "He's a peeping Tom," they say. "He's spoiled." "He doesn't care about anyone but himself." In a story as long as this one, students may lose track of some elements, so in response to the criticism of Charlie that usually arises, I like to call their attention to a couple of passages that indicate that the older Charlie recognizes some of the weaknesses of his younger self. (One occurs in the section of the story shortly after he arrives at the farm, with the paragraph beginning "Most days it was so hot that the very idea of fun boiled out of me and evaporated." Another occurs near the end of the story, when the narrator explains his unwillingness to identify the Ogden brothers on Thompson's behalf in the paragraph beginning "He had no business begging me.")

Once we've established who Charlie is and the perspective from which the story is being told, we can begin looking at what happens to him during his eleventh summer. While Charlie's father tries to make the prospect of a summer with his grandmother seem enticing, the reality is not very appealing. The farm turns out to be a ramshackle operation with not one hoped-for dog or pony but only a few chickens and a nervous rooster. His father's car hasn't yet faded from view when Grandma lets Charlie know she's willing to "belt" him if he misbehaves. His grandmother's profanity, her disrespect for his mother, and her apparent lack of concern for his comfort and entertainment are all a shock. Until recently, Charlie has been a much-favored mama's boy. But Charlie's real initiation doesn't begin until Aunt Evelyn and her boyfriend Thompson show up.

Most of the important webs of the story after this arrival are revealed in a series of observation or "snooping" scenes. It may be helpful for students to make a list of the various things Charlie sees and hears that he is not supposed to know about. Working from this list, students will be able to identify some common threads in each of the scenes and recognize that all of them involve a sex / violence / power nexus of some sort. By snooping, Charlie learns that his aunt, according to her mother, has "elevator panties." Charlie also witnesses Thompson's abuse of Aunt Evelyn while he's following the two on a walk. Awakening in the night to loud sounds that he mistakes for sounds of violence, Charlie goes to his aunt's room and sees Thompson and Aunt Evelyn making love.

After discussing these scenes, I like to turn to the passage in which Charlie kills the rooster and ask students to explain why he does so. Some will mention the dreadful heat that clearly works on everyone's nerves that day. Others will mention how bored Charlie is and how frustrated that the rooster is afraid of him and will not act like a pet. If all goes well, prior discussion of the snooping scenes will enable students to recognize Thompson's influence on Charlie—despite the fact that Charlie "has his number" in most respects—and the sense in which Charlie's experiences on the farm have prepared him to kill the rooster.

Charlie is a self-acknowledged "watcher"—an observer more than a doer. I like to ask students why the narrator, the older Charlie, is so adamant about labeling himself in this way. It is true that Charlie's only real action in the story is the killing of the rooster. His other significant action—his refusal to identify Thompson's assailants—is really only a passive denial. Perhaps one purpose of the story is for the narrator to explain—to his audience and to himself—why he killed the rooster and why he lied about Thompson's attackers. It may be that the summer he spent with his grandmother has changed him in ways that he is still struggling to reconcile and understand.

Questions for Discussion

1. Does the older narrator ever revise Charlie's initial harsh judgment of his father?

2. Do you like the young Charlie or the older narrator by the end of the story? Why or why not? Do you sympathize with either?

3. Why does Charlie kill Stanley the rooster? What feelings and experiences have led up to this act? It is a violent act. Is it in any way a sexual act?

4. In the end, the grandmother resorts to violence to get Thompson out of the house and away from Evelyn. Is the grandmother justified? Do you think Thompson has, in some sense, corrupted her —tempted her to sink to his level—or does her hiring of the Ogden brothers simply show that she is more than a match for Thompson in the end?

5. Were you surprised when Charlie refused to testify for Thompson? Why does he say he does so? Why do *you* say he does so?

6. Thompson has a goatee like a stereotypical portrait of the devil. Is there some sense in which he tempts people at the farm to do evil? (Is he *really* a "goddamn freak," as the grandmother calls him?) Do you think Thompson believes in evil? in sin? What role does Thompson's interest in psycholanalysis play in the story?

7. What is your characterization of Evelyn? What part does she play in the summer's events? To what degree, if any, is she responsible for her own troubles? for Thompson's beating?

8. What do you think Charlie learned during his summer at the farm?

Writing Assignments for Chapter 7

1. Write a personal essay about someone who has had an influence on you but about whose influence you have had doubts.

2. Read Erdrich's book *Love Medicine*, of which the story "Love Medicine" is only a chapter. Write an analytical essay in which you argue whether "Love Medicine" is more effective as a short story or as a part of the larger book.

3. Do some library research on Allen Ginsberg, the Beat Generation, and the word "beatnik." Then write an essay arguing whether it was silly for Grandma to call Robert Thompson a "beatnik" or not.

▽ ▽ ▽

Exploring
Contexts

8 THE AUTHOR'S WORK AS CONTEXT

While this text is designed to introduce students to a number of different writers and a variety of ways of looking at the world and responding to it, this chapter narrows our focus to two authors and offers an opportunity to explore the unique vision of each. Two stories by D. H. Lawrence and two stories by Flannery O'Connor provide the basis for such discussion, and passages from the writers' essays and letters at the end of the stories offer insights into their ideas about life and art. Teachers may chose to teach both authors and all four stories as a way of introducing students to the uniqueness of a writer's vision by way of comparison. (A D. H. Lawrence story is emphatically *not* a Flannery O'Connor story, and students who study the stories of each offered here will readily see this.) Teachers who prefer to focus on one of the two authors exclusively may want to add a novel or short story collection to their syllabus and spend more time fitting these stories into the larger context of the author's oeuvre.

Planning Ideas

• Assign Lawrence's *Sons and Lovers* or O'Connor's *Wise Blood* to be studied in conjunction with the stories or to serve as the subjects of analytical essays that students work on independently.

- Ask students to read the two selections by either Lawrence or O'Connor and to jot down a list of similarities and differences between the two stories in regard to subject matter, style, setting, use of symbolism, etc. (You may want to use these as a starting point for class discussion.) Later, have the students read the **"Passages from Essays and Letters"** for the appropriate author and ask them to use this material to annotate their list of comparisons and contrasts. (This exercise could provide the foundation for an essay on the author's approach to fiction.)

D. H. LAWRENCE

Odour of Chrysanthemums

In my experience students like this story a great deal, though they find it, and properly so, strangely moving and even disturbing. They have a tendency—confirmed, alas, by many critics—to insulate themselves from the applicability of the story to their own lives by overparticularizing the situation, that is, by attributing the isolation of Mrs. Bates from her husband only to the infelicity of that particular marriage. Though this may be true to a degree—inferring the reasons for the unhappiness of the marriage can be an interesting classroom exercise—it seems to me the implications are broader than that, and that's what makes the story greater and more disturbing: Lawrence may well be suggesting that we are all ultimately alone, separate even from our loved ones. This may not be a very startling or original truth, but it is given great impact in the story. Moreover, he seems to infer something about proper behavior from that truth: the recognition of our separateness, our individuality, should prevent us from defining for others their role in relation to ourselves—if they, whether spouse or child, are other, they must be free. This does not mean, of course, that there cannot be love and relationship, but rather that it is relationship between free, independent selves. We're all willing to accept this freedom for ourselves, but it gets a little sticky when our parents or children, husband, wife, girlfriend or boyfriend want to stand alone. (Students may want to push this to mean only sexual freedom, but the Lawrence story clearly involves fuller kinds of ultimate integrity.) That, and the loneliness of separateness, might be what some readers find disturbing here.

But who's Lawrence to say? It is true that he won't let us disengage ourselves from his fiction very readily, that we have a hard time talking about Lawrence stories in terms of focus or symbol or structure, but why should we pay any more attention to him than we do to Ann Landers, say? It is here that Lawrence's power of observation, particularly of natural detail, and his ability to describe that detail in words count. His presentation and control of sensory detail convince us he knows what he's talking about, and if he knows what he's talking about when it comes to trains and flowers, the reader tends to feel that he's more likely to know what he's talking about when it comes to love and marriage. That's why it might be useful to tell the class about how Lawrence was "discovered," especially since the anecdote involves the opening of "Odour."

Before World War I, a young woman sent to Ford Madox Ford, then editor of the *English Review*, three poems and a short story written by a schoolmaster friend of hers, the then-unknown D. H. Lawrence. Ford's comments are reprinted in the text.

It should be mentioned that the final paragraph in the story as Ford read it was later replaced, by Lawrence, with a new conclusion (the final seven paragraphs in our version). That paragraph puts Elizabeth in a less favorable light than the final version seems to: originally she seemed to have preferred her husband dead—dead, beautiful, helpless, like a baby. She can then possess him, have power over him. (Some living men want to regress, Lawrence says elsewhere—Gerald Crich in *Women in Love* and the paralyzed Sir Clifford in *Lady Chatterley's Lover*, for example—and certain kinds of women, or certain "lesser" drives in all women, want men to be such, just as there are comparable men or drives within all men that would reduce women to objects or slaves.)

I've always had trouble with the final sentence of the story, for I'm just not sure what it says or implies. Elizabeth tidies up the room because she submits to the necessities of living, of everyday life; she winces or shrinks from death, the idea of her own death, with fear. But why shame? The "and" makes it difficult to read this as shame of the fear of death. Perhaps, though, the sentence says that death is her ultimate master. It is not primarily or immediately the thought of her own death that she winces from in fear and shame, but the whole concept of death, even the death of another. Or she might be ashamed of the fact that another's death, particularly that of her husband, is really a convenience to her and that she feels something like relief.

Some instructors, in courses where novels are assigned in addition to short fiction, will want to read *Sons and Lovers*, and of course the relationship between the Morels in that novel is quite close to that of the Bateses here (as well as, apparently, quite close to that of Lawrence's parents—see some of the excerpts from Lawrence's nonfiction in the text). In the novel, Mrs. Morel dies before her husband, though he is injured more than once in mine accidents. To read the story in the light of the novel or vice versa raise an issue: is the author's canon cross-referential or interdependent (with or without regard to time of composition, development, etc.)? I do not think there are right or wrong answers to this question, though I think all critics, teachers, and students ought to face the question, answer it for themselves, and make the answer clear. So I'll start: I think there is a story called "Odour of Chrysanthemums" that exists in approximate isolation, separated from Lawrence and all his works (but not, of course, from the English tradition—thus "approximate"), just as a frieze can exist as a work of art separate from its building, a song from its play, a short story like "A Pair of Tickets" outside its context in *The Joy Luck Club*. Perhaps the first stage of reading should or must be to see works as free-standing forms, as isolated on the page. But whether you want to or not, you cannot read Lawrence or "Odour" for the first time twice, and once you read *Sons and Lovers*, you cannot read

"Odour" as if you have not read it. Works exist in relation to other works, the most obvious relation being to other works of the same author, and there is a kind of literary ecology or ecological balance in which every work to a greater or lesser degree affects every other work. . . . Now it's your turn.

I must add, finally, that I am embarrassed to have to admit that I don't fully understand the final sentence of "Odour," a story I've read countless times, and taught a number of times, by an author whose works I've based whole courses on. There are many things about many of these stories that I do not fully understand or have not finally made up my mind about. In my experience it's good, though it may be initially embarrassing, to admit these gaps and uncertainties, publicly, in class. It may shock the students at first—"You're not omniscient? What are you doing posing as a teacher then?"—but not only does it get the students to participate more actively and seriously in discussion (so much so that it's tempting to fake it, even when you have decided about a story, but I've found that disastrous), but I think ultimately gives them greater respect for you and your subject matter and opens them up to education as opposed to, or in addition to, mere "training."

Questions for Discussion

1. What sensory details do you find in the opening paragraph? later in this story? in later Lawrence stories? What expectations are aroused by the opening paragraph of the story? How are they fulfilled? Do the first four paragraphs of detailed description lead you to expect something other than a story of outcome? When do you first begin to suspect that Walter Bates is not off drinking somewhere? How does Elizabeth's assumption that he is in a pub affect expectation? tone?

2. What is the focus of narration? How does Elizabeth respond to her father's intention to remarry? How do we know? Can we conjecture more confidently after having read the rest of the story? on what basis? At what point do we first enter Elizabeth's mind? What shifts of focus are there? How does the movement from preponderantly dramatic presentation to Elizabeth's centered consciousness and into her mind relate to the development of the action?

3. What is the major dramatic irony in the story? What related ironies are there? what other ironies? In a Greek tragedy the audience knows the outcome in advance and so can immediately identify ironic statements and actions; the irony seems therefore directed primarily against the character, with the audience having something of the advantage of the gods. Here, however, when Elizabeth says, "I won't wash him. He can lie on the floor," or, "they'll bring him [home] like a log," though you may already have suspicions, you are no more certain of the outcome than she is. What is the effect, then, of such passages?

Does the insistence on or repetition of such phrases alert certain expectations or a range of expectations? Do you recall the phrases when you learn about the accident, realizing that they have lingered somewhere in your mind? What seems to be the purpose of such potentially ironic hints? What is the effect of such hints when you read the story a second time? (The answer to this last may be more complex than it seems at first. Is there any difference, for example, in watching films of a game you know ended 14–13 and one that ended 42–0?) What is the difference in effect between the earlier ironies and Elizabeth's telling her awakened daughter that her father has been brought home and is asleep downstairs?

4. How do the numbered sections structure the story?

5. How is Walter's mother's selfishness indicated? Elizabeth "fastened the door of the little parlor, lest the children should see what was lying there." What is implied by the use of "what" rather than "who"? Faced with the dead body of her husband, what failures of her own in their relationship does Elizabeth come to recognize? Was Walter's isolation and separateness the result of their inadequate relationship? Does this final passage suggest something beyond the particularities of the Bateses' marriage relationship, something more universal? Does it imply a view of proper human relationships, including love and parenthood? What is Elizabeth's attitude toward her husband's death? toward death itself? What does the last sentence of the story mean? Lawrence is often accused of being a didactic writer, of preaching. Would this story substantiate such a charge? Compare the presentation or embodiment of meaning or of a view of reality in "Odour of Chrysanthemums" and "Love Medicine."

6. Compare the use of chrysanthemums here with that of photographs in "A Pair of Tickets." Are the chrysanthemums ever used figuratively or nonliterally? How do they gain or accrete meaning?

D. H. LAWRENCE

The Rocking-Horse Winner

This is an oft-anthologized story, one of Lawrence's most popular. More than one person has told me that it is the only story they remember from their introductory fiction class of ten or fifteen years ago. And yet it is not a typical Lawrence story.

Achsah Barlow Brewster remembers hearing Lawrence tell the story (quoted by Edward Nehls, *D. H. Lawrence: A Composite Biography*, Madison: University of Wisconsin Press, 1959, 3:43–44):

> Out on the terrace of Quattro Venti [on the Isle of Capri], sitting in the spring sunshine, we were talking about the curse of money. He related his story of "The Rocking-Horse Winner," bringing money, but the little boy's death. The tale was told of a woman's inheriting a fortune, whereupon she bought herself a close collar of pearls; soon afterward a bee stung her on the throat, which swelled before the collar could be removed, choking her to death. Someone else recounted that a poor farmer inherited forest land which he sold for ten thousand dollars. When he was told it should have brought twenty thousand, he was so chagrined that he hanged himself on one of the trees. There seemed no end of such tales. Lawrence decided at once to write a volume of them under the title of *Tales of the Four Winds [Quattro Venti]* from which the proceeds should be divided equally among us, that the curse of the riches should be shared by us all.

The story was first published in Lady Cynthia Asquith's *The Ghost-Book: Sixteen New Stories of the Uncanny* (1926). The story might be read, then, as something of a jeu d'esprit, more at home among the collected ghost stories then in the collected Lawrence.

For just this reason, however, it may be a good story to use in order to discuss canon or the author's style or fingerprint. Here, in this most atypical story, Lawrence cannot help but write like Lawrence. The flat, fairy-tale-like or late-Tolstoy opening can be found in other Lawrence stories of the period, like "Two Blue Birds." Vintage Lawrence too is the reality that lies beneath appearances, beneath words, even beneath actions: "Everybody else said of her: 'She is such a good mother. She adores her children.' Only she herself, and her children themselves, knew it was not so. They read it in each other's eyes." You might ask the students about their own experiences: whether there are things they know without words, despite appearances, underneath actions. The theme of money or materialism versus love and life is also familiar in Lawrence's work, as is the perception that the lust for money is insatiable, and that even too much is not enough. Family tensions, deftly handled, are common in Lawrence's "Odour of Chrysanthemums" and *Sons and Lovers*—even though the suburban setting may seem unfamiliar.

The idea that this story is about masturbation for some reason has great currency—better not to inquire the reasons, perhaps. Riding even a rocking-horse may, it is true, be assumed to involve a certain amount of genital excitation; Paul's frenzy may be translated sexually and getting the secret name of the horse may suggest for some sexual climax. But a Freudian reading of this story is a reading out of the story. That is, the masturbation is not in the story, part of the story, demonstrable in detail in the story: it is a translation of the details of the story according to another formula or system than that contained within the story. This may be legitimate if you want to talk about Lawrence's sexuality or attitudes toward sex—conscious or, especially, unconscious. It may be legitimate, too, in trying to explain reader response. Readers may respond to this story because it parallels or embodies the rhythms or structures of masturbation; maybe that's why some students remember it more vividly than other stories they read at the time. But that's a study of responses and the reasons for them, conjectural and fascinating, and it seems to me that this is quite a different thing from saying that this story is about masturbation.

Questions for Discussion

1. If you did not know that this and the preceding two stories were by the same author, what internal evidence (elements, views, language within the story) might suggest it? How does this 1932 Lawrence story differ from his earlier one? Describe the continuity and the change or development in his work, assuming these stories to be typical of that work at the time of publication.

2. Compare the opening sentences of the Lawrence stories. In what ways might the opening of this story prepare you for the surreal or supernatural events later in the story?

3. What expectations are aroused by what precedes the first dramatic scene? by the divulging of Paul's luck? by the "secret within a secret"? When did you first guess how Paul learned the names of the winning horses? When did you first begin to suspect the eventual outcome of the story? Why is Paul's mother anxious about him? What is implied about feeling and common sense? Is Paul's mother's anxiety part of the realistic or of the supernatural aspect of the story? What are the implications? tone? emotional effect? of Oscar Cresswell's final remarks?

4. What is the focus of narration? How would you characterize or identify the narrator?

5. The "center" of Paul's mother's heart is cold and hard, she is incapable of love, but other people think she is a loving mother; she knows it isn't so, and she knows her children know it isn't so because they "read it in each other's eyes." What does this suggest about appearance or behavior and reality? about different kinds of reality? about different kinds of knowing? To what extent does this prepare you for the strange nature of the events that follow? How does the vagueness, for example, the absence of names on the first page or so, prepare you for those later events? How does the relationship between inner and outer reality here resemble or differ from that relationship in the other Lawrence stories? in "The Lady with the Dog"? How do the different kinds of reality here compare to those implied in "A Souvenir of Japan"?

6. What kind of literal sense do you make out of the children's hearing the haunted house whispering? their seeing in each other's eyes that they all hear it? that the rocking-horse hears it? What does Paul's mother mean by luck? How does he interpret it? Why doesn't Paul want his mother to know he's lucky? What happens when he does tell her? What is the irony of Paul's claiming luck? What does the story imply about luck?

7. Why do the voices in the house get louder or more insistent after Paul's mother gets the five thousand pounds? What is the effect on Paul? What does the story suggest about money needs?

8. In what sense may this story be considered symbolic or mythic? If mythic, and if myth is social or communal, of what social group or community is this a myth? Compare it as myth to "How Much Land Does a Man Need?" Compare the focus of narration, the kinds of detail and lack of detail, the sentence structure and diction, and the mixture of the real and the surreal in "The Rocking-Horse Winner" and "How Much Land Does a Man Need?"

FLANNERY O'CONNOR

The Lame Shall Enter First

College students are a difficult group to startle these days. If they haven't experienced all manner of shocking things before they arrive on campus, they have certainly seen them on television and at the movies, often from a very young age. They are a tough group to shake up, and yet many of my students admit to being shaken up by this story. I must admit that I, too, find it deeply disturbing. Like O'Connor's "A Good Man is Hard to Find," it's not a story one easily forgets and not just because of the ending.

Perhaps it's the implacable bluntness with which O'Connor presents her flawed and troubled characters: the smugly self-righteous Sheppard, his woebegone and neglected son, and the fiendishly malign but often amusing Rufus. Maybe it's that there is no one in the story to like. All of the characters are in some degree grotesques, "large and startling figures," as O'Connor would have it, created—as she says—as a means of speaking to the "almost blind" ("The Fiction Writer and His Country"). We sympathize with Norton, and we sometimes applaud Rufus's actions out of our own malice toward Sheppard, but we find no one with whom we want to identify, nor can we feel completely comfortable with our own reactions. By leaving us so much outside the story, O'Connor forces us into the position of judges. It is easy—perilously easy—for example, to recognize Sheppard's self-righteousness and to condemn him, but in the process we may be lured into an uncomfortable smugness of our own.

O'Connor's handling of Rufus's club foot is surely another reason the story disturbs us so profoundly. Ours is a culture deeply ill-at-ease with physical disability, and I have found students reluctant to talk about Rufus's foot, even though its ugliness is something he clearly enjoys flaunting. Sheppard observes that Rufus is "as touchy about [his] foot as if it were a sacred object." Rufus doesn't want the clerk to touch his foot, but he makes certain when Sheppard interviews him that the counselor cannot avoid looking at it. In O'Connor's work, bodily disability almost always accompanies spiritual disability. (Students familiar with her "Good Country People" will note the parallel to Hulga's false leg.) Talking about what Rufus's foot represents moves the discussion quickly into some key issues in the story because both for Sheppard and Rufus and for O'Connor it is a symbolic as much as a physical entity.

Sheppard, secure in his training as a counselor ("his credentials were less dubious than a priest's"), believes Rufus's club foot "explains" the boy's destructive behavior. In a rather Adlerian way he concludes that Rufus is trying to compensate for his handicap when he gets into trouble. On the contrary, as we discover near the end of the story, because of the training Rufus has received from his fundamentalist grandfather, he takes literally the biblical proclamation that at the gates of heaven "the lame shall enter first." He doesn't see his foot as a disability (as Sheppard does) but as a special admission ticket to paradise — even though Rufus realizes he will have to repent of his sins before he can take advantage of his position of privilege. In the story, the foot represents Rufus's pride in his ability to carry out evil acts and get away with it. His bodily disability is emblematic of his spiritual disability. He flaunts his leg as he flaunts his sin. Like the Misfit in "A Good Man is Hard to Find," Rufus understands the basic teachings of the Christian faith, but in him the knowledge has become twisted and ugly. Unlike the Misfit, who wishes he knew for certain whether Christ is worthy of his belief, Rufus believes Christian teachings are true. But for him they offer the opportunity to enjoy being evil for a while before he repents and is saved.

O'Connor does something very clever with point of view in this story. She keeps us very close to Sheppard, making us privy to his thoughts and offering us ample opportunities to criticize him and feel superior. We recognize that Sheppard is wrong about Rufus, but we may not suspect how tragically wrong until the very end of the story because we're hearing Sheppard's thoughts, not Rufus's. A smug do-gooder who ignores and abuses his son makes a fine target for our dislike (I'm reminded of Mrs. Jellyby in *Bleak House*), and while we know Rufus isn't the boy Sheppard imagines him to be, we may wonder if he might not be a better influence on Norton than is his father. O'Connor plays fair with us; she doesn't turn Rufus into a child of Satan suddenly at the end. From the very beginning of the story, Rufus overtly allies himself with evil ("Satan," he says, "He has me in his power"). He combs his hair "Hitler fashion." He "hisses" like a snake. Yet most of us, I think, are shocked to discover the depths of Rufus's evil. Perhaps we are so busy enjoying the many ways he frustrates Sheppard's plans that we ignore O'Connor's characterization. Perhaps it is that our imaginations can scarcely encompass the evil of which he is capable, which may be one of the points (at us) of the story.

One exercise I like to use with O'Connor stories works especially well with "The Lame Shall Enter First." The eyes in her works are almost always windows to souls. You might have your class skim through the story, marking all the references to eyes, sight, seeing, etc., then ask them to talk about how these references provide insights into each character's way of viewing the world. You might ask want to ask them what they make of Sheppard's eagerness to buy

Rufus a telescope—and then a microscope—of Norton's fascination with the former.

In the world of O'Connor's fiction we confront ultimate issues—love and hate, truth and falsehood, sin and redemption, life and death. O'Connor makes it clear she sees these issues from the perspective of orthodox Christianity. I like to ask students whether they believe a reader must share O'Connor's beliefs to appreciate her vision. Is O'Connor's vision comprehensible to an agnostic? to someone outside Judeo-Christian culture?

Questions for Discussion

1. At the beginning of the story, we see the world from Sheppard's perspective. When does your sympathy begin to move away from Sheppard and toward Norton? Why do you think O'Connor has Norton prepare such a disgusting breakfast? What do you make of Sheppard's diagnosis of why Norton threw up? What name does Norton use for his father?

2. Sheppard believes Norton sells seeds because he's greedy, materialistic, and selfish. Can you provide another explanation? What might the seeds symbolize? Why is Norton described as looking like a larvae?

3. How does having Rufus in the house change things for Norton? Why does Norton become absorbed in using the telescope? Why does Sheppard refuse to tell Norton that his mother has gone to heaven? Why does Norton want to believe she has?

4. Rufus spends a lot of his free time reading encyclopedias. What is Sheppard's reaction to this activity? Why do you think O'Connor describes Rufus as ravaging each subject that he reads about? When Sheppard uses the words "truth" and "light," what does he refer to? When Rufus uses these words, what does he mean?

5. O'Connor says each of her stories depends upon the success of a "gesture"—"some gesture of a character that is unlike any other in the story, one which indicates where the real heart of the story lies" ("On Her Own Work"). Is there such a gesture in "The Lame Shall Enter First"? If so, can you explain its importance to the story?

6. Why, at the end of the story after Rufus and Sheppard have their last confrontation, does the policeman say, "Well, they seen each other now"? Why does Rufus allow himself to be caught?

7. Why does Sheppard repeat to himself, "I did more for him than I did for my own child?" Do you find any significance in Sheppard's name?

FLANNERY O'CONNOR

Everything That Rises Must Converge

Among all O'Connor's stories, this one contains some of her funniest dialogue and reveals O'Connor's fine ear for the rhythm, nuance, and banality of everyday speech, particularly southern speech. After talking about the devastating conclusion of "The Lame Shall Enter First," I find the class needs a little comic relief, so I like to begin discussion of "Everything That Rises" with language. O'Connor always pays particular attention to the ways the language we use reveals us. If you've discovered some talented readers in your class, you might want to have two of them read a passage from the story (just the dialogue)—perhaps the section from Mrs. Chestny's comments at the end of paragraph 10 through Julian's comment—"Doubtless that decayed mansion reminded them." Mrs. Chestny's cliché-ridden conversation shows her to be unreflective, uninventive, and unable to escape either the verbal locutions or the mental landscape of the past. (Yet occasionally she speaks the truth, however unintentionally, as when she observes that what Julian calls "true culture" is "in the heart.")

Students will often note that Julian's use of language is no less revealing of character than his mother's. He doesn't converse with his mother so much as emit exasperated retorts more appropriate in tone to those of a sulky adolescent than a grown man. Because O'Connor presents the story from Julian's perspective, we are also privy to the "language" of his thinking. I like to ask students what they make of the way Julian is described in paragraph 2—what they make of the perspective presented in paragraph 10.

O'Connor's use of point of view in "Everything That Rises" is very similar to the way she uses it in "The Lame Shall Enter First," so you may want to ask your class to compare O'Connor's presentation of Julian's perspective and Sheppard's perspective in each story. Both men have great faith in their own judgments, although one is wrong about the others he judges and one is basically right. Both men are also portrayed in such a way as to prompt readers to judge them harshly. Do we in a sense condemn ourselves by adopting the same role as O'Connor's protagonists? Or is there a distinction between the judgments Shepperd and Julian make about others and our own about them?

In "Writing Short Stories," O'Connor emphasizes the importance of conveying the social idiom in which her characters move: "When you ignore the idiom," she writes, "you are very likely ignoring the whole social fabric that could make a meaningful character." This comment can provide a neat entry into a discussion of the social milieu of "Everything That Rises" and its importance to our understanding of Julian, his mother, and the African-American woman Mrs. Chestny angers. Julian claims his mother doesn't understand where or who she is. He believes that she lives in the past, that she ignores the changes in her status and in the status of African-Americans and pretends that little has changed since her great-grandfather owned "a plantation and two-hundred slaves." I like to ask half of the class to provide support for Julian's contention that his mother doesn't face the world as it is and the other half to offer evidence that Julian can't face the world either.

O'Connor wrote that she used violence to wake her characters up, to return them to reality and prepare them "to accept their moment of grace," and to reveal who they really are ("On Her Own Work"). The conclusion of "Everything That Rises" reveals who Julian is, a man-child still deeply dependent on his mother. Whether the death of his mother will cause him to see himself clearly is left indeterminate, as is the question of his ability to confront his "guilt and sorrow" about her violent end. The final paragraph of the story has the surreal quality of a nightmare: Julian runs, but he seems to be getting nowhere. I must confess that the final sentence of the story remains something of a mystery to me—perhaps as O'Connor intended. It would appear that the "tide of darkness" that seems to pull Julian back to his mother would cause him to make "his entry into the world of guilt and sorrow." Instead, somehow this tide allows him to postpone it, "moment to moment."

Questions for Discussion

1. What similarities do you observe between "Everything That Rises" and "The Lame Shall Enter First"? How would you know, if the author's name were missing from these stories, that Flannery O'Connor wrote them?

2. "Everything That Rises" depends far less on overtly religious imagery than does "The Lame Shall Enter First." Does "Everything That Rises" "work" better or less well because of this? Do you find one story more accessible than the other?

3. Describe as fully as possible what you believe Mrs. Chestny feels when she recognizes that the African-American woman on the bus is wearing the same hat she is. Describe the other woman's feelings. Why is she so enraged when Mrs. Chestny offers her son a nickel?

4. What does Julian think about when he is inside his "bubble"? What do you understand the bubble to represent?

5. Julian considers himself far more enlightened in his attitude toward African-Americans than his mother. What do you think?

6. What do you make of the change in language Julian uses to his mother when he realizes she may be dying?

7. Examine the references to eyes, sight, etc. in "Everything That Rises." What do these references tell us about Julian's perspective through most of the story? at the end of the story? What do you make of O'Connor's description of Julian's mother's eye raking his face before she dies?

8. Does Mrs. Chestny's encounter with violence prepare her "to accept her moment of grace"? Or is Mrs. Chestny simply doomed because of her bigotry?

Writing Assignments for Chapter 8

1. Write a personal essay describing an encounter with racism. The essay could be about racism directed toward you or toward another person. It could even be about racist impulses you have had yourself. What prompted the incident? How did it end? How did it make you feel? Were there any "aftershocks?" What sense did you make of it?

2. Using the appropriate "Passages from Essays and Letters," write an essay about either the two Lawrence stories or the two O'Connor stories, exploring the degree to which the author's statements about writing conform to the author's practice.

3. Research the background of either O'Connor or Lawrence and write an essay discussing the influence of the author's background on the situations and settings of his or her work.

4. Write an essay comparing and contrasting Lawrence and O'Connor's use of characterization, setting or symbolism.

5. Carter's "A Souvenir of Japan" and Lawrence's "Odour of Chrysanthemums" have in common female protagonists who feel alienated from their mates. Write an analysis of the way each author handles this topic.

9 CULTURE AS CONTEXT: BORDER STORIES

The actual border between Mexico and the United States plays a role in two of the three stories in this chapter—Richard Dokey's "Sanchez" and Denise Chávez's "The Last of the Menu Girls"—but shifting borders less easily traced on a map are the subject of all three selections. In Anaya's "The Water People," Toni tries to negotiate the blurred or blurring boundaries between the Catholic faith in which he was raised and the herbal medicine, legends, and magic that are elements of his native culture. While Richard Dokey's "Sánchez" is partially about journeying across the border from Mexico into the United States, it is also about generational borders, the desire for a better life, and the longing for a home. The relations between Chicano citizens of the United States and illegal immigrants form part of the backdrop to Rocío Esquibel's story in Denise Chávez's "The Last of the Menu Girls," but in the forefront are Rocío's experiences in her first summer job—her exposure to pain and suffering, her friendships with a diverse cast of characters, and the gradual flowering of her ambition.

Teaching literature from outside one's own cultural context can be a fraught undertaking. There are those who assert that we should never do so—that stories by African-American women should be taught by African-American women, that only Native-American teachers should teach Native-American writers. If you are a non-Chicano teacher tackling this chapter—or a teacher approaching any story in the text about a culture other than your own—I offer the following by way of caution and advice. One of the ancient verities of Western literary criticism has been the insistence that truly great art is "universal"—that it treats subjects and offers truths that are shared across the boundaries of race, nationality, and culture. Recent multicultural criticism has called into question whether such universal truths exist for all cultures without exception. Certainly anyone teaching literature today should take care not to presume too far along such lines. What is considered deceptive practice in one cultural context may be understood as legitimate cleverness in another; familial power structures condemned in one culture may be components of religious doctrine elsewhere. I have found that it is best never to presume that students share my assumptions in regard to what is universal or true—or that they necessarily share such assumptions in common with each other. This does not mean that we can find no areas of agreement nor does it mean that I ignore my own cultural values, or that I encourage students to ignore theirs. It does mean that I take care to acknowledge that our values may differ and that I encourage my students critically to examine the cultural values revealed in the stories we study in an atmosphere of mutual respect.

Planning Ideas

- Ask each student to bring to class a one-page essay describing the cultural context in which he or she feels most at home. Have each include at least three of the following elements: ethnic culture, geographical culture (urban, suburban, rural; state, regional, national), religious culture, educational culture. Before discussing Anaya's **"The Water People*,"** ask students to share their statements of cultural identity and to explore any tensions they may feel between one aspect and another.
- Assign Anaya's novel *Bless Me, Ultima*, of which the story **"The Water People"** is a chapter.
- Bring in several objects that evoke different reactions from people of different cultures, perhaps an American or Confederate flag, a copy of the Koran, a cross, a picture of Malcolm X (depending on what seems most appropriate for your class)—or ask students to bring in objects they consider cultural icons that they feel people from other cultures may not understand. Use these objects as a basis for discussing cultural divides and the degree to which it is possible to cross them.
- Show the Spike Lee movie *Do the Right Thing* and ask students to comment on the movie's portrayal of the various ethnic groups it features.

RUDOLFO ANAYA

The Water People

Toni bears the name of a Catholic saint and his mother has brought him up to follow the teachings of the Roman Catholic Church, yet the beliefs and practices associated with his Native American heritage also have a strong appeal for him. In this story, which is also a chapter of the novel *Bless Me, Ultima*, Toni's loyalty to the Catholicism is strained and tested. Already, as the story opens, Toni is wondering why the healing power of the old native woman who has come to live with his family has cured his uncle after the efforts of doctors and priests failed. It seems to Toni that God himself (herself?) has failed.

One way to begin talking about the religious and cultural tensions with which Toni struggles is to focus on the temptations Toni confronts that threaten his Catholicism. You may want to give students some time to skim back through the story and compile a list of challenges to Toni's faith and practice, beginning with Ultima's healing of Toni's uncle and including the visit to the garden, the sighting of the golden carp, the mermaid story, and Toni's concluding dream. Once students have identified the tensions Toni is struggling with via these temptations, you can lead them to analyze his responses to each.

Flannery O'Connor, among others, has suggested that people reveal their true characters under pressure, and among the admirable features of Toni's character revealed under the pressure of temptation are his integrity and his loyalty to the precepts of the Church, teachings he knows by heart. Toni refuses to lie about his beliefs or to ignore them in order to gain access to the golden carp, even though he is patently eager to see the magical fish.

In the course of the story, Toni retains his Catholicism but also uneasily accommodates some of the magical ideas and beliefs to which Cico introduces him. I ask students to locate these moments of accommodation in the text— Toni's oath not to kill carp, for example, or his eating the carrot from Narciso's garden—and to suggest to what degree they believe these accommodations are workable compromises. To what degree do they observe similar accommodations of different traditions and beliefs in their own cultural and religious situations? What about Toni's clear sense that the appearance of the golden carp in the hidden pool is a miraculous event? Toni seems to feel that his awestruck reaction to the golden carp is a sin. I like to ask students if they agree.

Cico's story about the Hidden Lakes and the mermaid who supposedly lives there calls to mind the Sirens in Homer's *Odyssey*, and Narciso's garden seems a real-life Garden of Eden. Are there other parallels in the story between Native American beliefs and aspects of other religions or myths? Why might Anaya have included such parallels?

Toni's dream at the end of the story is both a nightmare vision of magical judgment on the sinners of his town and the embodiment of the tensions he feels between his father's heritage and his mother's. At the end of the dream, Ultima appears, calms the raging storm as did Christ on the Sea of Galilee, and delivers a pronouncement reconciling the conflicting beliefs of Toni's mother and father. Anaya's story concludes with Toni resting and at peace.

I like to ask students how they interpret this dream. Is it Anaya's response to cultural and religious conflict—"The waters are one. . . . You have been seeing only parts . . . and not looking beyond into the geat cycle that binds us all"—or is Ultima's appearance and message only wish-fulfillment? Depending on the composition of the class and how readily your students respond to such questions, you might want to expand the discussion to talk about whether all religious and cultural conflicts can be resolved in the way that Ultima suggests in the dream.

Questions for Discussion

1. What evidence do we have that Toni is a good Catholic—that he knows the teachings of the Church?

2. Is it intolerant to believe that your cultural or religious values are right and another's are wrong? What does it mean to be tolerant of another's beliefs?

3. What do you make of the golden carp? Does Anaya intend us to believe it is a magic fish? How do you explain the appearance of a golden carp as big as a boy?

4. How does Cico account for the stories about the mermaid? Does he

believe there is an actual mermaid? What is Ultima's response when Toni tells her the things he has heard from Cico? How does her response affect your view of the stories?

RICHARD DOKEY

Sánchez

Because the story opens in Stockton and because most students will have had the experience of seeing their parents react negatively to something to which they are attracted or about which they are proud, I like to start discussion by asking about the different reactions Juan and Jésus Sanchez have to the town. Jésus clearly sees in his new situation an opportunity for independence, adventure, and economic advancement. He guides his father proudly through the place he envisions as the site of his future success. But Juan sees Stockton differently. He sees the squalor of Jésus's rented room, the ugliness of a place where all seems uprooted. Ultimately, he declines to visit the canning factory where his son will work, his disappointment in his son's vision of the future as palpable as his love for him.

Students who have read closely will remember that Juan knows Stockton, has visited the town repeatedly in the past. If no one brings it up, I ask what memories Juan has of the town. (See par. 43.) Responses to this question usually lead us to talk about Juan's dreams and ambitions as a young man and to contrast these to the hopes of Jésus. At this point, I ask students to explain the reasons for Juan's disappointment in Jésus's choices.

We are told that Juan left his parched homeland when he was a young man "because he feared the land, believed almost that it possessed the power to kill him—as it had killed his mother and father, his aunt, was, in fact, slowly killing so many of his people." He felt he was compelled to change his situation as a matter of survival. In comparison, his son's motivations for moving to Stockton—independence, the chance to work in the canning factory and make money—must seem woefully inadequate. In addition, Stockton has unpleasant associations for Juan. When he was a much younger man, he traveled to the town in the company of other immigrant workers who got drunk, visited whores, and fought. He didn't join in their revels, however, but instead stood on the corners of Stockton's skid row and thought about what he had lost. At the time his dearest hopes for the future had been cast down by the tragic outcome of his wife's most recent pregnancy. Desperate to assure that she would not become pregnant again, he had recently had a vasectomy and given up, as he then believed, all hope of ever having a family.

Stockton's ugliness, both remembered and observed anew during the tour with his son, contrasts sharply with the beauty of place in the Sierra Nevadas where Juan doggedly pursued his own dreams as a young man. It must seem to him, when his son rejects that place for a rented room in Stockton, that his struggle to establish a home in the midst of loveliness for his family has come to nothing. The son whose life was so costly to La Belleza and to Juan remains Juan's *querido*, his dear one, but Jésus's rejection of all his father has labored to attain breaks the older man's heart and makes him realize that the home he established first for his wife, and later for his child, is no longer home to him either.

Questions for Discussion

1. Have you ever tried to share something that you are proud of with a parent and found him or her unable to appreciate what you appreciate? How do you account for the differences in your perceptions?

2. In paragraph 47, Juan Sánchez gets up in the night and looks at the stars, and "as always he was moved by the nearness and profusion of their agony." Why does Juan associate the stars with agony? What do the next few lines tell us about Juan's view of life?

3. Richard Dokey spends a good portion of the story suggesting how beautiful the area in the Sierra Nevada Mountains is where Juan eventually makes his home. Why does he begin the story by describing the ugliness of Stockton, where Jesús will work for the Flotill Cannery?

4. How does Juan account for the racism of the people of Twin Pines? What does Juan's explanation tell us about him? How is this racism expressed?

5. What do you believe happens to Juan at the end of the story? Does he go home to Mexico, called back to his homeland by the "embracing love" that he felt "lowing across the mountains from the south"? Or does he commit suicide, seeking out the love that "must all still be alive somewhere" by joining La Belleza in death?

6. Define the two kinds of love Juan discovers that are described in paragraph 71. What is the love that "wanted him for his own"? Does this kind of love have anything to do with the way the story ends?

DENISE CHÁVEZ

The Last of the Menu Girls

By the time they come to college, most students will have filled out at least one job application; some will have completed many. Chávez's story takes the form of an employment application—a fact that may puzzle some readers—so I like to get students thinking about the similarities and differences between the applications they have filled out and the one we read over Rocío's shoulder, so to speak, in this story. The form Rocío is in the act of completing has caused her to reminisce about her first (and only) job as a "menu girl" at the Altavista Memorial Hospital. Instead of providing information about the job in a brief, business-like way, as most of us do when filling out forms, Rocío begins thinking about the events and lessons of the summer. (Whether Rocío actually writes down all of what we read in the story on the form might be a matter for debate. In any case, the process of application calls up myriad memories.)

The nature of the application process and Rocío's response to it tells us at least two important things about her summer experiences: (1) despite her early embarrassment about the trivial nature of the job, it has had an important impact on her, and (2) despite her vehement declaration in the fifth paragraph— "I never wanted to be a nurse, ever" and similar declarations elsewhere in the text—the job has led her to apply for more work having to do with the sick and dying, probably a position as a nurse or a nurse's aide.

Chávez conveys the process by which Rocío comes to change her mind about hospital work and begins to develop real ambition both effectively and realistically. I suggest to my students that, like most of us, Rocío alters direction slowly and by fits and starts. Sometimes I divide the story into sections of a few pages, assign the sections to different discussion groups, and ask each group to find evidence suggesting the status of Rocío's ambitions and feelings about hospital work at various stages of her employment. For example, in the section labeled "Mr. Smith," Rocío reveals that her first reaction to her employer and the position of menu girl is repulsion and embarrassment: "Was I to work for this gnome? I wanted to rescue souls, not play attendant to this crippled, dried up specimen. . . ." And yet, while Rocío thinks about the lofty task of rescuing souls (whatever that means to her at this juncture), she also longs for the freedom of previous summers when she didn't have to work: "Senior year had been the happiest of my life; was it to change?"

Although we are never told so directly, by the end of the summer, Rocío is transformed. The girl who couldn't stand the sights and smells of illness eagerly fills in as a nurse's aide. The girl who dreamed vaguely of being sexy and important and of having fun has gained a new sense of ambition and appears on her way to fulfilling Arlene's vision of her as a latter-day Florence Nightingale.

Questions for Discussion

1. Does it seem appropriate that Rocío is the "last of the menu girls"? Why or why not?

2. What do you make of the ending, of Rocío's experience of being a patient? Could it be that this experience was, in some respects, the one she had always most dreaded? In what way might this experience be considered a preparation for the future?

3. Why does Chavez have Rocío recall and describe at such length the disgusting illnesses she has seen and been told about? What does this opening contribute to the story?

4. What clues do we have early in the story that Roscío will change her mind about nursing?

5. Why does Rocío say she can't remember whether Arlene plans to major in biology or home ec? Do you accept her explanation? Might there be some other reason that Rocío makes this mistake?

6. What does Rocío mean when she says "That week I fell in love"? In love with what? with whom?

7. What do we know about Rocío's father? Does what we find out have any relevance to her decision?

8. Why are the Chicano nurses so contemptuous of the illegal alien who got his nose bitten off in a fight? What is Rocío's response to the man?

9. If you had to point to one passage in the story that explains Rocío's change of heart about nursing, could you? If so, what passage would it be?

Writing Assignments for Chapter 9

1. Write a personal essay about a job you have had that brought you in contact with people from cultural backgrounds different from your own and / or forced you to view your cultural background in a new way.

2. Do some library research on the 1848 Treaty of Guadalupe Hidalgo between Mexico and the United States. Write a research paper explaining the circumstances and provisions of the treaty and exploring why some Chicanos might see the treaty as justification for ignoring the border between Mexico and the United States.

3. Compare the mixture of Catholicism and Native-American magic in Erdrich's "Love Medicine" with the similar mixture of influences in Anaya's "The Water People." What similarities and differences do you see between the protagonist's responses to the mixtures? What are the authors' views insofar as you can determine them?

10 LITERARY KIND AS CONTEXT: INITIATION STORIES

Students seem to respond well to initiation stories, perhaps because student life is a series of initiations—or because many students are not so very far from the initiation experiences of childhood—or (more mundanely) because initiation stories are a genre they are familiar with from high-school literature courses. I think of this chapter as one that can be used rather late in the course, as placement in the text indicates, or quite early in the term. Some classes respond better to literature when their first engagement with it is familiar (and thereby reassuring), and—if I sense that I have a group of such students (science majors uncomfortable about their verbal and literary skills?)—I sometimes teach these stories before moving on to the chapters that focus on particular fictional elements.

Planning Ideas

- Assign *Dubliners*, the short story collection of which **"Araby"** is a part, and use the work to explore Joyce's fascination with moments of initiation and epiphany.
- If you want to discuss tone as a separate element of fiction, "Araby" provides a good opportunity to do so and could be linked with other stories in the anthology—**"The Country Husband," "The Loons," "A Souvenir of Japan*," "The Watcher*,"** and **"Boys and Girls,"** among others—to form a unit.
- Ask students to bring to class a short personal essay (1–2 pp.) in which they describe an initiation experience—either an experience of first love, an experience of disillusionment, or an initiation into a different sense of self. Ask several volunteers read their essays as an introduction to the initiation theme.

JAMES JOYCE

Araby

Joyce seems to have been one of those writers for whom the short story meant the initiation story. His epiphanies, or moments when the reality or inner nature of things "shines forth," are almost the same as the "illumination" in most initiation stories. "Araby" is a fine example of this. Brief, almost diagrammatic— and, one may hope, close to the experience of the students—the story should present little initial difficulty in reading or discussion, even though its perfect, almost chiseled form may seem static to some.

I like to start with the obvious here, and I have had some success in class in getting students to list the romantic elements—the paperback books, the boy's bearing his "chalice safely through a throng of foes" with tears and prayers, the name of the bazaar. Another list, a list of the "realistic" or antiromantic elements—the rusty bicycle pump and odor of ashpits, the drunks on the street, the uncle's stumbling homecoming, the banal banter at the bazaar—will then graphically suggest the basic contrast in the story. It is then not difficult to show, from the end of the fourth paragraph ("my foolish blood") to the final "vanity . . . anguish and anger," the nature of the illumination and its relation to that contrast.

I also like to begin something of a counterthrust by asking whether the description of Mangan's sister holding a railing spike and leaning toward the boy, her hair, neck, hand, dress, petticoat illuminated by the lamp, is a romantic or realistic "painting." (Curiously there's a rather similar piece of chiaroscuro in "The Dead," as you may remember.) But the issue soon becomes the relationship of focus and voice. The focus is on the young boy, obviously; the voice is that of the man who was that boy. Calling his young self's blood "foolish," and describing his walking through the market on Saturday in chivalric terms, describing his desire as wanting to "veil" his senses, and such alliterative inflated phrases as "prayers and praises," suggest the emotional distance between focus and voice, between the innocent and initiated. I feel there's a great deal of affection for the boy-self in the narrator, and a bit of nostalgia both for the lost innocence and the intense—if foolish—feeling. There's a much stronger streak of the Romantic in tough-thinking Joyce, I believe, than most critics admit.

I think, then, the tone of this story is not simple, and this might be a good time to bring up the subject of tone (which is not done in the text). Also, I like to call attention to the complexity of tone in the story before I get into the personal experiences of the class—so that the students don't feel too uneasy about their own "foolishness" in puppy love. But I can see that with some classes you might want to get a personal paper first, take them to the edge of embarrassment, or to the edge of that sophisticated contempt that eighteen- or nineteen-year-olds have for the childish actions of fifteen- or sixteen-year-old puppies, and then spring the complications.

Questions for Discussion

1. Whose language is the final sentence with its alliterative pairs "driven and derided," "anguish and anger"? And what of the rest of the flexible, beauti-

fully polished, rhythmic prose? By whose voice is this prose conveyed?

2. In what sense is the boy's initiation a loss? In what sense is it a discovery?

TONI CADE BAMBARA

Gorilla, My Love

One might say there are at least two initiations—or perhaps better, transformations—going on in Bambara's story, and I like to begin discussion by asking students to describe them.

(1) Hunca Bubba plans to get married, and as part of this new beginning, he changes his name. Changes of name often accompany such initiations in our society. (For example, when Catholics are confirmed—that is, when they ritually confirm their faith and accept the obligations it entails—they take on a new name. Marriage in our society often entails a change of name for the bride and, more recently, sometimes for the groom.) Hunca Bubba's change of name—or return to his official name—indicates an impending change in his status. In a sense, the new name suggests that he is taking on a new identity.

(2) Scout / Hazel also experiences an initiation. She had already been aware of the duplicity of adult society, as the movie theater anecdote tells us. The anecdote also tells us that she is willing to fight such mendacity through means simultaneously comical and alarming. But there is something particularly disturbing to her about the "change-up" Hunca Bubba pulls on her, and I like to ask students why this is so. The text seems to suggest that her previous experience of adult lying has been outside the family. But Hunca Bubba is an *uncle* who deceives her, a member of the us-versus-them club. (It is revealing that when Baby Jason joins Scout / Hazel in crying, it is in part "Cause he is my blood brother. . . ." Blood is thicker than water and should be, correspondingly, more reliable. But from a child's point of view this, heartbreakingly, turns out not to be the case.) Beyond lashing out verbally at her uncle, there is little Scout / Hazel can do.

This experience is for her an initiation into the breadth and depth of adult mendacity; it is also an occasion for the acquisition of transformative wisdom. Appropriately, she marks this transformation with a change of name. Henceforth, she will go by Hazel, her proper, even adult, name. And she will not permit Hunca Bubba, the betrayer, to call her by any of the pet names that she has acquired within the family. Hazel has moved into a new phase of life, a phase initiated (like so many others in the process of growing up) by a painful realization and the dispelling of the comforting illusions and fantasies of childhood.

Questions for Discussion

1. We do not know for sure that the narrator is a girl until well into the story. Did you assume from the first that the narrator was a girl or a boy? Explain your assumption. On what evidence or impressions was it based? Discuss your assumptions in terms of the text and in terms of gender expectations.

2. Do you find the children's reaction to the religious movie somehow irreligious or even blasphemous? How is the fact that the narrator and her companions are children relevant to this question? Can we discern anything about the narrator's religious convictions from this story?

3. Are comforting illusions and fantasies, no matter how untrue in the adult world, essential to childhood? How painful has the dispelling of childhood illusions and fantasies been for you? (Will you tell your own children that Santa Claus exists or not? Why?)

4. What do you make of Hunca Bubba's reaction to Hazel's sense of betrayal? Why does he apologize for misleading her?

ALICE MUNRO

Boys and Girls

If, in what my students call "in the present day and age of these modern times of today," you have trouble getting a discussion started on this story, you'd better call for an investigation by the narcotics squad or hang up your mortarboard. In my perverse way, if I detect the proper intensity of seethe and the lid of indignation about to blow, I try to get their noses (in or out of joint) back into the text. I sometimes start them off with the second sentence: what's going on there with beautiful silver foxes besides killing and skinning them? Does this have anything to do with that more central killing, the killing of the horse, and with the more central concern of differentiation of the sexes? (No, no, don't get too far ahead of me. We'll talk about that issue more fully a little later.) And now the third and fourth sentences: the heroic calendars sent by fur companies (irony anyone?), and what does one of those calendars show? European heroes with "savages" serving as beasts of burden, all against a background of a rather hostile nature. Are we getting a picture of where the narrator stands on social, political, economic issues? Any relation to. . . . Well, we'll get on to that in a minute.

Now, in the second paragraph, there's the girl's mother, who doesn't like the killing and skinning or the gruesome play of the hired man, or the smell. But the girl finds the smell "reassuringly seasonal, like the smell of oranges and pine needles." How could she associate those? Would this be the time to begin to talk about responses "innate" and "learned" or "acculturated"? The "feminine" responses of the mother and the "masculine" responses of the girl here and through much of the story may be looked at in these terms, mightn't they?

It might be impossible to keep "the issue" out of the discussion, but one good in-class written or oral exercise might be character descriptions of the mother and of the father, of Laird, of the hired man. Can the students sketch the character of the narrator as a girl as well? An alternative assignment would be an analysis of the relationship between the girl and her father, the girl and her mother, her brother. You might want to call attention as well to the age as well as sex division, to child versus grown-up and the narrator's perception of grown-up versus child.

But sooner or later, and quite properly, the discussion will turn to the subject indicated in the title, the subject that dominates even if it does not exclude other subjects in the story. This may be a good story in which to stress "development" or the sequential and temporal ordering of the material, for the first and second halves of the story may suggest different emphases, and to "spatialize" the story or take evidence without regard for its place in the story may be misleading. To show the differences, you might want to ask the students to look at the contexts and implications of the two appearances of the phrase "only a girl." You might want to call attention to the narrator's differing roles in her earlier and later dreams. The turning point comes when she is eleven and involves the horses, yet that section is introduced by "I have forgotten to say what the foxes were fed." How could so significant an element in the story be "forgotten"? There would be no initiation story—at least not in these terms—without the horses, you might suggest. You might point out that the trigger to the memory is the father's bloody apron, as if she were just remembering her childhood up to that point. You might ask the students whether this suggests anything about the older narrator's—the voice's—attitude toward the innocence of her childhood (the first part of the story), and toward her initiation into youth if not adulthood. Do these attitudes tell them anything about why certain details were included in the first part of the story, why they were treated the way they are there, and why quite different details are selected and why they are treated quite differently in the second half of the story?

There is no sense in denying the force of theme in determining much of the content and structure here, so I find it just as well to get it out on the table—though not necessarily first. You might want to ask in what sense the characters are representative: Father, Mother, Little Brother, Average Male, Girl? Do the students see any thematic relevance in the characterizing of the two horses? Would the girl have opened the gate wide for Mack? Is there any theme wider than the sexist theme implied by the burdened savages, by Henry's Stephen Foster song, by the slaughtered foxes and horses?

Still, you might want to ask to what degree the particulars of the story transcend the theme in interest and import. Are the details of fox farming and of life in rural Canada only interesting in their thematic implications? (You might here want to relate childhood and rural life—innocence / Eden / garden—as a common American theme.) Putting up the curtain between her brother's bed and hers may have thematic import, but are all the specific details of the unfinished upstairs bedroom, its contents, the children's superstitions about security, their songs interesting only in terms of the theme? (And, by the way, to what degree is "boys-and-girls: childhood" just as good a rendering of the implications of the title, as "boys-versus-girls: sexism"?) Why does the girl put her brother on the rafter in the barn, endangering his life? How is it similar and how quite different from the freeing of Flora?

You may want to ask your students to compare this story to "Araby," perhaps with the handle of romance-of-childhood versus realism-of-maturity, and with some attention to the prose and use of detail. Since in some ways this story may give women students a bit of a hard time, if that's the way your class goes, you may want to ask the question (for discussion or paper) whether there is any significance in the fact that the initiating act here—regardless of outcome—is the liberating of an animal.

Questions for Discussion

1. What is the nature of the initiation in the story? Is there more than one initiation?

2. How do you read the final paragraph of the story?

3. What kind of story might this have been *without* the horses?

Writing Assignments for Chapter 10

1. Compare the tone of the narrators in "Araby" and "Boys and Girls." To what degree do the narrators' views of their experiences seem to have changed over time?

2. Write a personal essay about a time when you felt that assumptions about gender created discomfort or restrictions for you. Whose assumptions were they? How did you respond?

3. "Translate" a page of "Gorilla, My Love" into standard, academic English prose. Then write an essay describing what is gained and lost in the translation.

11 LITERARY FORM AS CONTEXT: THE SHORT SHORT STORY

As the text suggests, this chapter can provide occasions for exploring and even celebrating the marvelous flexibility of the short story form, and, despite the brevity of its selections, can test the analytical abilities of even the most seasoned and sophisticated reader. The "short shorts" provided here can also very usefully be assigned at the beginning of the term, perhaps in conjunction with the short selections that make up the "Reading, Writing, Responding" chapter. I find that if I have a class of students relatively untutored in the methods of literary analysis, it can be helpful to assign a number of very brief works during the first week or two of the term and to spend a significant amount of time (at least a week or two) showing students how to read closely and effectively. When I use these stories in this way, I pay more attention to conveying ways to glean signficance from the text than to studying particular elements, imparting terminology, or suggesting theoretical approaches. In these sessions, we tend to study a story's opening paragraph(s) for hints about its conflicts and concerns, to look closely at the possible implications of the title, to note repeated patterns, and to jot down questions that the text provokes. In other words, we work to gather the raw material of analysis and then try to make sense of it. After several such sessions, I find that the class has a better understanding of what it means to read a text, and students are ready to tackle the work of the semester with some degree of confidence.

Planning Ideas

- Show the class a videotape of the BBC film "Five Stories of an Hour," which offers a straight reading and four film renderings or "translations" of the work in a mere thirty minutes. Divide the class into groups and have each group analyze one of the translations of the story, taking care to comment on which parts of the story the filmmaker emphasizes, which parts are changed, and to what apparent purpose and effect.
- If you are using poetry in your course, you might pair one of these very short stories with a narrative poem of about the same length and use the pairing as a basis for discussing the similarities and differences between reading a poem and a very concentrated short story.

- Assign different stories from this chapter to different groups of students. Have the students draft a plan for expanding the story into a longer work—a full-length short story, a novel, or a screenplay. Ask each group to share the plan with the class, to explain what additions would be made, why they chose to expand the story as they did and to suggest the strengths and weaknesses of the expanded form in comparison to the original.
- Bring in a copy of *Life's Little Instruction Book* so that you can compare some of the father's suggestions to his son in that work with the mother's suggestions to her daughter in **"Girl."** You may also want to discuss why one work is classified as a nonfiction "how to" book and the other is called a short story (i.e., is labelled literature).

KATE CHOPIN

The Story of an Hour

Chopin's story concludes with what has come to be called an "O. Henry ending," and so I sometimes ask students how the author sets us up for this ending. Since we know from the beginning of the story that Mrs. Mallard suffers from heart trouble, how is it that we are surprised (if we are—and I was the first time I read the story) when her husband unexpectedly returns and she dies of a heart attack? Clearly Chopin takes particular care to put us off the scent. Early on the narrator assures us that a family friend, Richards, has inquired closely into the matter of Brentley Mallard's death and convinced himself by way of "a second telegram" that Mallard truly has perished in the railway disaster. He goes to this trouble because he wants to make absolutely sure of the truth before bearing the news to the ailing Mrs. Mallard.

Such careful craft is evident throughout the work: in the upstairs/downstairs, private/public dichotomies Chopin sets up and in the way she sustains suspense as she gradually allows Mrs. Mallard—and the reader—to discover her own possibly "monstrous joy" at her husband's apparent demise. One way to examine Chopin's masterly use of suspense is to read the story aloud, pausing at several junctures to imagine what revelations might be up ahead. (If you show the videotape suggested above, you can simply stop the tape at several points during the actress's reading.) For example, the glorious spring day so beautifully described in paragraphs 5 and 6 might be expected in a more conventional story to suggest the tragic contrast between the liveliness and beauty of the season and the desolation and loss that are Mrs. Mallard's lot. However, as we soon discover, the birds twittering and the mottled vista of clouds and sky suggest, less predictably, that a new, freer life is opening up for Mrs. Mallard. Similarly, when we read that the lines of Mrs. Mallard's face "bespoke repression and even a certain strength," we may at first believe that she is repressing her grief, trying to be strong and maintain her composure despite the loss of her husband. Later we realize that she is probably repressing recognition of her joy—and perhaps that the lines of repression also suggest something about her history within the marriage.

Some students may jump to the conclusion that Chopin's is a story about a woman subdued and perhaps abused by her husband—a story implicitly critical of the "western patriarchal hegemony." But a closer look at the text suggests that assessing blame is not the story's aim, and in this regard, of course, paragraphs 12 and 13 are key.

In paragraph 12 the narrator describes the husband's hands as "tender" and acknowledges that his face "never looked save with love upon her." More importantly, in paragraph 13 the narrator suggests that the repression Mrs. Mallard has felt is experienced by women *and* men: "There would be no one to live for her during those coming years; she would live for herself. There would be no powerful will bending hers in that blind persistence with which men and women believe they have a right to impose a private will upon a fellow-creature. A kind intention or a cruel intention made the act seem no less a crime. . . ."

Chopin here seems to suggest that, by its very nature, marriage encourages people to impose their wills upon one another. To explore this idea a bit more pointedly, I like to ask my students to think about their dating experiences. I ask them if they *always* get to go to the movie they most want to see when they go out on a date. (And I suggest some serious self-examination may be in order if they answer in the affirmative!)

Questions for Discussion

1. What examples of irony do you find in the last five paragraphs of the story?

2. Why is it appropriate that Richards try to screen Brently Mallard from his wife's view?

3. Do you believe the Mallard's marriage was a loveless one? How would you describe the marriage, based on what the story tells you?

ERNEST HEMINGWAY

A Very Short Story

The story of a sad love affair recounted in a page and a half, this work contains as much plot as television might use to sustain a two-hour movie of the week. To get across to students how many events Hemingway packs into this brief story, you might lead them in compiling a list of plot elements on the blackboard. A wounding, an operation, convalescence, lovemaking, a prayerful visit to a church, frustrated lovers, battle, long-distance love, lovers parting, lovers quarreling, a tearful goodbye, a seduction, a rude a awakening, a broken heart, a tawdry affair, a ruder awakening—all these elements are part of one very short story. How, I sometimes ask, does Hemingway manage to squeeze it all in, and what keeps this story from seeming like a mere list a plot elements like the ones Atwood strings together in "Happy Endings?"

Hemingway has been quoted as saying that he worked on the "iceberg principle." That is, he tried to write so that one-eighth of what happens in the story is revealed and the other seven-eighths is left below the surface for the reader to discover. He said he felt this made the reader participate in the story, so that the story became part of him (or her). I like to spend some time with the class talking about what is left out of Hemingway's story that we must fill in for ourselves. For example, there is no unmediated dialogue, we learn very little about who the characters are or what they look like, we never know the woman's full name, and the man is nameless. After we have discussed what is missing from the story, I like to ask whether the story suffers from the omissions—or whether something is gained by leaving these things out.

Questions for Discussion

1. Does the story simply recount the experiences of two presumably fictional characters, or can their experience be somehow generalized? Does Hemingway's style of presentation suggest an answer to this question?

2. What does the story suggest about the nature of love and romance? About love and romance in wartime? Does the spareness of its telling affect the nature and / or effectiveness of its wisdom?

3. If Hemingway had chosen to tell the tale in a thirty-page story or a two-hundred page novel, would its significance change? Would its effect change?

GABRIEL GARCÍA MARQUEZ

A Very Old Man with Enormous Wings

The best defense, we're told, is a good offense, so I like to be offensive in teaching "Very Old Man" and ask students whether they can take a story like this seriously. If credibility doesn't come up, I ask if they believe the story. Then, do they "believe" the people in "Sánchez" or "Boys and Girls" ever really existed or if the events happened as they are told? With luck, we're off and running on issues like probability and telling the truth by lying. Why should a probable fiction be better or more serious or more valuable than an improbable one? Aren't they both, after all, fiction—i.e., false? Well of course you can learn about people and life from probable fiction, but how often do you run into a very old

man with enormous wings? But do you learn anything about Pelayo and Elisenda? about provincial culture and provincial Latin American culture? about
crowd behavior? about human response to the unknown or extraordinary?
Indeed, you can argue, you may be able to learn more about response to the
unknown here than in, say, "Everything That Rises Must Converge." There you
know about the limited perspectives of Julian and his mother and can feel superior to them, but here the extraordinary man is as strange to you as it is to the
villagers.

This may be a good time to bring up symbol once more: is the old man a
symbol? As a symbol, if he is one, does he "stand for" something? if so, what? if
not, can he still be a symbol? We're back to symbols as nonparaphrasable units
of meaning.

As usual—or perhaps more than usual—you of course must be prepared to
handle quite different responses and to bring them back to areas you want to
discuss at this point in the course. If credibility doesn't come up right away, you
may want to listen for interpretations of what the old man stands for, begin with
symbol, and work around to meaning in terms of the way people in the story
act. Or someone may begin by saying that what García Marquez is doing is
recounting a folk tale straight, as if the narrator is as credulous as the villagers
and that it is a kind of patronizing tale whose subject is human credibility. How
do we deal with folk tales? Do we dismiss them? interpret them psychologically
or anthropologically? accept them as a vision of reality from an angle quite
different from ours but more or less common to a significant number of people
in the world? You might want to compare the folklore element here with that
in "How Much Land Does a Man Need?" or "Love Medicine."

At some point in the class discussion the realistic (some would say disgusting) detail in the story is sure to come up. It's easy to dismiss this merely as
a device for achieving credibility or willful suspension of disbelief in an evasive
half-truth, I think. I'd rather think of the details as part of the imagination or
vision of the story, as if Garcia Marquez had said to himself, "What would happen if a very old man with enormous wings were found here in the village?" and
had then imagined the consequences as precisely as he could.

One hopes someone will mention the humor—the neighbor woman who
knows everything about life and death and who identifies the old man as an
angel; Father Gonzaga's testing him with Latin; the villagers' plans for him,
including his being "put to stud in order to implant on earth a race of winged
wise men." I hope you don't have to explain why such details are funny; or why
funny details don't disqualify the story from serious consideration.

Questions for Discussion

1. The story is full of rather off-putting realistic details, cruelty, greed,
humor: what is it we feel reading this story? Does the mixture of real and fan-
tastic have its analogue in the potpourri of emotions?

2. And what, finally, do we feel about the old man — pity? fear? disgust? wonder? Do we want him to turn out to be a hoax? stay and play with the children and make Pelayo and Elisenda rich? die (to rid the world of monstrosity)? soar off into the sun?

3. How are we to take the subtitle, "A Tale for Children"?

JAMAICA KINCAID

Girl

It might be interesting to approach this story as an example of "wisdom" or "didactic" literature. The earliest wisdom literature we know of is the Sumerian "Instructions of Suruppak," parts of which date to as early as 2500 BC. We know of Egyptian, Aramaic, Hebrew, African, Greek, Irish, and Norse versions, among others. The genre is as old and widespread as literature itself. Generally, wisdom literature offers advice as to conduct and supports this advice with truisms and general pronouncements usually offered in a fictitious setting wherein a father addresses his son.

Traditional "didactic" literature — and there is much that feels and is traditional in "Girl" — offers practical advice on some aspect of life. For example, the Greek poet Hesiod in his *Works and Days* and Thoreau in *Walden* offer practical suggestions about farming and rural life. Yet, almost invariably, mixed in with this practical advice and / or subtly suggested by the advice are ethical admonitions as well. These authors are not merely interested in teaching people how to farm but how to live and what to value.

It can be useful to give this background information to students and then ask them to what degree "Girl" fits in with the genres of wisdom and didactic literature and to what degree it departs from them. Is it, in effect, an antiwisdom or antididactic work in which the advice harms rather than edifies? The most obvious difference between "Girl" and the works I have mentioned is its brevity. I sometimes ask the class whether a series of suggestions of this length can hope to impart much (positively or negatively), or whether so short a story, because it *does* consist of a series of straightforward admonitions, is likely to be more effective than a story that tells a tale.

Questions for Discussion

1. How might the advice be different if the addressee were a boy or young man? What advice might a mother give to a young man? What advice might a father give?

2. Why, amidst all the practical advice about how to iron, set table, etc.

does the speaker include the admonitions about not becoming a slut? Does the inclusion of these admonitions suggest that not becoming a slut is no more or less important than ironing correctly, or does it suggest just the opposite? Is there an inner coherence or logic to these pieces of advice?

3. Who is speaking? How can you tell?

4. Is this really a story? If so, why do you say so? What makes it a story? If it is not a story, what is it?

5. Why does "Girl" end with dialogue about feeling bread? Is this somehow a conclusion to what has come before? Why does the author end where she does?

YASUNARI KAWABATA

The Grasshopper and the Bell Cricket

The narrator's approach to the events of "The Grasshopper and the Bell Cricket" transforms a rather simple, children's adventure into a lovely prose poem about love, the assessment of value and the gifts of memory and innocence. The story also presents a parable about art and artistry, and it is with that aspect of the story that I like to start. In paragraphs 4 and 5, the narrator explains the origins and evolution of the beautiful lanterns that the children carry each evening in their search for grasshoppers. The lanterns, which were first bought or made as practical tools for the hunt, have become over time, lovely and elaborate works of art, with each child vying to produce a more beautiful version than the last. I encourage students to discuss what views of art and the artist the narrator seems to suggest in his telling of this part of the tale.

The last half of the story introduces the subject of youthful attraction. The boy who has found a grasshopper keeps offering it to the children at large, but he waits until the girl he fancies expresses her wish for the insect before making a present of it to her. Students are sometimes puzzled at this introduction of young love into the story. I like to provoke their thinking about this element in a somewhat roundabout way, by asking why the narrator feels "slightly jealous" of the boy. In the course of exploring this question, students often come to perceive that the narrator envies the boy and the other children their innocence, their unexperienced pleasure in the grasshoppers, the bell cricket, and each other. He knows that time will change all this—that, figuratively speaking, they will probably catch common grasshoppers more often in their adult lives than they will catch rare bell crickets—that life will be full of disappointments as yet unimagined. When he sees the names of the boy and girl projected by serendipity on each other's clothes, he appreciates the chance beauty and rightness of the picture before him. He imagines that if each could carry that picture into the future, it would provide pleasure and solace in the midst of adult dissatisfactions and failures.

Questions for Discussion

1. What does the part of the story involving the artistry of the children have to do with the ending of the story—the narrator's desire that the boy and girl remember the beauty of their names projected onto each other's clothes? In what sense is this part of the scene, which is temporary and which only the narrator observes, a work of art?

2. Why do the children make new lanterns every day? What are their motives?

3. What do the narrator's musings reveal about his experience of life and love? Would it make any difference in your perception of the story if you found out that the narrator only imagines the creation and evolution of the lanterns, building this part of the story on the evidence of the lanterns with which he sees the children playing?

Writing Assignments for Chapter 11

1. Write your own short story "Boy" modeled on Jamaica Kincaid's "Girl," or write your own version of "Girl," accounting for your inclusions and omissions. Do this either from your own point of view or from the point of view of an unwelcome adviser.

2. Do some library research on Hemingway's theories of fiction, and write an analysis of "A Very Short Story" in which you measure his success in following his own precepts with that story.

3. Write an essay on the role of the artist as suggested in "The Grasshopper and the Bell Cricket" and "The Hunger Arist" or "The Zebra Storyteller."

∇ ∇ ∇

Evaluating Fiction

For most students, a "good" story is a story that they enjoy—good literature is literature that entertains them—even though they sometimes suspect that their teachers' notions of "good" literature is just the opposite (literature than doesn't entertain but instead bores, depresses, or confuses them). Part of the job of courses like this and teachers like us is to expand students' horizons and enlarge the realm of literature that students are *able* to enjoy. But, along the way to doing that, I find I can't push too hard when it comes to evaluation. I find, for example, that many students respond enthusiastically to Connell's "The Most Dangerous Game" and are extremely resistent to analyses that would devalue the story because of its formulaic qualities. I have had much more success with stressing the positive aspects of the very best stories we read, realizing that many students will come to a more sophisticated understanding of literature as they learn to read closely and to understand works of greater complexity.

As far as my own evaluative standards are concerned, I try to mention them repeatedly during the term but in an unobtrusive way. I often talk about how certain stories have grown in richness for me over the years, standing up to repeated rereading and yielding new insights over time. I talk about the difference between a book or story that one reads merely to find out what happened and the work that rewards one's attention long after one *knows* what happened. I also stress the degree to which writers offer new ways of looking at age-old problems, the degree to which the best literature offers the unpredictable, the unexpected.

Planning Ideas

- Show the PBS American Short Story film version of **"Barn Burning,"** (with Tommy Lee Jones as Abner), and ask students to (1) compare and contrast the written and the film versions, and (2) evaluate which version is "best," taking care to define what they mean by "best."
- Spend some time asking the class to evaluate the selections on your syllabus they have read thus far. Which stories did they find most memorable?

least? Which stories do they think will still be anthologized and read one hundred years from now? Why? Which stories would they recommend to someone else? Why?

RICHARD CONNELL

The Most Dangerous Game

Many students will have read this story before, perhaps in high school, and in my classes the vast majority still like it a good deal. As a matter of fact, it fairly consistently scores in the top three or four when I ask students to rank the stories they've read in order of preference. For many instructors this will be a little surprising, and for some more than a little disappointing. But it is a "rattling good" adventure story with a good plot that is well structured. I have to be very careful in teaching this story not to be patronizing or off-putting. This is not, after all, a poor story.

Assuming considerable student response, then, you can plunge right in, to the structure or the means by which the excitement of the story is controlled and heightened. Students who have not read the story before might be asked to stop reading at the first break and write down their expectations about how the story will develop and what in that section gives rise to such expectations. It may be well at this point to suggest that almost all plots involve false expectations as well as "true" ones, or foreshadowings, just as a good mystery story will involve false clues leading to false suspicions. The "true" expectations make the ending of the story appear, when looked back upon, "inevitable," and the false ones, cleverly used, make that inevitable ending appear nonetheless "surprising." As I suggest in the text, the best reader is not necessarily the one who guesses the outcome correctly, but the one who is most sensitive to all the possibilities, all the expectation—a point that bears repetition.

There are two common, related, widely held, and often unexpressed assumptions that might be challenged in discussing this story. One is that "mere adventure" stories or slick stories are devoid of themes or thematic scope; the other is that "real literature," as opposed to popular literature, is cerebral or intellectual—literal detail in such stories being only the embodiment of the abstract "idea" of the story. "The Most Dangerous Game" has a rather clear theme that is announced in the first few paragraphs; if its call for sympathy for the "huntee" in a world divided between hunters and huntees is not necessarily outright condemnation of hunting or killing for any purpose, it is surely an appeal for sympathy for the underdog and against violence, urging the reader to put himself in the place of the victim. That the story is set just after World War I and the Russian Revolution, and that Zaroff and Ivan are Cossacks (the most ferocious and loyal of the adherents to the czar) does not seem wholly accidental. The story thus has political and moral thematic scope. Indeed the plot is almost too contrived to illustrate that theme, too pat: Rainsford, the hunter who believes in his total difference from, and superiority to, the game he hunts, is forced literally to put himself in the position of the hunted. If this story falls short of "literature," one might argue that it is not because of its lack of "ideas," but because it is too cerebral: the fiction or fable, the plot and characters, being too dominated by theme, too abstract and unlifelike.

The precise detail, including details of character and characterization, and the precise language in which the story is written are not highly significant here. That's why the story can be (and repeatedly has been) made into good movies and TV plays, and why it can be retold in other words with relatively little loss of power. This is not necessarily a flaw, of course. It is, for one thing, testimony to the strength of the story-line. And in this respect it is typical of the yarn or tale, a story that can be retold, can be transmitted orally with great variation in words and sentence structures. It is, in fact, an excellent illustration of history existing in large measure independent of structure, and might be useful in class for just that purpose.

Questions for Discussion

1. What expectations are aroused by the first few sentences of dialogue in the story? How is each of these expectations continued or reinforced, fulfilled or disappointed? Once the nature of Zaroff's "game" is clear, how is suspense maintained? Do you ever really doubt the outcome? If you are reasonably sure who is ultimately going to win the "game," how do you explain the "excitement" or appeal of such stories? Is "suspense" or "expectation" a better word for describing your responses? How do you know (by what means do you know) who is going to win in this story? (How do you know who will win in a John Wayne movie?) Can you tell with the same certainty who is going to win an election? a football game? an Olympics competition? Does you relative certainty about the outcome of this story imply a "view of reality" that you detect here? Can you discover any specific evidence within the story of that view? How much of your certainty of outcome derives from evidence within the story and how much from previous reading or film-watching experience?

2. Are there any details or actions in the story (such as Rainsford's falling overboard) that seem hard to believe? How do these affect your enjoyment of the story while you are reading it? your judgment of the story afterwards? Have you ever seen a film which you enjoyed until you thought about it later? until you saw it a second time? To what extent are "second thoughts" and second viewings or readings valid criteria for judging a work?

3. The first scene is presented almost entirely through dialogue. Are there any passages there that seem unnatural as conversation, as if they were clearly

intended for the reader and not for the person spoken to? What is gained and what lost by this dramatic presentation?

4. In the first scene the discussion of hunting, the actual purpose of the trip, seems to be introduced casually into the conversation. Did it alert your expectations? In the light of later events, should it have? How is that discussion related to what happens later in the story? To what extent does the conversation define the specific theme of the story? How does Rainsford's dismissal of superstition and of "mental chill" as "pure imagination" relate to his theories of hunting?

5. Zaroff says that "instinct is no match for reason" and that "life is for the strong." How do these statements relate to Rainsford's earlier description of hunting? What are his reactions to Zaroff's statement? Is Zaroff's position logical? Are Rainsford's objections logical? Is there any significance in the fact that Zaroff's clothes fit Rainsford?

6. What does "game" in the title mean? To what extent is Zaroff's hunting a sport? Could he make the hunt more "interesting" by evening the odds, by giving the quarry more weapons or advantages? Does the fact that he does not do so throw any question on the validity of his arguments?

7. Zaroff is a Cossack and considers the overthrow of the czarist regime by the communists a debacle; he is a gentleman, a gourmet, a connoisseur. How do these details relate to his "game"? to his arguments? to the theme? Are there, then, political implications in the hunting-hunter theme of the story?

8. In a story that involves a considerable amount of action, the climactic action, the final fight between Zaroff and Rainsford, is not described. Can you think of any reasons for this omission? For the paragraph leading up to the fight, the focus of narration shifts for the first time from Rainsford; why?

WILLIAM FAULKNER

Barn Burning

This is a good story to use late in the semester with students experienced in analysis who have the basic elements of fictional presentation firmly under their belts. "Barn Burning" works well in the sections of the course emphasizing point of view, characterization or setting, or as part of a study of the initiation theme. I find it works best—and I'm most pleased with class discussion—when I teach it after students have the tools in hand to appreciate its richness and complexity. Since the introduction in the text focuses on style of presentation, I like to start discussion by asking the class to compare Faulkner's narrative presentation in two paragraphs of "Barn Burning" to the "suspended time / animation" scene in Ambrose Bierce's "Occurrence at Owl Creek Bridge." I sometimes read aloud (or ask a good student reader to read aloud) the passage in which Faulkner uses something between a freeze-frame and a slow-motion technique similar to Bierce's to describe Sarty's sensations in the pause between the judge's question and Harris's response (pars. 10 and 11).

In "Occurrence at Owl Creek Bridge," Bierce suspends time to call attention to the differences between imaginative wish fulfillment and reality, and in doing so, he experiments with an early type of psychological realism. Faulkner's use of psychological realism is similar in that the scene in the make-shift courtroom juxtaposes the "reality" of the pause between the judge's question and Mr. Harris's answer and the simultaneous imaginative sensation Sarty has of swinging helplessly out over a ravine. Some members of the class, I hope, will see a qualitative difference between the ways Bierce and Faulkner employ this technique. If you can get your students to talk about this difference—one accomplishes little more than an interesting plot twist, the other helps to create the portrait of a deeply divided soul—the class will be well on its way into an evaluation (and, I hope, an appreciation) of "Barn Burning."

Once we've begun to talk about Sarty and Faulkner's portrayal of his conflict, I like to ask how the story would be different had Faulkner made Sarty the narrator. Clearly the boy isn't capable of telling a story nearly as complex as the one Faulkner presents through the shifting focus of a third person perspective—and it's not just that he's a boy, or that he's ill-educated. Sarty neither knows nor understands a number of important things about his father's history and motivations—for example, Abner's activities during the Civil War and his attitude toward fire—that we learn about through the third person narrator. Much of the social context of "Barn Burning"—the suggestion that the old southern hierarchy of plantation aristocrat over poor tenant farmers and slaves remains intact after the war—would be lost without this outside, authoritative voice. Much of the irony of the ending—Sarty's despairing, desperate attempt to assert his father's bravery as a counter to all his father's wickedness—would be lost without the authoritative voice.

As it is, Faulkner manages to have it both ways, and after stating this, I sometimes ask students to speculate about what I mean. What I'm getting at is that Faulkner's shifts in perspective, however confusing, enable him to present Sarty's plight with all its personal urgency and to present the larger context in which Sarty's struggle is only one of many struggles. By taking us into Sarty's mind, Faulkner causes us to feel the powerful tug of war within the boy between the pull of "blood" (product of genetics, nurture, loyalty of kinship?) and the pull of justice. He does this both through the narrative description of Sarty's feelings and through the italicized words that convey Sarty's thoughts in his own words. The details about setting and history (paragraph 15) fashion a much larger perspective. And the curious statement near the end of the story, "The slow constellations wheeled on," simultaneously suggests the vastness of the new world Sarty faces alone and the insignificance of his decision (and even of all human endeavor) in the face of an indifferent, impersonal universe.

If style hasn't come up in our discussion of focus and narrative technique, I like to get the class to look at a couple of passages from the story in which Faulkner uses some of his notoriously long sentences: perhaps the paragraph describing Sarty's fight with the older boys after the first trial and the paragraph near the end of the story describing his wild flight away from De Spain's house after he's carried the warning. While Faulkner is deeply concerned with the inward life of his characters, his prose is often extremely cinematic. You might ask your students to describe the way they would film both these scenes using whatever techniques of filmmaking—montage, jump cutting, voice-over, etc.— seem appropriate. If your library has the PBS film version of "Barn Burning" from The American Short Story series, you might have the class watch the film and critique it. If your students have thought about filming the two scenes mentioned above, they will probably be eager to suggest how the film they've seen could be improved to convey more of Faulkner's vision. I find this approach very effective as a way to call attention to Faulkner's narrative virtuosity (students can see how much he packs in that the film leaves out) without seeming to preach about it.

Faulkner's characterization of Sarty seems to me quite different from his characterization of Abner. Students usually find Abner a somewhat mysterious character, as Sarty himself does. You might want to instruct half of the class to write a paragraph explaining why Sarty finally breaks away from his father— providing evidence from the story about what events lead up to his decision— and instruct the other half to write a paragraph explaining why Abner Snopes habitually burns barns. Which group is able to come up with the most definitive explanation?

Questions for Discussion

1. Why do we feel we know Sarty better at the end of the story than we know his father? What does Faulkner gain by characterizing Abner as he does?

2. To what degree does the end of "The Most Dangerous Game" offer closure (a sense that all loose ends are accounted for and tied up)? What about the ending of "Barn Burning"? If a story ends somewhat inconclusively, is this good or bad, or does your answer depend on the story? Which story leaves you with more to think about?

BHARATI MUKHERJEE

The Management of Grief

When Judith Templeton asks Shaila Bhave to help her communicate with the other Indian people in Toronto who have lost relatives in the airplane bombing, she does so because Mrs. Bhave is reported to have responded to the accident "more calmly" than the others. Indeed, in the first half of the story, the narrator seems reliable and steady—especially in contrast to her neighbor Kusum, who threatens suicide and makes it cruelly clear that her older daughter is a burdensome responsibility in contrast to the beloved younger daughter who has been killed. I like to ask students whether at any point in the story they begin to question Mrs. Bhave's reliability. Students usually come to class wanting to know what they are to make of the mysticism in Mukherjee's story, and this question gets us into the issue. When midway into the narrative Mrs. Bhave reports that her dead husband Vikram appears to her in a temple, we may question whether this is a mystical experience or a delusion brought about by grief and longing. You might want to ask your students whether the story seems to support one interpretation over the other.

"The Management of Grief" is a story about how one group of people responds to loss. It is also about being different or "other"—about living outside the dominant culture. Pretty early in the discussion I like to get students to talk about the cultural groups represented in Mukherjee's story. There are the Hindu Indians who have settled in Canada, like Mrs. Bhave; the Sikhs, represented by the elderly couple in Agincourt but also by the radicals accused of bombing the airliner; the native Canadians, represented by Judith Templeton, the provincial representative, and the white neighbors who attend Satish's and Kusum's housewarming; the Irish men and women Mrs. Bhave and the others meet during their trip to the crash site; and perhaps also the Americans, represented by the white-haired TV preacher and his audience. Conventional wisdom would have it that universal experiences, especially tragedies like death, transcend cultural differences. You may want to ask your students if Mukherjee's story supports this view.

Who, besides the other relatives of the deceased passengers, offers sympathy that Mrs. Bhave is able to believe and accept? Why are the gestures of the Irish welcome while Judith Templeton's best efforts ultimately are not? It may be a question of proximity to the tragedy. Judith Templeton is an ocean away from the bombing site. The TV preacher and his audience are also miles away, seemingly oblivious to suffering amidst "potted palm trees under a blue sky." But the Irish are intimately involved in dealing with the gruesome aftermath of the disaster. They see grieving relatives wandering their streets and haunting their shores, and they mourn with them.

On the other hand, it is hard to avoid the suggestion that the gulf between the Canadians and Americans and the immigrant Indians exists because those who are part of the dominant Western culture refuse to accept the Indian way of handling grief, to admit the validity of another way of mourning. Could it be that the Irish are more accepting, not just because they are close to the scene of tragedy, but because historically they have always been outsiders, too?

Perhaps at some point someone will suggest that cultural differences are not the only barriers to accepting another's way of grieving and that cultural similarity does not necessarily guarantee understanding. (If no one does, I bring it up myself.) One recurring motif in the story is the idea that "a parent's job is to hope." Mrs. Bhave, her neighbor Kusum, Dr. Ranganathan, and the elderly Sikh couple share this belief. It is perhaps the main thread that links them as Indians in their response to the tragedy, but it is notable that the experience of loss itself is their strongest tie. The granddaughter of a devout Hindu and the daughter of rationalists, Mrs. Bhave has no firm spiritual or cultural anchor. When she goes to India, she travels for months with her family "courting aphasia," but as Dr. Ranganathan says, the survivors have "been melted down and recast as a new tribe." Only those who have suffered this particular loss can share its particular anguish—yet even those in the "tribe" cope with grief in very individual ways.

At some point in discussion, I like to bring up the implications of the title. The coldness of the term "management" would seem to hark back to Judith Templeton's well-meaning but rather clinical approach to helping the bereaved immigrants. Although I'm tempted to dismiss the idea that Mukherjee' story is an indictment of white / Western / American / Canadian insensitivity toward minority cultures—especially given the discussion above—I'm not certain the notion will go away. What are we to make of Mrs. Bhave's defection from Ms. Templeton's crusade? Of Judith Templeton's name and its associations with Judeo-Christian culture?

Questions for Discussion

1. What of the ending? Does the story seem incomplete? Does Mrs. Bhave receive instructions from the spirits of her family—and if, so what do we make of them—or does she descend into utter madness? If we believe the latter, do we do so out of Western skepticism?

2. Is the ending in some sense a means of confronting and frustrating readers who reject mysticism? Readers who like pat endings? Do you believe any audience would find the ending completely satisfying? If so, what kind of audience?

Writing Assignments for Evaluating Fiction

1. Evaluate the ending of "Barn Burning" and the ending of "The Management of Grief." Does each story have an effective ending? Is one ending better than the other?

2. Write an essay in which you evaluate one of the stories assigned this term and explain why you believe it is the best short story among those assigned for the course.

3. Write a personal essay describing the experience of reading a story that had a significant personal impact on you, then evaluate the story on the basis of its literary qualities.

∇ ∇ ∇

Reading More Fiction

I've often felt that sections like this were places where editors dumped the stories they wanted to include but didn't know what to do with, though I've known that the intention was supposed to be to give instructors a free hand with a certain number of stories and to demonstrate to students that a story in a chapter on plot is not necessarily a story that can be approached only through plot, etc. So now I'm faced with a dilemma: I want to shut up and let you get on with your teaching, and I want to make some helpful suggestions—and show that I at least think I know some things a teacher can do with these stories. So let me have it partly both ways: for "The Real Thing" and "The Summer My Grandmother Was Supposed to Die," I'll do the whole thing; for the others I'll just tell you where in the text proper I was tempted to put the story.

- "A Hunger Artist," would work very well with the stories in "Symbols," as would "Into Night." (I don't believe the meaning of the Kafka story is paraphrasable, by the way, despite the strong elements of allegory about art.) You might also consider using "A Hunger Artist" as part of a discussion on the role of the artist, along with "The Zebra Storyteller," "The Real Thing," "The Grasshopper and the Bell Cricket," and maybe even "Happy Endings."
- "Great Falls" is an initiation story and might profitably be taught with "The Watcher" or any of the stories in the initiation chapter. It could also be taught as part of the "Symbols" chapter or the chapter on point of view.
- "The Yellow Wallpaper" is a good story to add to the "Setting" or "Point of View" chapters, but it could also be paired with "Shiloh," "The Odour of Chrysanthemums," or "The Story of an Hour" as a way examining different approaches to gender roles and troubled marital relationships.
- "Into Night" would be a fine addition to the chapter on point of view, but it would also work well as part of a thematic study of children and parents along with "Personal Testimony" and "A Pair of Tickets." "Into Night" would also be a good selection to use along with "Sonny's Blues," "Gorilla,

My Love," and "Girl" in creating a unit on African American writers, or it could be paired with "The Managment of Grief" for a discussion of indeterminate endings and the use of magic or mysticism in the short story.

HENRY JAMES

The Real Thing

If "The Cask of Amontillado" is a story about plot or plotting, "The Real Thing" is a story about character and characterization, and that, plus its quality, is why it is here. The chapter suggests how I read the story—real ladies and gentlemen are useless as models for or representation of ladies and gentlemen precisely because they are real, and reality is made up of stereotypes. Major and Mrs. Monarch are only useful as models for stereotyped stories. You might want to point out that this paradox is prepared for in the first paragraph by the "paradoxical law" that people who looked famous were never famous and vice versa. Both these paradoxes are debatable, and sooner or later—though perhaps later, toward the end of your discussion of the story—you may want to raise the issue of the truth of the story, whether it is the real thing, but by that time you may also have laid the groundwork for discussing the reliability of the narrator.

Something you may have to clear up first is the whole conception of class. I find that my students have great trouble with this concept, particularly as it appears in James or Trollope or any late nineteenth- or early twentieth-century English work (the American-born James being in many ways more English than the English). Many know better, but they insist on using "rich" and "upper-class" as synonyms. They have to be reminded about "the vulgar rich" and the "impoverished genteel" and it is news to many of them that anyone who works for a living, no matter how rich—or mannerly—is, at best, middle-class. It is possible that without some discussion of class the full poignancy of the story (as, in the final paragraph, "it was dreadful to see them emptying my slops") will not fully come across. Not that this poignancy will go unchallenged—someone may ask, "Why shouldn't they empty slops? Somebody's got to do it. Why are they better than anyone else? If they have to make a buck and they have no other skills, then they just have to do the best they can." Can an egalitarian read with sympathy this apparently elitist story? (We are back to whether a 1990s feminist or civil libertarian can read "A Rose for Emily" with sympathy.) How one deals with different, especially unacceptable, political, social, and moral values in reading and appreciating literature is an issue that must be confronted in any course treating literature, especially that of other times or cultures. I want my students to take values and literature seriously, as I am sure most of you do as well, so too latitudinarian a position may subvert our purposes. On the other hand, I do not want to reinforce what I find is an already entrenched bias against appreciating or applauding anything that fails to confirm our own vision and views, for this clearly works against the understanding and sympathy that the study of the humanities and especially the study of literature are meant to encourage. This is a very shadowy area, but the issues are real and important, and, if we are not to sterilize our discipline, I believe we must get it out in the open, in front of the class, with all our prejudices and uncertainties hanging out. What do you think?

When I feel I've sufficiently discussed character and characterization, stereotypes and class distinctions, art and reality, and perhaps literature and values, and life, I like to turn to the very end of the story: "my friend Hawley repeats that Major and Mrs. Monarch did me a permanent harm, got me into false ways. If it be true I'm content to have paid the price—for the memory." That the story is a "memory" of the somewhat distant past is suggested in the very first sentence of the story—"in those days." I am not sure what the value of the memory is that has made it worth so much to the narrator. The memory surely is not pleasant—he hated seeing them empty slops, he had to turn them away after about a week, he does not know whether he did them any good, what their fates were. He does not seem to mean that the memory was in the "lesson"—that art is the illusion of reality and not the representation of it— for the price he has paid apparently is a lessening of his artistic ability ("permanent harm," "false ways"). I'd like to think that James, being James, is turning the screw of the paradox once again, so that if the real thing is not a good model for art, then perhaps what is good for art is not good for our real lives, our humanity. That experience which weakened his art made him a better human being (or "real person"). As I say elsewhere in this text, I do not mind parading my uncertainties before the class when they are real and earned—that is, when I have at least worked at resolving them.

Part of the "earning" here may be trying to come to terms with the character of the narrator himself. He is not successful enough not to want or need paying "sitters" and commercial work doing book illustrations, yet he is quick enough to point out that his professional judgment is not that of a barber or tailor (that he is not merely commercial, a tradesman). His mind is subtle enough to see things paradoxically, shrewd enough to recognize that since Claude Rivet only painted landscapes he would sacrifice nothing in recommending the Monarchs to him for their portraits, and tactful enough not to say so. After you have done so to your own satisfaction, you might want your students to go through the story carefully and thoroughly, searching for details that characterize the narrator. They can then report their results in a paper or discuss them in class.

One question that you may want to raise yourself is what, precisely, is the narrator's attitude toward the country-house class—or toward the Monarchs, for that matter. Why can't the artist—who, if he is not a successful portrait artist, seems to be a skilled illustrator—use his imagination to alter the Monarchs? Why do they always appear so large in his drawings? Could it be that the artist is less confident, less sure of the value of his work and his position in society than he realizes? His distress at seeing the Monarchs down on their luck and emptying slops notwithstanding (or is distress his full feeling?), isn't there a kind of contempt, even hostility in his attitude? Perhaps a kinder way of getting at this is to ask the students to try to deduce from the story exactly what the narrator believes is the value of art and the role of the artist in society. You might also ask them if our narrator seems comfortable with this role and sure of his ability to fulfill it.

MORDECHAI RICHLER

The Summer My Grandmother Was Supposed to Die

This may be one of the few stories in the anthology to deal with an experience that many students will think of as close to or potentially close to their own, dealt with in a way that they think they might be able to emulate. Though the elements of revenge, cruelty, courage, and imagination may be extracted from the first stories and related to the student's own life, "The Summer My Grandmother Was Supposed to Die" seems to cry out for a personal narrative from the student.

I don't like to teach this kind of story first in a course because it gets us (and I really mean to include myself) using stories to talk only about ourselves, reducing them to our terms instead of going out to meet them on their own and thereby broadening our own perspectives. But I do want to treat personal narrative fairly early to make sure that our reading and discussion are not merely cerebral exercises or academic games. I am an un-re / de-constructed referentialist in dealing with most stories.

So after I have talked about literature for a week or so in a more or less "objective" way and had the class write at least one paper critically treating a more or less technical aspect of narrative structure, I like to ask the students to read a personal narrative like Richler's and to write one of their own, suggesting that it might be well to choose a real episode to write about. And I ask them to be very conscious of the questions they are asking, the choices they are making, the problems they face. How do you select an experience to write about? What makes it seem like good material for a story? Where do you begin? How do you get your reader's attention? How do you decide what to put in and what to leave out, what to tell when? How do you tell a story?

You might apply some of these questions to the Richler story. The opening of that story may seem easy to explain: he begins with the doctor's decree that the boy's grandmother has less than a month to live. Though she lives on for more than four months, the story seems bounded by diagnosis and death. But very soon the story shifts back seven years to the death of the grandfather, the grandmother's stroke soon thereafter, and her coming to live with the narrator's family. The seven years prior to the gangrene are divided by the mother's illness, the temporary removal of the grandmother to the home, and her return, precipitated by the narrator's blunder. It is not until near the end of the story that we learn the full force of the title and that the structure of the story is justified from "supposed to die" in the doctor's terms back to the story of the grandfather, his first marriage, second marriage, and death, and forward to the death of the grandmother and the new gloss on the phrase "supposed to die." If the title does not tease us into attention, the third brief paragraph should: isn't it unnatural, monstrous, for Muttel's mother to want her own mother to die?

Some discussion might be generated by asking students at first to point out the realistic detail in the story (the Jewish milieu, the streets of Montreal, the apparently digressive details of the thoughts and activities of small boys from peeping to scatology, to popular culture, sibling rivalry, baseball) and how that contributes to a sense of actuality. But, you might ask the students, isn't its apparent actuality undermined by artful structuring, the rearrangement of the chronology, and such "literary" devices as the verbal play in the title that defines the structure?

How about the students' own narratives? Have any of them rearranged the time sequence of the history? Are the details selected or arranged to "make a point" or embody a theme? Does "telling a story" mean distorting reality?

The story would not be the same if its narrator could have told it moment by moment or at least episode by episode as it happened (though of course he was only seven when his grandfather died and younger than our students when his grandmother finally died). Doesn't memory inevitably distort? When we know how things turn out, we can go back and select those things that were important in making it turn out that way (like film clips from a game). That, we must agree, is distortion. Surely, then, things written down immediately, such as Pamela's letters (so we can't say "in the heat of the moment," can we?), are truer—they tell things more as they really are. Perhaps one of the students wrote a narrative that he or she remembered but that was also recorded at the time in a journal or diary. Isn't the immediate, personal account the more accurate? Knowing others won't read it, we tell our diary the truth, don't we? You might ask if any students are embarrassed by their old diaries, if they can see their self-deception, or "acting." Isn't the writer of the diary really a persona or two personae we construct for the purposes of writing and reading the diary? Isn't the self projected in the diary a fiction of sorts, someone we would like to be, or someone like fictional characters we admire? Isn't the writer an "interested party"? There may be ways, then, in which disinterested or inquisitive memory may be more rather than less accurate than the immediate transcription.

A good deal of this has to do with focus and voice. The voice in a remembered story is the older narrator, the focus the younger acting character. Even in a diary, focus and voice may be to some degree different, depending on how much we make ourselves the heroes of our own lives.

▽ ▽ ▽

Teaching Poetry

How to begin teaching poetry? The arrangement of the poetry in *The Norton Introduction to Literature* suggests one way; in fact, it suggests a beginning, middle, and end for a course in poetry—moving from some of the simpler issues of interpretation to more complicated ones. Still, you have a lot of choices to make, for few courses offer enough time to raise all of the questions and problems that are built into the textbook. And probably no course offers enough time to discuss adequately all of the poems in the text. The introductory section, *Poetry: Reading, Responding, Writing*, addresses some of the issues on students' minds when they begin a course in poetry, and I hope that the discussion there will defuse for you some of the objections that students sometimes raise when they first face the serious study of poetry. For many students, the experience with poetry that you provide them will be the first serious exposure that they will have had, and choosing the right poems for them to study in detail is crucial.

I like to wing it a little in the early class meetings, trying out three or four poems with students before committing myself completely to a syllabus (although that flexibility may not be possible in large, multisection courses with a preset syllabus). But if you have flexibility, use it. Ask your students to talk the first day about poems they have already read and liked, and have them fill out a card indicating how much formal training they've had and what their nonliterary interests are. With such information and with the experience of three or four class meetings, you will be in a better position to choose poems that will interest your students, as each chapter offers a variety of good poems, some dealing with fairly sophisticated issues, and to keep interested those students who may be ahead of the average in your class.

The poems at the ends of chapters give you a chance to do two things in class: (1) read individual poems closely in order to see what they say, what they do, and how they work; and (2) compare poems that have things, such as subject matter, in common so that individual differences begin to show up very early, even before your students have terminology adequate to describe them fully. Each group of poems, those that are discussed and those that aren't, contains a variety of modern and traditional poems, a sufficient variety to raise many kinds of questions for class discussion, and there are enough poems in each that you can skip any poems you don't like or would rather not discuss. I myself usually do fewer than half the poems in each group, changing the selection every time I teach the course. I raise some technical questions early (it's hard to get far without mentioning, for example, questions of speaker or word choice), but I raise them as the issues come up in particular poems, saving systematic discussion for later.

The eight chapters in *Understanding the Text* systematically introduce technical problems—tone, speaker, situation and setting, words and word order, figurative language, structure, sound and sight, and stanzas and verse forms. Not every teacher will want to take up all these issues, and in the chapters themselves I have tried to say the most basic and elementary things so that, if you like and if you have time, you can take up some more difficult problems in class, using either the examples I discuss in the chapter or those in the selection of poems at the end of each chapter. You may find, too, that you would rather choose some of your examples from elsewhere in the text (I often do that myself; I don't like to use the same examples every time I teach the course, and besides it is good for students to recognize that any poem can be used as an example of a lot of different things). You may also prefer to teach these chapters in a different order; I like to bring up the issues in this order because it works for me, but I've tried to make it possible for you to move the chapters around to suit yourself. Even when one of my comments looks back at another poem, it could just as easily look ahead.

Exploring Contexts remains, as in earlier editions of this book, the most innovative section. The five chapters here introduce more complex issues of context: questions of time, place, and authorship, and issues that go beyond the work on the page and into the cultural milieu from which it comes. The issues here are of several different kinds, and you will want to choose which ones best fit the aims of your course. Many courses, I know, start running out of time at just the moment they arrive at this section, but I hope you will find time to tackle some of these contextual problems. Your best students will especially appreciate it, and often the reluctant poetry readers discover there what poetry is for. Besides, this section is often the most challenging and rewarding one to teach, or so it seems to me.

I have put quite a number of poems in a *Reading More Poetry* section at the back, taking them out of groups and categories altogether. I hope that here you will find some poems you want to teach in one unit or another early in the course; the "open" grouping is intended to suggest more flexibility and invite you to shop for poems you want to teach in a particular way. But there's another reason for the large open group, too: many of these poems are particularly challenging and could well be appropriate at the end of the course when your students will have acquired a variety of skills. It's not a bad idea to see if they can do "everything" with a few of these poems at the end of the course as a kind of review. It is a good confidence builder.

Whether you make up your own syllabus or conform to one already set, one of the toughest decisions involves how to distribute class time. Basically, the decision comes down to the question of intensiveness versus extensiveness; you simply cannot discuss as many poems in class if you do each one thoroughly. Compromises are of course possible: you can vary the pace depending on the difficulty of individual poems, you can assign study questions on poems you don't have time to discuss, you can assign four or five poems for a given class meeting and pick only one for discussion, or you can have exceptional days in which, if you usually discuss one poem intensely, you instead teach briefly seven or eight poems (or vice versa). It seems to me helpful to retain some flexibility, perhaps even putting "open" or "catch-up" days in your syllabus or occasionally scrapping a planned assignment in favor of something that has become crucial to the class. I usually spend the better part of a class on one poem, especially early on, but I almost never (except for the first two or three class meetings, when I am emphasizing how much there is in every poem and how closely one must read) assign only one poem. Asking students to read one poem five or six separate times probably involves noble intent, but an assignment that consists of only one poem (a few pages of reading at most) doesn't look like much to any student and probably sets a bad class expectation. Often I choose three or four short poems for a day's assignment, discuss the most difficult one in class, and either point to one or two specific problems in the others or (more profitably if there is time) ask students to raise questions that troubled them. Clearly, the key to good class discussion is good preparation (theirs as well as yours), and anything you can do to stimulate sensible preparation is a real help. Getting the whole class involved in discussions seems to me crucial, but sometimes it is difficult, partly because some students seem to be shy of poetry and partly because others get excessively enthusiastic and sometimes want to dominate the discussion. It may take your whole bag of tricks to keep balance and order in the classroom, but you can help yourself somewhat by insisting on the kind of careful and precise preparation that has everyone think deeply about certain problems before class. Sometimes this is best done by a last-minute, looking-ahead comment at the end of a class, sometimes by study questions handed out ahead of time, sometimes by quizzes, and sometimes by assigning brief minireports to individual students for a future class meeting. (See the Planning Ideas at the beginnings of each chapter. Which ones you try will depend on the make-up of individual classes and upon particular opportunities and problems that arise, and I don't know any general rule to use except to keep a close watch upon the class dynamics, especially in the beginning.)

One thing that does practically guarantee—at least in the long run—close attention to class discussion is the assignment of challenging and frequent papers. (See the Writing Suggestions and Assignments at the ends of the chapters in the text and at the ends of chapters in this *Guide*.) What you can do in this area—as distinguished from what you'd like to do—will of course depend on the size of your class and the number of weeks you have to devote to poetry. The very nature of writing gets students to think deeply and formulate their thoughts and feelings articulately. I think it's especially important to assign papers early (I usually assign a very short one for the third class meeting), and I prefer many short papers to fewer longer ones; that way you can help students more quickly with problems, and they can have several chances to prove and improve their skills. Papers on one specific aspect of a poem—papers that can be done in 400–500 words—still almost inevitably ask students to confront the whole poem, and I find that classes become more lively after each paper—at least as soon as the initial disappointments wear off. Papers are, of course, time consuming for you; to be effective they deserve extensive comment on both good and bad features, and individual conferences are usually necessary. The ideal is probably a paper a week and a conference a week, but unless your class is restricted to a very small size, you will have to adjust the ideal to fit reality. Wherever you begin and at whatever pace you proceed, it is almost always a good idea occasionally to sum up and occasionally to set up something for future use. If you begin as I do by holding back as much as possible on technical problems, you may nevertheless want to mention some terms as an issue emerges in a particular poem and perhaps sometimes assign (or point toward) the Glossary or part of a later chapter. I like to give a sort of impression of disorder at first (so much to learn, so little time), and then do some summarizing when we formally consider a particular technical issue, often asking my students to look again briefly at poems we have already discussed. This tends to provide a cumulative feeling about learning, with the added benefit of showing students that they've made real progress in learning to approach poetry analytically and experientially. If you can do it unobtrusively (without playing "What do I have hidden in my hand?" too crudely and obviously), it gives the class a relaxed flow and a quiet sense of direction. A number of the suggestions that follow will (I hope) point you toward other strategies of putting things together; I have made quite a number of suggestions about ways of teaching specific problems, and you may wish to skim through the Guide before looking in more detail at the comments, suggestions, and questions on individual groups and individual poems.

∇ ∇ ∇

Poetry: Reading, Responding, Writing

In talking about the relations of readers and poetry, the introductory chapter of the text stresses the interconnections between the reader's personal emotions and experiences and the reader's response to a poet's words. It may be useful to emphasize and clarify the nature of this complicity between poet, poem, and reader so as to avoid a problem I sometimes encounter in my classes: the tendency of some students to let their experiences control their readings of some works. (For example, a student who found her volunteer stint in a hospital repulsive may focus on the disgusting images in Sharon Olds's "The Glass," recall similar scenes from her time as a candy striper, and seem unable to recognize how Olds transforms the image into a symbol of love and affirmation.) I try to caution students that, while their experiences and feelings will inevitably enter into their responses to poetry (the poet's voice may sometimes seem to speak to them in a very personal way), the poet's experience rarely duplicates the reader's exactly. Readers must take care to study the details of each poem closely, attempting to understand the emotions and experiences the poet strives to convey—whether similar to or different from their own.

Planning Ideas

- I like to begin the study of poetry by showing Part II of the six-part PBS video series *The Power of the Word*, moderated by Bill Moyers. In the series, Moyers interviews practicing American poets who also read from their works. Part II of the series explores the poetry of James Autry, a white business executive whose inspiration and subject matter come from the business world and his southern boyhood, and Quincy Troupe, an African-

American poet who teaches nontraditional students and writes about his native St. Louis. This segment also explores how the language and subject matter of poetry grow out of the personal experiences of the poets. (Galway Kinnell and Sharon Olds are among those featured in Part I; Li-Young Lee* is one of the poets featured in Part IV.)

- a. Before classtime, I ask five students to practice acting out Tom Wayman's **"Wayman in Love"** as though all of the characters who appear in the poem really exist. (One student serves as narrator.) Then I have them "perform" the poem for the class—in costume (or at least with Marx and Freud appropriately bearded). I find this is a good way to establish that poetry can be amusing and fun but also to initiate discussion about the strategies various poets employ to convey states of consciousness—thought, memory, dream states—and to discuss Wayman's skill in addressing serious topics in a humorous way.

  b. Another entertaining way to introduce Wayman's poem is to show the brief scene from the Woody Allen film *Annie Hall* in which the two main characters think about how dissatisfied they are with their sex life. Those who know the movie will remember Allen's technique of having the female lead seem to rise from their shared bed and talk to the audience, followed by the male character doing the same. After showing the film clip—easily obtainable on video tape—I like to ask students if they see any parallels between Allen's technique for conveying his characters' thoughts and Wayman's.

- I sometimes ask students to choose among the poems in this chapter the work that evoked the strongest response in them. Then I have them bring to class a paragraph describing their responses and explaining what details in the poem contributed to them. In class I ask a few students to read their paragraphs and use these as a starting point for discussing the poems the students have found most striking. (If you have followed the strategy of keeping your syllabus flexible early in the term, as suggested above, in the Teaching Poetry chapter, this exercise may help you to determine what poems should make up the rest of the syllabus.)

MARY, LADY CHUDLEIGH

To the Ladies

Students rarely have trouble understanding the message of this poem, but they may need help in appreciating the skill with which the poet expresses her— or the speaker's—feelings about a wife's place in the world early in the eighteenth century. One way to start is by asking students to locate the many absolutes sprinkled throughout the poem: "nothing," "all," "never." These not only emphasize the speaker's complaint that women who marry are utterly imprisoned but also help to create the speaker's desperate and angry tone. Aspects of form also contribute to the poem's sense of constriction: the exact end-rhyme, the tight precision of the iambic tetrameter.

Questions for Discussion

1. Given that in 1703, married women had almost no legal rights, might you still take issue with the speaker's pronouncements about the status of wives in her time? What statements might you dispute?

2. If the speaker overstates her case to a degree, why might she do so? What possible purpose(s) might she have?

3. Could this poem have been written in the 1990s? What details would you need to alter to update the speaker's complaint and advice?

RITA DOVE

Fifth Grade Autobiography

The title of this poem tells us that the speaker is a fifth grader, but the photograph she describes was taken when she was just four years old. Sometimes I ask the students to imagine under what circumstances the speaker would construct such an autobiography—while completing a school writing assignment? during show-and-tell? I also try to get them talking about what kind of people usually write autobiographies—and why the writer / speaker of this particular autobiography is different from the usual, the expected. Certain details—the brother's Davy Crockett cap, his sailor suit—suggest the time-period when the photograph was shot. If my students are too young to remember the fads and styles of the late 1950s and early 1960s, I provide the footnotes. I also like to ask them what sense—taste, smell, hearing, sight, touch—evokes the strongest memories for them as a prelude to discussing how sensation helps to provoke the speaker's memory in the poem.

Questions for Discussion

1. What devices does the poet use in the poem itself to suggest the age of the speaker?

2. The speaker is describing a photograph, not constructing a linear narrative. How does the description of the visual images in the photograph tell us more about the speaker than simply looking at the picture would?

3. How do the memories triggered in the speaker by the photo make the photo itself clearer to us?

4. Is it difficult to distinguish between description and memory?

5. What makes this an autobiography?

EDNA ST. VINCENT MILLAY

[I, being born a woman and distressed]

In this poem the speaker is concerned with what she perceives as a conflict within herself between passion and reason. Millay skillfully employs the Italian sonnet form to set up the situation in the octave (the proximity of the man she addresses stirs her senses and confounds her brain), and to respond to the situation in the sestet (whatever her bodily response to the man, her heart and brain reject him). Students are sometimes reluctant to discuss their own experiences in handling tensions between passion and reason when the focus is sexuality, but I can often get them to talk about their mixed responses in some other area of their lives, e.g., the tongue says "eat more of this German chocolate cake" while the brain says, "you are going to feel bloated and overweight if you indulge."

Questions for Discussion

1. What does the speaker feel is the relationship between being a woman and being "undone, possessed" (line 8)?

2. What do "stout blood" and "staggering brain" suggest in the context of the poem, and how does the former commit "treason" against the latter (lines 9–10)?

3. What are the assumptions the speaker is challenging in the person she addresses? Do these assumptions differ by gender?

AUDRE LORDE

Recreation

If you are teaching this poem early in the course, your students may not hear the pun in the title, and you may need to point them to the theme of creation (lines 12, 17–18, 22) and re-creation; you may also want to remind them that the original meaning of recreation is a renewal or remaking of oneself.

Questions for Discussion

1. What is the "leash" referred to in line 11? Why does it need to be cut?

2. Lorde creates a comparison between writing and making love. In what senses are the act of writing and the act of love similar?

LI-YOUNG LEE

Persimmons

This poem is in one sense about the imprecision of language as contrasted to the precision of images, yet particular words connect the events in the speaker's life and the parts of the poem. It is also a poem about ignorance and intolerance—and the way that the meaning of words or signs varies from person to person, based on their perspectives and experience. Stanzas four and five address these issues in ways students often find quite moving, and so I tend to start discussion there. In stanza four, we discover why different-sounding words have close associations in the speaker's mind because of his personal experiences, and in stanza five we discover that the teacher's experience and knowledge are not in all ways superior to her student's (a development my students tend to relish).

Questions for Discussion

1. How does translation work as a theme in the poem?

2. How does the ability to paint while blind compare to the poet's ability to express himself in a language other than his own?

Writing Assignments for Poetry: Reading, Responding, Writing

1. Compare the attitudes toward childhood and adults in "The Fury of Overshoes" to those in Rita Dove's "Fifth Grade Autobiography" and in Audre Lorde's "Hanging Fire" (p. 718).

2. Do some library research on the circumstances of Mary, Lady Chudleigh's life, and write a paper in which you theorize about the experiences that might have led to the composition of "To the Ladies."

3. Write a paragraph exploring the meaning and importance of one significant line or sentence from a poem in this chapter.

Examples: a. "Knowing / it wasn't ripe or sweet, / I didn't eat / but watched the other faces." ("Persimmons")

b. "Who the hell did my cousin marry." ("Thirteen Years")

▽ ▽ ▽

Understanding the Text

1 TONE

"Don't use that tone with me!" "What tone?" my teenage son replies, feigning innocence. He knows, of course, that I'm objecting not to *what* he says but to *how* he says it. Tone is that elusive quality that allows us to make subtle alterations in the gap between what we say and what we mean. In short, tone makes irony possible. It also provides a way of making poetry seem alive and human to students whose previous experiences with poems have left them cold. Since we have all felt anger, fear, elation, sadness, desire, and frustration, students can learn to experience poetry fruitfully by learning to recognize that a poet has felt the same things—and has found just the right tone to make the experience come alive for the reader.

Planning Ideas

• A good way of helping students recognize varieties of tone is to save a few of the poems in the section to be read during class. Before having the students read them, I list on the blackboard isolated phrases or lines that could carry a variety of tones, depending on the context. Examples: "Doesn't she look pretty?" (**"Barbie Doll,"** line 23); "That's all." (**"Leaving the Motel,"** line 25); "He had been our Destroyer . . ." (**"Hard Rock Returns,"** line 34); "I think I may well be a Jew." (**"Daddy,"** line 35). I divide the class into small groups and assign one of the lines to each, asking each group to construct several imaginary contexts in which the line might appear. Each context should imply a different tone. I then ask a student from each group to explain to the whole class how the line might be delivered in at least one of the more interesting contexts. The class then plays "Name That Tone," generating a series of nouns or adjectives to identify the tone. Next, the students read the poem from which the line has been taken. In clarifying the differences between the tone of the line in the poem and in its imaginary context, the ensuing discussion gets students not only looking closely at an isolated passage but also thinking about how the part fits into the whole.

- A related exercise: before students have read Dorothy Parker's **"Comment,"** distribute on a handout the first three lines of the epigram. Have each student come to the next class with an appropriate fourth line. Then reveal Parker's line. The exercise makes it clear that the tone of an isolated passage alters that of surrounding passages.
- Another option: at the end of the class preceding the one on tone, have each student draw an adjective from a hat (examples: *gentle, worried, eager, frustrated, cynical, joyful*). The student writes a four-line epigram that conveys the tone. The epigrams can be turned in or discussed in class.

MARGE PIERCY

Barbie Doll

Certain word choices in this poem readily lend themselves to a discussion of tone. Examples: *"as usual"* (line 1), *"magic of puberty"* (line 5), *"wore out / like a fan belt"* (lines 15–16). This last image also works to introduce not only the concept of the simile but also the relation of rhythm to meter. Rhythm is the actual pattern of stressed and unstressed syllables in a line; meter is the prevailing pattern of stressed and unstressed syllables. Rhythm, then, is variable; a line in a Shakespearean sonnet may well depart rhythmically from the poem's meter. Needless to say, good poets provide rhythmic variations for good reasons. Lines 15–16 of "Barbie Doll" do not sound "poetic" in part because of the simile (how poetic are fan belts?) but also in part because of the rhythm. As imagery affects tone, so does rhythm.

Questions for Discussion

1. Why is it that "Everyone" sees "a fat nose on thick legs" (line 11) only after the speaker's image of herself has changed?

2. What does the title add?

SYLVIA PLATH

Daddy

This poem alternates between the particular and the general experiences of oppression. The person speaking in the poem is a particular woman, remembering her childhood and her father. She feels sympathetic toward others who have suffered, but beyond that, she begins to lose her own identity: "I began to talk like a Jew. / I think I may well be a Jew" (lines 34–35). She sees her pain as the pain of every woman: "Every woman adores a Fascist, / The boot in the face, the brute, / Brute heart of a brute like you" (lines 47–50). What she perceives as a woman's love of pain accounts for her trying to get back to (or get back *at*) her dead father.

Questions for Discussion

1. To what is the speaker referring in line 58? in line 67?
2. Why does the speaker say, "Daddy, I have had to kill you" (line 6)?

THOMAS GRAY

Elegy Written in a Country Churchyard

In addition to affording a chance to introduce the word *lugubrious* into students' vocabularies, this poem lends itself to a discussion of the relation between sound and sense. From the long vowels of the first quatrain to the strategy of delayed negation in the fifth and the sixteenth (we are given images of vitality before we learn that "No more" can the inhabitants of the churchyard partake in them, that "Their lot forbade" fame and glory), the poet impresses on the reader a profound sense of loss, of unfulfilled potential (lines 20, 65). The speaker's tone is understandably sorrowful as he contemplates the departed villagers' common lot.

Questions for Discussion

1. What might be the message of the "uncouth rhymes" and the scriptural passages mentioned in lines 79 and 83?

2. Some say the poem would be better unified and more effective if it ended after line 92. Do you agree?

3. Who is the "thee" of line 93? Why does the poet employ this strategy?

WILLIAM BLAKE

The Tyger

What is the "fearful symmetry" of lines 4 and 24? Why is it a *fearful* symmetry? This complex and evocative concept is central to Blake's thought—and to his habits of composition. For one thing, the poem itself employs metrical and stanzaic symmetry. For another, it seems to have been meant as a companion piece to "The Lamb" (p. 979). ("The Lamb" is from Blake's *Songs of Innocence* and "The Tyger" from his *Songs of Experience*.) A discussion of the parallels as well as the differences between the two poems can prove fruitful.

Questions for Discussion

1. Why does the poet describe the activity of the tiger's creator in anthropomorphic images?

2. What is the effect of altering just one word in the first and last stanzas?

Writing Assignments for Chapter 1

1. Compare the hate / love relationship between daughter and father in Plath's "Daddy" to the relationship in Sharon Olds's "The Glass" (p. 662) and "The Lifting" (p. 715).

2. Using as many details from Gray's "Elegy Written in a Country Churchyard" as possible, either defend or refute the following thesis: The speaker longs to be part of a community—either that of the famous or that of the unlettered dead—but he is ultimately unsuccessful in joining either.

2 Speaker

The speaker of a poem might be thought of as the voice of the poem. Students (and some critics), following what we might call the biographical impulse, often confuse the voice of a poem with the poet's voice, and sometimes, of course, this identification is justified. Living in an age of confessional talk shows and made-for-TV self-exploitation, we are constantly bombarded with the sounds and images of public self-exposure. In this atmosphere, it is good to remind our students that while a poem may in part be an exercise in self-revelation—and certainly confessional poetry of one sort or another has been a dominant form since at least the arrival of the Romantics—it is just as likely to speak through an imaginary person or thing as through the voice of the poet. (Indeed, even the most avowedly personal poem is conveyed in a voice modulated by artifice, one never precisely equivalent to the poet's voice.) In discussion, students will slip and use the poet's name instead of "the speaker" (as on occasion I do), but it is well to maintain the distinction as much as possible so that students do not go astray when they move on to analytical writing assignments.

Planning Ideas

- You might want to open your discussion of the "speaker" by assigning one of the poems in which the speaker clearly is not the poet—**"In a Prominent Bar in Secaucus One Day,"** perhaps, or **"In Westminster Abbey*."** Then turn to some poems that could be autobiographical—**"Hanging Fire," "The Lifting," "Twenty-year Marriage*."** If you include Atwood's **"Death of a Young Son by Drowning"** in your discussion of apparently personal poems, you can help the students to see how complicated this issue can be (see discussion in Guide [p. 134]).
- Several of the poems in this section deal in one way or another with the speaker's gender (e.g., **"Sudden Journey," "Hanging Fire," "The Changeling," "[My mouth hovers . . .]*"**). You might assign students to read these works and bring to class a one-page essay comparing and contrasting the treatment of gender in two of them.
- Before classtime, ask the students to look up the word "changeling" in the *Oxford English Dictionary* (OED). Have them note the history of the word and several examples of its usage over time. Take this exercise as a starting point for discussing the ways in which the speaker of the poem might be considered a "changeling."
- If you plan to discuss the biblical allusions in the conclusion to Sharon Olds's **"The Lifting,"** have students look up two biblical passages—Hebrews 9 and Acts 9: 1–22—in a King James Bible and bring brief synop-

ses of both passages to class. Since students often have trouble with the seventeenth-century English of the King James Bible, exposing them to the verses that Olds alludes to and asking them to work out what the passages mean can make discussion more fruitful, even if you still must provide some help in translating the biblical passages into modern English.

SHARON OLDS

The Lifting

This is a poem about a single, fleeting experience. In the first line, the poet recreates her own surprise and brings the reader, without introduction, into a particular situation: "Suddenly my father lifted up his nightie." How does the speaker surprise herself by her own response? Notice how Olds moves from the specific to the general in the course of the poem. You might ask students to compare this to the progression of her poem "The Glass." Ask them to define the various feelings the speaker has toward her father in these two poems. How effective is the poet's use of shocking images in this poem and disgusting images in "The Glass"? Do these images become less shocking and disgusting by the end of the poems? Why?

It may be useful to explore the allusions embedded in the concluding lines of Olds's poem. The ending of the poem metaphorically conflates the raising of the father's nightgown and several biblical images. The nightgown is compared to a "veil" that will rise after one dies. (See Hebrews 9 in the King James Version of the Bible.) The writer of Hebrews describes the veil that covers the "Holy of Holies"—the sacred place in the temple beyond which the ark of the covenant lies, where only the High Priest may venture. In this New Testament passage, Christ metaphorically becomes the High Priest, the one privy to the truths behind the veil. To move beyond the veil is to gain access to the revelations that Christ will give to those who accept him and thereby receive the promise of eternal life.

Veils do not actually fall from anyone's eyes in the Bible—despite Olds's statement—but in Acts 9:1–22, "scales"—or something like them—fall from the apostle-to-be Paul's eyes after he has been struck blind on the road to Damascus. Paul's archetypal conversion experience transforms him from a persecutor of Christians into a missionary, a martyr and, eventually, a saint. In biblical terms, he is portrayed as being blind to the truth of Christianity until the scales fall from his eyes.

Olds's use of biblical allusion is complicated and by no means clear cut. She doesn't say the veil *will* rise; she says "we were promised" it "would" rise. You might want to ask students why they think Olds alludes to these biblical images. You might also want to ask how the speaker equivocates in her evocation of them and why.

Questions for Discussion

1. Can we assume that Olds is a Christian because she alludes to passages in the New Testament in her poem?

2. Is the speaker making fun of Christianity by comparing her father's self-exposure to Christ's revelation?

3. What is Olds's purpose in employing these allusions at the end of this particular poem? Does the speaker have mixed feelings about the promises to which she refers? Why might these promises seem appealing, whether or not the speaker believes they will be fulfilled?

HENRY REED

Lessons of the War: Judging Distances

My students often argue with each other about whether there really are two speakers as such in the poem, or whether, instead, the poem is a reverie in someone's mind, a reverie in which two voices recreate a kind of scene. The lack of quotation marks may contribute to the latter view, but either way of reading comes to much the same thing. (All dramatic dialogues are, in one sense, similarly reveries in a poet's mind.) In any case, it's important to emphasize the extreme differences of language between the two voices: the jargon-spouting, thoroughly "army" drill instructor who dogmatically, ungrammatically, nonsensically (see especially lines 10–11), and rudely badgers his pupils in lines 1–22 and 31–36, versus the recruit who rejects the army way for a highly metaphoric (and perhaps too dreamy and "poetic") mode of speech that, however, leads him to common-sense conclusions in lines 25–30 and 37–42.

Questions for Discussion

1. What is accomplished by describing distance as time in the last line? How does it relate to the poem's title? Where else in the poem is space regarded as time?

2. What passages would you emphasize if you were considering the poem as (a) an antiwar statement? (b) an account of military mentality? (c) an analysis of ways of perceiving natural landscape? (d) a dialogue between stereotyped articulation and instinctive feeling? (e) a description of man's relationship to

nature? (f) a contrast between things that endure and temporal or temporary things? What passages would you have to omit or deemphasize in order to regard the poem in each of these ways? Does having to ignore part of the poem invalidate the thesis?

JOHN BETJEMAN

In Westminster Abbey

The gender of the speaker is indicated here by the end of the first stanza, and the "lady" is characterized very quickly, mostly through her own words and attitudes. Having students detail how she is characterized and what precisely is implied by each of her self-righteous, self-centered, and bigoted statements can be the basis for a good discussion of how characters reveal themselves through language. A thorough discussion of characterization here almost makes a discussion of "speaker" as such superfluous, for everyone will recognize that poetry sometimes dramatizes a character as in a play instead of presenting an authorial voice speaking directly.

Questions for Discussion

1. Where is Westminster Abbey? How does the setting of the poem contribute to the characterization of the speaker?

2. Do you agree with the speaker that, although she is a sinner, she has "done no major crime" (lines 25–26)?

GWENDOLYN BROOKS

We Real Cool

The speaker in this poem purports to speak for a group. I try to get my students to notice how the collective nature of the poem's statement is emphasized through the form Brooks imposes on it. The word "We" dangles unexpectedly at the end of each line except the last. The speaker is never identified as an individual. While the collective character of the speaker's group is partially revealed through the group's actions, the form and meter of the poem also contribute to its characterization. The "We" of the poem share certain behaviors and expect to share an early death. The title suggests that "coolness" involves doing what others do—being part of the crowd—or of a particular crowd. The conclusion of the poem suggests where such behavior can lead.

Questions for Discussion

1. How does the rhythm of the poem contribute to the characterization of the speaker(s)?

2. What does it mean to "Strike straight"? To "Thin gin"? To "Jazz June"? How do these phrases help to characterize the speaker(s)?

3. Is the speaker's idea of what is "cool" and the poet's idea of what is "cool" the same? (Are the poet's perspective and the speaker's perspective the same?)

SIR THOMAS WYATT

They Flee From Me

This poem seems to me deceptively difficult, and often I assign it early in the course, do little with it in class, and then return to it later in the course when students have more fully developed their analytical skills. On a first reading, its themes of loneliness and betrayal are quite evident, and it fits well with the poems about speaker because it provides a revealing self-portrait. What seem to me interesting about the poem's complexity are two things: 1) the delicate tonal control, the move from the boasting of the first stanza to the dreamy nostalgia of the second to the anger and self-exposure of the third; and 2) the portrayal of a speaker who comes to seem more and more bitter and out of control.

Class time on both of these issues can be well spent, especially since the poem is an older poem, and students often have trouble with poems not in a modern idiom. But here even the unfamiliar words ("newfangleness" for example) are emotionally loaded; working with the OED (this can be a good early library exercise) can become part of the analysis of tone and feeling. Very good discussion can be generated about just what words and structural strategies in the poem create the abrupt mood and tonal shifts which contribute to the portrayal of the speaker. Ask your class exactly what was "special" about the experience of stanza two, and get them to articulate exactly what the speaker objects to in the behavior of this woman. Then get them to analyze the speaker's own behavior and attitudes and compare the two "characters" in the poem.

(Note: Students of Wyatt sometimes argue that the speaker in the poem is someone very much like Wyatt himself, and there may be a question here as to how self-conscious the portrait of the speaker is. It takes a very sophisticated group of readers to get into the question of intention here, but you can get at the character of the speaker well enough through the text of the poem without having to get into historical or biographical issues. Save those for later, perhaps returning to this poem when you do consider them.)

Questions for Discussion

1. What is the implied metaphor in lines 3–7? What does the metaphor suggest about the speaker's attitude toward the women he has known?

2. In what tense(s) is the poem written? Trace the changes in tense from line to line.

3. Characterize the speaker. Do you think he has a right to be bitter? Why or why not?

MARGARET ATWOOD

Death of a Young Son by Drowning

I've had very good luck with students' writing on this poem. It is difficult but clear, and the final image of staking out new territory by planting a flag (in this case psychological territory for the recovering speaker) brings the events and images of the poem together very nicely. Close analysis really pays off here, and the "character" of the speaker reliving the child's death and her experience in coming to terms with it becomes clear when the poem is read and reread several times.

Students usually assume, I find, that the "speaker" here is Atwood herself and that she is writing about a personal tragedy. Some of that assumption is probably generic—whatever we say about speaker, many readers believe that writing is narrowly autobiographical, in any case—and some stems from the sheer vividness of the poem, from the repetition of the child's birth journey in his death journey to the "claims" made on new land by the speaker at the end. There is so much precise detail, such a powerful sense of loss. It is therefore very useful to put the poem in its proper context, a context that makes clear why it is important to distinguish poet from speaker. This poem is from Atwood's book *The Journals of Susanna Moodie* (1970); all the poems in the book are written as if spoken by Susanna Moodie, a real person (1805-1885) who emigrated from England to Upper Canada and wrote several books about her experiences. In these poems, Atwood fictionalizes the life considerably but bases many of the poems on actual incidents recounted by Moodie. "Death of a Young Son by Drowning" is from Section II of the book, which recounts incidents in Moodie's life between 1840 and 1871.

Questions for Discussion

1. Does Atwood's poem provide any internal evidence to suggest it is not a personal, confessional poem? How might one discover that Atwood based the poem on another's experience?

2. Does the knowledge that Atwood based her poem on incidents in the life of Susanna Moodie change your reaction to the work?

WALT WHITMAN

[I celebrate myself, and sing myself]

In the preface to *Leaves of Grass* (1855), Whitman makes clear that he considers the work a personal, poetic manifesto defining what American literature should be if it is to embody the national character as he perceives it. I sometimes like to introduce this first section of that longer work by telling my students Whitman's stated aim (without adding much biographical or literary-historical detail). Then I ask them what sort of speaker Whitman invents to convey this new, quintessentially American poetry. The egotism of the speaker is readily evident to them from the outset, but some students will notice that the overweening self-confidence of lines 1 and 2 is complicated and softened by the easy egalitarianism of line 3: "For every atom belonging to me as good belongs to you." At this point, I try to draw them into a brief discussion of how notions of ego and equality combine in our perceptions of our American heritage.

Once we've established that, in celebrating himself, the speaker also means to celebrate the uniqueness and complexity of all things American, I ask the class to look for details in the poem that suggest what Whitman's vision of America might be.

Questions for Discussion

1. The speaker is portrayed as leaning, loafing at his "ease," and observing "a spear of summer grass." If the speaker is the author of a new American poetry, what "American" qualities are suggested in this description?

2. What does the speaker mean when he says he "now thirty-seven years old in perfect health [begins]"? What is he beginning?

3. What characteristics—of the speaker, his poetry and things American— are revealed in the final stanza?

Writing Assignments for Chapter 2

1. After reading Audre Lord's "Hanging Fire," write a personal essay describing in some detail the frustrations of being a fourteen-year-old girl or boy.

2. Go to the library and look up Henry David Thoreau's letter to H. G. O. Blake, dated November 19, 1856, in which he talks about Walt Whitman and

his poetry. Write an essay describing Thoreau's opinion of Whitman and his work, based on the information you gain from this letter.

3. Read two or three of Sharon Olds's other poems in conjunction with "The Lifting." Write a paper describing the speaker in each of the poems and discussing whether the same speaker seems to be speaking in all of the selections.

3 SITUATION AND SETTING

This chapter asks students to focus on three questions: What is going on in the poem (what is the situation)? Where does the situation occur? When does it occur? Some discussion about how these issues intertwine may be helpful. For instance, a couple arguing loudly about money troubles will evoke one reaction if they are portrayed arguing in their own kitchen—another perhaps if they are in bed—a different reaction still if they are in a grocery store, or just outside the office of the husband's or wife's boss. We view a spot of blood in one light if it appears at the tip of a hunting knife held by a hunter, in another light if it appears on the same knife held by an abused spouse. The spot of blood may take on entirely different associations if it appears on bedclothes following a wedding night.

As in the case of James Dickey's "Cherrylog Road," the time of day and the time of year may also contribute significantly to the situation. In Dickey's poem, the heat of high noon in summer suggests the passionate heat of the coupling that took place between the speaker and Doris Holbrook and intensifies the sense of lustful excitement the poem conveys.

Planning Ideas

- Bring in pictures or show slides of several very different settings. Spend a few minutes discussing each, asking students to determine the location, the time of day, and the season represented. Then ask them to choose a scene and write a couplet describing as much about the setting and situation as possible. Have volunteers share these with the class, and then discuss the variety of responses evoked by each scene.
- To convey the idea that setting and situation are often inextricably linked, ask students to describe in a paragraph a setting that they ordinarily associate with peacefulness and calm. After they have written the description, ask them to write another paragraph describing a situation in which they would no longer feel relaxed in that same place.
- If you use novels in your course, you might assign students to read Emily Brontë's *Wuthering Heights*, creating a teaching unit on situation and setting using Brontë's poetry and prose and some biographical detail about the moors on which she grew up (see Writing Assignment #3). Hardy's *Return of the Native* and selections from his poetry would also work well.
- If you plan to teach Susan Musgrave's **"I Am Not a Conspiracy . . . ,"** you might show a brief clip from David Lean's 1946 film of *Great Expectations* (available on video)—the scene in which Pip, who has stolen food for the

escaped convict, encounters a herd of cattle and imagines them looking accusingly at him. Pip's paranoia has amusing similarities to the speaker's in Musgrave's poem.

ROBERT BROWNING

My Last Duchess

In this poem there is no commentary at all and no obvious reflection; this poem is an almost pure example of a straight dramatic situation. Because it is spoken by a single character, this kind of poem is often called a dramatic monologue (see the Glossary). Characteristic of the dramatic monologue is a gradual revelation of the situation and the speaker's character. The speaker gradually gives himself away, creating in the reader a stronger and stronger sense of horror at the duke's past actions, his present intentions, and his character. Some students will decipher the syntax of this poem with relative ease, but don't be surprised if some need help.

Questions for Discussion

1. Describe the dramatic situation. Characterize the speaker in detail. How is each aspect of his character suggested? What do his descriptions of the painting and statue tell you about him? When do you begin to sense his role in the earlier events he alludes to?

2. Characterize the duke's "last duchess."

3. What is the auditor like? How can you tell?

4. What information is withheld for dramatic effect? Describe the effects of timing in disclosing the information. How important is the precise time of disclosure? Evaluate the structure here against traditional descriptions of dramatic structure.

ELIZABETH ALEXANDER

Boston Year

Alexander's poem describes a year spent in Cambridge, the township across the Charles River from Boston proper that is considered part of Greater Boston. Some students will know that Cambridge is home to Harvard, Radcliffe, and MIT and will wonder, given the narrator's interest in bookshops and museums, whether she spent her "Boston year" as a student or perhaps as a research scholar. I like to ask students to characterize the narrator's year in Cambridge as a positive or negative experience. After a brief period of discussion, the class may divide into diametrically opposed camps, but usually a number of students will observe that her experience included a liberal sprinking of both the good and the bad.

In Cambridge the narrator suffered the indignities and loneliness of being considered different or "other" and searched in vain for people like her to make herself feel at home. Neither the usually welcome nor the usually unwelcome visitor knocked at her door. Yet she also explored communities that were exotic and "other" to her in the city, discovering new sources of delight and experiencing acts of kindness at the hands of the immigrant inhabitants of the city. Depending on the nature of your class, you may want to devote some time to discussing the students' own experiences of feeling like outsiders and of learning the ropes in a new place.

Questions for Discussion

1. What does the narrator mean when she reports in lines 7 and 8: "I ate stuffed grape leaves and watched my lips swell in the mirror"? Are her lips really swelling (did she have an allergic reaction to stuffed grape leaves?), or is it only her perception that her lips are swelling? Explain.

2. Why does the narrator care that her apartment floors won't come clean? To what stereotype or slur is she perhaps reacting?

3. Why does the narrator mention that Harriet Tubman, an historical figure long dead, never came to her door? What does she mean to suggest?

4. What is the meaning of the last phrase of the poem: "Red notes sounding in a grey trolley town"? What experiences are associated with "Red notes"? what experiences with the "grey trolley town"?

EMILY BRONTË

The Night-Wind

Setting and situation merge in this poem as the speaker imagines a part of the natural world, the wind, beckoning her outside into the night. The poem takes the form of a dialogue or discussion between the narrator / speaker and the wind. Although the speaker asks to be left alone, the poet gives the wind the last word, and the speaker, for all her protest, seems complicit in her own seduction. Students who have learned something about Emily Brontë's love of the outdoors may note the special care with which the dialogue is crafted to suggest how compelling she finds the countryside at night.

Questions for Discussion

1. What is the speaker's relationship with nature? Where do you find evidence about this relationship?

2. "The Night Wind" ends inconclusively with the wind still making its appeal. Do you think the wind succeeds in tempting the speaker out into the dark night? Explain your answer.

SUSAN MUSGRAVE

I Am Not a Conspiracy . . .

The speaker in Musgrave's humorous poem appears to be a poet who is undergoing an "image makeover" at the hands of someone named Paul, a photographer with whom she may or may not have an intimate relationship. Whatever her relation to Paul, it is clear that the speaker is uncomfortable to the point of hysteria with the new image Paul has in mind for her—understandably, since it involves her being photographed standing naked in high heels in a cornfield(!) Her discomfort with Paul's vision of her is evident when she says, "What Paul sees is something different from / me."

I like to ask my students to find where evidence of the speaker's hysteria first appears and to talk about the meaning of lines 5 and 6. There may be disagreement about the significance of the references to the corn-god whispering about whiskey and cocaine (lines 14 and 15). Perhaps whiskey and cocaine seem appropriate accoutrements for the wild, new image Paul wants the speaker to project. Perhaps the speaker is tempted to escape from her discomfort with the new image through alcohol or drugs. Perhaps the speaker actually uses drugs recreationally and, under the strain of the "makeover," becomes paranoid about the chance that she will get caught.

There is likely to be more agreement about another aspect of the speaker's situation—her discomfort at being naked under these circumstances. I like to ask students where in the poem they find evidence of this discomfort. Generally they are quick to note, in line 29, the echo of the word "shuddering" from line 13 and to make the connection between her horror at the notion of purses being made from the skins of unborn calves and her horror at standing before a camera naked in a cornfield.

Paul is trying to make the speaker into a saleable image, into a consumer product. The last verse of the poem suggests the degree to which his effort causes the speaker to feel disassociated from herself. In her paranoid fantasy, her very work, one source of her identity, becomes suspect.

Questions for Discussion

1. Why does the speaker imagine the cows interrogating her? What state(s) of mind does this fantasy suggest?

2. Why might the speaker associate her poems with illegal drugs?

3. Is this a poem about image-making and advertising, or a poem about the nature of poetry, or both?

WILLIAM SHAKESPEARE

[Full many a glorious morning have I seen]

This sonnet takes several turns marked by the words "Anon," "Even so," "But," and "Yet." In this sense, the poem itself imitates what it describes—clouds passing in front of the sun and blocking its light, then moving by and letting the light shine again. How is this inconsistency accentuated by the poet's choice of words such as "Flatter," "Gilding," and "mask'd"? By the reference to alchemy? What is the importance of the final distinction between "Suns of the world" and "heaven's sun"?

JOHN DONNE

The Good-Morrow

This is a poem about waking and discovery. How many different kinds of discoveries does the speaker describe? What is the parallel between exploration of "new worlds" and the way the speaker feels about his new love? What does the speaker mean by "got" in line 7? What does he mean by "possess" in line 14? What might the fear in line 9 refer to? What is the ideal of love expressed in the poem? To what is it contrasted?

MARILYN CHIN

Aubade

Morning in this poem is rejuvenating to individuals and to generations. What is the relationship between the individuals waking and the natural and historical events described? The poem juxtaposes two sources of light—the sun and a candle. What is the contrast suggested? How does this sea compare to the sea in Matthew Arnold's "Dover Beach"?

JONATHAN SWIFT

A Description of the Morning

Unlike the last three morning poems, this poem is not concerned with private feelings but with creating a sense of place. Although the poem is called "A Description of the Morning," it describes only people, not nature. What do the brief descriptions of morning routines tell us about the individual people? the neighborhood?

SYLVIA PLATH

Morning Song

Morning in this poem has both a metaphorical and a literal meaning. A child is born and thus enters the morning of its life. Mornings have changed for the mother who must rise to care for her crying child. How does the birth of the child fit into the mother's conception of nature? Of her own life? Why doesn't she feel responsible for the birth of the child (lines 7–9)?

Writing Assignments for Chapter 3

1. Write an essay exploring the use of color in Dorothy Livesay's "Green Rain," Elizabeth Alexander's "Boston Year," and April Bernard's "Praise Psalm of the City Dweller" and explaining how the colors in each poem contribute to the depiction of setting.

2. Craft your own dramatic monologue in which the duchess of "My Last Duchess" is the speaker and responds to the duke's charges against her. Take into consideration how her age, position, and situation might influence the way she expresses herself.

3. Research the setting in which Emily Brontë grew up and skim entries from Emily Brontë's journals for references to Haworth and the moors. Write an essay exploring her relationship to the landscape surrounding her home.

4. After rereading Elizabeth Alexander's "Boston Year," write a poem or short essay describing a time and place that you felt like an outsider.

4 LANGUAGE

If in earlier classes you have been emphasizing—from time to time, at least—the significance of individual words, shifting the focus to language in this section will be natural and easy for the class. In my own classes, I usually teach the poems at the end of this chapter by asking the students to isolate some key words in the poems, and we discuss each of these in detail—for precision of word choice, for the connotations of each word, for the multiple suggestions (or "ambiguities") that some words usefully provide, for allusions to other literature or traditional ideas, for references to specific facts and events, and for the placement of the word in relation to the larger emphases of the poem. Written exercises can be especially useful in this group; they can be focused on a single word in a poem or on a group of related word choices.

Planning Ideas

- Before class, give students a series of sentences to complete by supplying an extended simile. Encourage them to use their imaginations and to employ vivid language. (Sample sentences: My first date was like   ; When I get angry, I am as   as a   ; The building this class meets in is like   .) Ask them to share these in class.
- Ask each student to come up with a word to describe how one might enter a room ("dash," "saunter," "sneak," etc.); then discuss the connotations of the words supplied. What is suggested about a character if she is portrayed "skipping" into a room? "racing"? "slinking"?
- Bring to class several small objects, and pass a different object down each row of desks. Have the students in each row list as many possible symbolic associations for their object as they can. (Good objects include keys, light bulbs or candles, a single flower, an apple, a white piece of cloth, an object bearing the school insignia.) Have students share their lists with the class. Then focus on one of the objects, and discuss how it might be used in a poem as a personal symbol—suggesting a concept (or concepts) with which the object is not usually associated.

Precision and Ambiguity

SHARON OLDS

Sex Without Love

Students tend to fall roughly into two camps in their responses to this poem. One group views the speaker's portrayal of those who have sex without love as sneakily judgmental but accepts that, in some cases, her judgment might be correct. The other finds in the speaker's metaphors evidence of a shrillness, almost a hysteria, that suggests the speaker's approach to sexuality may be considerably more skewed than that of those who have sex without love. It seems to me that both views can be supported, and since the commentary and questions in the text tends to bolster the latter interpretation, I offer here some notes exploring the former.

Students quickly recognize that the metaphors and images the speaker uses to describe those who have sex without love become increasingly disturbing as she piles them one on one. The graceful image of dancers gives way to the chilly reference to ice-skaters and ice, which gives way to a grossly physical description of lovers "fingers hooked / inside each other's bodies, faces / red as steak, wine" (lines 4–6). Sometimes a student will note that the traditional elements of a romantic dinner (for nonvegetarians, at least) here become the basis of a distinctly unromantic and off-putting picture, one which concludes with a simile involving mothers who plan to give their children away. Students who believe that the speaker is unbalanced will point to this harsh and shocking comparison as evidence. Those who believe the speaker is making a valid point will sometimes interpret the metaphor as implying the unnaturalness and sterility of sex without love.

Some students will be reluctant to discuss lines 8–16, where the speaker develops her ideas using religious imagery—but in an unexpected way—suggesting through repetition and spacing (lines 8 and 9) the experience of sexual climax. If you have the nerve, and a little dramatic talent, this is a good passage to read aloud, even though it sometimes provokes embarrassed laughter. Some students have no trouble understanding the speaker's use of "God," "Messiah," and "priest" as metaphors. Others will be so conditioned to respond to these words in specific ways that they will need some nudging to recognize that the "God" for those who have sex without love is pleasure or orgasm (according to the speaker), and the "false Messiah" or "priest," who is not to be mistaken for the god, is the sexual partner.

Usually the extended runner / athlete metaphor developed in lines 18–24 of the poem is more easily decipherable, although there may be some controversy about whether the last three lines actually delineate a "truth" for the person who embraces sex without love or for the speaker of the poem.

Questions for Discussion

1. What do you make of the phrase "light / rising slowly as steam off their joined / skin"? Why does the speaker include this description? In what way does it contribute to the comparisons developed in the middle section of the poem?

2. What is the ambiguity in the phrase "its own best time"? How do the dual meanings of the phrase enrich the poem?

GERARD MANLEY HOPKINS

Pied Beauty

This poem is a celebration of beauty, but of imperfect beauty. Rather than searching for wholeness or perfection, Hopkins calls attention to those things in nature and in the human world that are unusual and unexpected. More than likely, students will need considerable help with the vocabulary of this poem. It may be well to guide them through a line-by-line paraphrase, giving special attention to the words Hopkins coins and the archaic words he resurrects. This is also a superb poem to study when you deal with sound effects.

Questions for Discussion

1. How does the poem itself fit the speaker's description of something "counter, original, spare, strange"? How do alliteration, assonance, and word choice make this into a strange and surprising poem?

2. What is the effect of the final "Praise him"? Does the poem lead you to expect such an ending?

WILLIAM CARLOS WILLIAMS

The Red Wheelbarrow

This is one of the most admired short poems of the twentieth century, and much of its force derives from its careful and precise choice of words and the way those words are deftly set into place. Your students may appreciate its art more fully if you ask them to try to rewrite the poem, keeping exactly the same visual objects (wheelbarrow, rainwater, and chickens) but presenting them differently. You can either set specific rules (change the opening phrase; keep the objects in the same order, etc.) or give them a free hand to try to create another poem with only the same basic materials.

Questions for Discussion

1. What are the advantages of a visual scene?

2. What is the function of the first four words? Why does the poem begin with a vague term like "so much"?

3. Does the poem's major effect depend upon an agreement between different readers on exactly what those words mean? Do the objects in the poem "stand for" anything? That is, are they "symbolic"?

E. E. CUMMINGS

[in Just-]

Cummings is famous for his unconventional manipulations of words and space on the page. I like to begin talking about this poem by asking students to explain the logic and effect of "eddieandbill" (line 6) and "bettyandisbel" (line 14). Then I ask them to explain the effect and force of "mud-luscious" (lines 2-3) and "puddlewonderful" (line 10).

Questions for Discussion

1. How does the interaction of the children and the old man relate to the tension between newness and tradition?

2. What are the implications of the allusion to Pan?

EMILY DICKINSON

[I dwell in Possibility—]

Like Cummings, Dickinson uses conventional syntax but substitutes unexpected words, giving the poem an element of surprise and ambiguity. How does the unconventional use of prepositions in this poem compare to that in other Dickinson poems you have read? Describe the relationship of the speaker to her house.

JOHN MILTON

From Paradise Lost

How does the poem generate the directional effect of lines 44–49? How much of the gravity portrayed depends on word order? How, exactly? Compare the tone and pace in Wordsworth's "Tintern Abbey." What factors account for the very different tonal effects achieved in blank verse here?

Metaphor and Simile

Metaphor can be very hard to teach if one tries to teach individual metaphors in isolation. To many students, individual metaphors often seem mere decoration (sometimes, of course, they are) and therefore rather precious and effete. Good basic metaphors are, of course, more vigorous and functional than that, and I think it is best first to emphasize poems that depend on metaphor, usually a single extended metaphor or at least a series of related ones. "That time of year though mayst in me behold" works well as an introduction because of its three closely related metaphors for aging and coming death. The first metaphor is expansive and rather general, and doesn't give much of a sense of urgency; its focus on a whole season of the year makes the aging process seem long and drawn out, but the other two metaphors are progressively more limited in time, and they project an increasing sense of urgency, as if, by the twelfth line, death were imminent. Because the poem is so carefully structured on the basis of the metaphors (four lines being devoted to each), it is easy for the students to work out and discuss, and with a little prompting from you they will be able to see the progress of the metaphors and their relation to the tone of the poem. Another poem that seems to me to work especially well in a discussion of metaphor is "The Death of the Ball Turret Gunner," which has the advantage of being very short and based on a single metaphor. Its birth metaphor (or rather prebirth metaphor—the gunner is hunched into a fetal position), although not altogether easy to see at first, makes for an especially lively discussion because of the irony of its use in the context of death; the metaphor takes the discussion quickly to the center of the poem. Other poems in the group use equally crucial and interesting metaphors, and it is probably a good idea to offer at least some variety in your selection of poems to discuss in class—choosing some poems that use more submerged metaphors and some that use multiple metaphors, as well as those that work from one central one. It may be useful, too, to go back to some poems you have discussed earlier, looking at the function of particular metaphors in the poet's conception of an individual poem.

RANDALL JARRELL

The Death of the Ball Turret Gunner

The introduction to this group (above) suggests some aspects of the poem to emphasize. Here is another line of questioning: What have "sleep" (line 1), "dream" (line 3), and "nightmare" (line 4) to do with the basic action of the poem?

HART CRANE

Forgetfulness

This highly suggestive poem is crafted almost entirely of similes and metaphors and appears to end with a paradox. I often start by asking students if they notice any difference between the comparisons drawn in the first stanza and the comparisons created in the second. If responses are slow in coming, I call attention to the words "song," "freed," "reconciled," and "unwearyingly" in the first stanza, which seem to have positive connotations, even to celebrate the liberating effects of forgetfulness. In the second stanza, the comparisons are more difficult to categorize. Is "rain at night" bad or good? Does it make one gloomy or lull one to sleep, for example? What are the connotations of comparing forgetfulness to "an old house in a forest"? Is the house peacefully secluded or woefully neglected? How is forgetfulness a "child"—in the sense that we associate a child with purity? with irresponsibility? The second stanza ends by suggesting that forgetfulness can have far-reaching effects for good or evil, an observation that helps to resolve the seeming paradox of the final line. You might ask students when in their own lives forgetfulness has been a good thing and when a bad.

Questions for Discussion

1. What do you make of the references to "white" in line 8? What connotations does the color white have, conventionally? Does the second mention of "white" in the line carry the same connotations as the first?

2. Explain how forgetfulness might "stun the sybil into prophecy." How might it "bury the Gods"?

3. What does the last line of the poem mean?

AGHA SHAHID ALI

The Dacca Gauzes

At the risk of murdering to dissect this lovely poem, I sometimes begin discussion by asking students to help me list on the blackboard the words and phrases associated with the Dacca gauzes. We begin with the descriptive names: "woven air, running / water, evening dew" (lines 2 and 3) and add "dead art," "heirloom," and "lost." If no one brings it up, I mention that the grandmother's comment at the end of the poem reemphasizes the notion that touching Dacca gauze was like touching air—in her comparison, the wonderfully fresh, "dew-starched" air of an autumn morning.

Against these associations, we set a list of phrases referring to the actions of the British imperialists, who diverted the cotton once woven into Dacca gauze to England for use in English cotton mills. That list includes references to amputation and silencing and shares with our other list references to death and loss. Placing the lists side by side throws into sharp relief the contrast between the loveliness, softness, and delicacy of the fabric the Bengali weavers once made and the coarse muslin that remains as a legacy of British usurpation. If, as most historians now attest, the story of the amputations is apocryphal, it nevertheless serves its purpose in the poem. The amputation of the weavers' hands symbolizes the amputation of a form of indigenous artistic expression and the brutal and wanton destruction of a culture for economic gain. The Dacca gauzes—and the remnants of the old culture—remain alive only in the memories of the old, who will soon perish as well.

Questions for Discussion

1. What do you make of the epigraph? What relationship does it have to the poem and its message?

2. Does it matter that the story of the amputations is not true? What is true about it? Why might the author have been taught this story in history class? Have you ever been taught something about your history that later proved not to be true?

JOHN DONNE

[Batter my heart,
three-personed God . . .]

How is the God in this poem characterized? What position does the speaker want to occupy with respect to his God? Do you find the sexual imagery shocking? What is the impact of the paradoxes in the last three lines? The poem suggests comparisons with different types of poems. Compare its language of conquest to Donne's "The Good-Morrow" (p. 750) Compare its violence to Angelou's "Africa" (p. 1005). Compare its religious fervor and its structure to Hopkins's "God's Grandeur" (p. 1100).

ANONYMOUS

The Twenty-third Psalm

The organization of the Twenty-third Psalm, like other Hebrew psalms, depends not on meter or rhyme, but on a structure of half-lines that repeat words, phrases, and cadences. This way of structuring a poem, called parallelism, is not common in poetry written in English (Walt Whitman's poetry is one exception). You may want to bring in some other psalms to read in class so that students can get a sense of how this structure works.

Questions for Discussion

1. What is the effect of the repetition of such phrasing as "He maketh," "he leadeth," "he restoreth," "thou preparest," "thou anointest"?

2. How is this structure appropriate to the themes of protection, safety, and peace in the psalm?

Symbol

"Symbols 'ray out,'" a teacher of mine used to say while flamboyantly striking off long rays or arrows in chalk on the blackboard. What she meant by the statement was that symbols and their meanings are rarely simple equations of object and idea. Good symbols tend to be richly suggestive, to have multiple "rays" of meaning. You may need to press your students a bit to make them move beyond the easiest or most readily evident symbolic associations. Eight poems mentioning roses are included in this section (five in the Shorter Edition) and one, Burns's "A Red, Red Rose," is placed earlier in the chapter to help students explore the many ways that a single symbol can be used.

EMILY DICKINSON

[Go not too near a House of Rose—]

How is a House of Rose like a House of Possibility in "I Dwell in Possibility" (p. 775)? What is the relationship between the first and second stanzas? What is "Joy's insuring quality?"

WILLIAM CARLOS WILLIAMS

Poem ("The rose fades")

Whereas Dickinson celebrates the fragile, ephemeral quality of the rose in nature, Williams celebrates the representation of the rose in poetry because a poem preserves its splendor. What does the poet mean by "naturally"? What is the poem's attitude toward nature? toward poetry?

DOROTHY PARKER

One Perfect Rose

The speaker is drawing on two romantic conventions—the rose as a symbol of love in poetry and the social custom of sending flowers to a woman. What does the speaker mean by "I know the language of the floweret"? How does she debunk both of these traditions in the poem?

Questions on the Rose Poems

1. In which poems is the figurative language used structurally, to build or unite a particular section or sections of the poem? When figurative language is used structurally, how is the transition made from one section to another? Which poems are based almost completely on one metaphor?

2. Which uses of figurative language in this group are purely ornamental? In what different ways does figurative language contribute to meaning? What other figures besides metaphor are illustrated in the group?

KATHA POLLITT

Two Fish

This poem sets up one image of love and then turns it into an image of death. The speaker is clearly responding to another person's attitude toward such images. What is the difference in attitudes toward love of the speaker and the person she addresses? In symbolic terms, who are the two fish in the title?

ROO BORSON

After a Death

I like to start discussion of Borson's poem by asking why the speaker symbolically replaces the person who has died with a chair. I try to lead students to brainstorm about possible reasons: the person who has died has literally left a chair empty—at the dinner table, in the living room; in addition, one can sit on a chair or curl up in it, as the speaker might have sat on the lap of the deceased; a chair is also a place to "rest," as the speaker suggests in line 8; the chair, in a sense, provides support. The poem also implies that—except when the speaker goes "out into the world" (perhaps to work, to buy groceries, etc.)—she sits and thinks about the one she has lost. For this activity, the chair is perfect.

Questions for Discussion

1. Given the evidence of the poem, what kind of relationship do you think the speaker had with the person who has died? Support your ideas with evidence.

2. What does the speaker mean when she says, "I can do what I do best"? What does she do best?

3. Why does the speaker need the chair? Interpret the last three lines of the poem.

Writing Assignments for Chapter 4

1. Rewrite Shakespeare's sonnet "That time of year . . ." to reflect your own time of year, your own age. Follow his practice of developing a different metaphor in each quatrain.

2. Do some library research on the history of British rule in what is now Bangladesh. Write a report discussing the aspects of Bengali culture that were altered or lost when the British seized control. Did British rule have any positive effects?

3. Contrast the God in the Twenty-third Psalm to the God in Donne's "Batter My Heart. . . ." The speaker in Donne's poem is driven by passionate desires, but the speaker in the psalm says that his God takes care of his needs: "I shall not want" (line 1). Contrast the forms of the two poems. How does the sonnet form make "Batter My Heart . . ." seem more urgent and harsh?

5 THE SOUNDS OF POETRY

Occasionally a student turns up in my office worried about the sheer amount of reading required for the course. The student is willing to put in lots of time but reads slowly. "Others can zip right through these assignments," I hear, "and they seem to do fine. But it takes me forever." More often than not I find that these students learned to read by subvocalizing rather than by visually processing the printing on the page. They may not move their lips when they read, but they might as well; since they hear each word in their heads, they can't read much faster than they can speak.

I try to encourage these students by explaining that while reading takes them a long time, there are advantages to subvocalizing: mentally hearing every word gives one, over the years, a fine feel for the language. I tell such students that they have the rhythms of English in their bones. Often, in fact, these students do better than their faster friends at reading aloud and at scansion. I tell them to look forward to this chapter; it should appeal to them.

Planning Ideas

- It always pays to have students practice reading poems aloud, but that is especially the case in this chapter. One way of getting students to respond to the nuances of oral performance is to bring in recordings of poets reading their own work. The class may decide that a student's rendition of a poem by, say, T. S. Eliot or E. E. Cummings is better than the poet's reading. Note: Norton makes available a videotape of Agha Shahid Ali, Judith Ortiz Cofer, amd Alberto Ríos reading from their work.
- Michael Harper's **"Dear John, Dear Coltrane"*** works better if the class has heard a recording of Coltrane's "A Love Supreme" and perhaps "Naima."
- Make sure early on that students understand about enjambment; many of them automatically pause at the ends of even unpunctuated lines. It can be useful to mark on the board both the placement and the length of pauses; a written exercise on how pauses are indicated and controlled by a poet can also be helpful.
- Galway Kinnell's **"Blackberry Eating"** (p. 1071) might well have been included in this chapter; the poem's sounds are clearly inseparable from its sense.

WILLIAM SHAKESPEARE

[Like as the waves make towards the pebbled shore]

Lines 368–69 of Pope's "Sound and Sense" read, "But when loud surges lash the sounding shore, / The hoarse, rough verse should like the torrent roar." What devices for imitating the sound of waves do Pope and Shakespeare share? How do their strategies differ?

ALFRED, LORD TENNYSON

Break, Break, Break

1. What metrical units does the poem use most frequently? How does the effect of line 13 differ from that of line 1? To what extent does the force of each of the two lines depend upon broken expectations? Upon repetition? Pause?

2. Compare Shakespeare's "Like as the waves make towards the pebbled shore" and the passage from Pope's "Sound and Sense" quoted just above. How do the different poetic purposes lead to different uses of sound and pause? Compare Arnold's "Dover Beach" (p. 741). To what extent is each poem's tone dependent on its rhythm and pace?

THOMAS NASHE

A Litany in Time of Plague

I like to begin discussing this poem by playing the devil's advocate. In my most sincere voice, I say, "Now, here is a poem that doesn't have much to say to us today; modern medicine has done away with things like the plague." It doesn't take long for students to think about HIV and AIDS. Perhaps someone points out that we may enjoy the benefits of first-rate medical technology, but most of the world doesn't. In any case, the discussion leads to the question of whether the poem would have anything to say to a society that had wiped out all diseases. Technology has changed, but has our basic human condition? Is the line "Earth's but a player's stage" less applicable today than it was in 1600?

Questions for Discussion

1. What is a litany? Why is it an appropriate form for embodying the speaker's concern with both his own impending death and that of all created things?

2. The poem's basic metrical pattern is iambic. How does the rhythmic variation from iambics in the repeated line "I am sick, I must die" make the line effective?

3. A book reviewer recently quoted Nashe's line, "Brightness falls from the air" (line 17) as if it described a world bathed in light. Is that what Nashe means?

JUDITH WRIGHT

"Dove-Love"

How would you characterize the three kinds of doves described in the poem? Why do the words "I could eat you" connect the three kinds of doves? Does the refrain "I do. I do" in this poem have the same connotations as the "I do. I do" in Plath's poem "Daddy" (line 67, p. 690)?

GERARD MANLEY HOPKINS

Spring and Fall

The speaker's vocabulary and syntax are anything but normal; little attempt is made here to capture the rhythms of ordinary speech. Words like "*wanwood*" and "*leafmeal*" are Hopkins's coinages, and a construction like "Leaves, like the things of man, you / With your fresh thoughts care for, can you?" takes some sorting out to yield a paraphrase like, "Are you able, in your youth, to care as much about the falling of the leaves as you do for humanity?" Why does the poet delay the "can you?" For most readers, Hopkins's suggestions for stressed syllables seem especially odd. What difference in meaning does stressing a word like "*will*" (line 9) make?

Questions for Discussion

1. Can you paraphrase the message of the speaker to Margaret?

2. Does the alliteration serve any special purpose?

3. How does the use of language in this poem compare to that in Hopkins's "Pied Beauty" (p.772)?

MARGE PIERCY

To Have Without Holding

Students tend to respond well to this poem, perhaps because many of them have struggled with the issue it addresses, but they often fail to recognize how adroitly Piercy matches sound and sense: the sense of line one—"Learning to love differently is hard"—is played out in the many hard and harsh sounds of the poem. This is a good poem to read aloud slowly or to have read aloud by an accomplished reader while the rest of the class listens and jots down or underlines the hard or harsh sounds they hear. It may be desirable to stage several readings: one to detect hard or harsh sounds (the many plosive *B*'s and *P*'s, for example), another to focus on instances of onomatopoeia, and yet another to pick up patterns of alliteration, assonance, and consonance.

Questions for Discussion

1. What is the difference between having and holding and "having without holding"?

2. Look at how Piercy places punctuation to create pauses and to mark off long runs of words ("to hold back what is owed to the work / that gutters like a candle in a cave / without air") or to create short phrases ("I can't do it"). How does punctuation contribute to the sense of the poem?

3. Are all of the sounds of Piercy's poem harsh ones? What do the sounds that are not harsh—the liquid *L*'s, for example—contribute to the poem?

4. This speaker thinks of love-making as a means of balancing "hunger and anger" (lines 33–34). How is this balancing act different from that concerning the speaker in "I being born a woman and distressed" (p. 670)? What internal indications are there that Millay's poem was written in 1923 and Piercy's in 1980?

EMILY DICKINSON

[A Narrow Fellow in the Grass]

How does the structure of the poem itself recreate for the reader the growing uncertainty and the element of surprise experienced by the speaker? What leaves the speaker frightened at the end of the poem? Is it fear of harm, or fear of uncertainty?

ROBERT HERRICK

To the Virgins, To Make Much
of Time

Several things indicate that Herrick does not intend this to be a straightforward *carpe diem* poem. For one thing, there are several echoes of the New Testament parable of the Wise and Foolish Virgins (Matthew 25:1-13), which places the advice to "seize the day" in a specifically religious context. That the title addresses not virgins in general but *the* virgins would perhaps not indicate an allusion to the parable if Herrick did not also include terms like "lamp of heaven," "prime," and "tarry." Besides, the speaker's advice to the virgins is hardly typical *carpe diem* strategy: the virgins are invited not to a tryst but to "go marry."

Questions for Discussion

1. Can the poem be enjoyed without picking up on the New Testament echoes? How does the poem change once the allusions are pointed out?

2. Does *coy* (line 13) seem to mean *coquettish* here or simply *shy* (its usual meaning in the seventeenth century)?

Writing Assignments for Chapter 5

1. Carefully read the commentary on "The Word *Plum*" in the text, and do your best to analyze in similar detail the sounds of any other poem in this unit.

2. Listen to as much of John Coltrane's music as you can find, and then reread Michael Harper's "Dear John, Dear Coltrane." Write an essay on the music that shows a different side of Coltrane from the one revealed in the poem.

6 INTERNAL STRUCTURE

As human beings we seem to be able to absorb experience only if we organize it in some way that conforms to previous knowledge. For poets, whatever they want to show us or tell us, a major problem is to formulate their perceptions in sequences to which readers can readily respond. Like other artists, poets have to depend not only on how their own minds organize experience but on how their audiences relate to that organization of experience. In one sense every element of a poem is part of its organization; every decision about craftsmanship leads to other decisions—and also proscribes other possibilities—so that considerations of word choice and word order, patterns of metaphor, and choices of speaker, situation, and setting are inevitably factors that go into the organization of a poem. But broader conceptions of aim and intention are involved too: often poets have some kind of structural model in mind as they construct their work— an accepted and familiar mode of perception (perhaps one adapted from another work or art), a structure that will provide the reader a flash of recognition and something to hang onto.

Teaching form and structure is always difficult, and it is easy for the discussions to become abstract, often slipping into arguments about definition and leaving individual poems behind completely. The crucial issue, most effectively addressed with specific examples before the class, is how the structures of one mind can be shared with another. For example, how do the details in the first and last lines of "Sir Patrick Spens" imply an organizational strategy? How about the stanzaic structure of "Sonrisas"? The choice of images in "Auto Wreck"? It seems to me important that the issue of structure be raised at several points in the course, not just in this unit. What I do with this group is raise the whole issue of how our minds sort things so that they can be grasped and shared. Then I try to note in other units the organizational implications of whatever artistic strategies are used.

Planning Ideas

- Like other medieval ballads, **"Sir Patrick Spens"** has come down to us in a variety of forms. Have students find in the library some variants and explain why a particular variant is more or less effective than the version in our text. A more ambitious project, one that could be done as a writing assignment, involves checking in a good dictionary to see whether the roots of the variants in several versions of a ballad are Latinate or Germanic and drawing conclusions about the poetic suitability of each version.
- Before having students read Williams's **"The Dance,"** show a slide of Brueghel's *The Kermess* (sometimes spelled *Kermis*). Ask the class to

159

describe what the artist seems to want the viewer to notice in the drawing. If the question has not come up after some discussion, ask, "Is Brueghel celebrating with the peasants or making fun of them?" Then read **"The Dance,"** and compare Williams's emphases to Brueghel's.

• A similar exercise can be done with a slide of *The Kermess* or any other work of visual art, especially one that does not depict a familiar scene. Divide the class into groups, and ask each group to discuss a particular organizing principle of the work: one group might answer the question, "How does the artist lead the viewer's eye from one spot to the next?"; another, "What patterns of lighter and darker areas can you find?"; another, "What contrasts other than light and dark can you find?"; another, "What emotional response does the work invite?"; another, "What story does the work tell?"; and another, "What is the point or message of the work?" The exercise should help students discover that organizing principles are various, that asking questions about structure helps one see things that one didn't see before—that one does not at first glance "get" a work of visual art any more than one "gets" a whole poem upon a first reading.

ANONYMOUS

Sir Patrick Spens

The situation calls to mind Shakespeare's *The Tempest*, written over three hundred years after this ballad. The first scene of Shakespeare's play stages the storm referred to in the title. As in "Sir Patrick Spens," part of the point is that when it comes to powerful natural events like a storm at sea, political rank means nothing—less than nothing, in fact, if the nobles allow their assumption that rank makes them invulnerable to cloud their judgments about practical matters.

There are, of course, differences between the play and the poem. The Boatswain in *The Tempest* takes command during the storm, ordering the noblemen to obey him. If a similar situation arises in "Sir Patrick Spens," the reader (or hearer: students need reminding that medieval ballads made the rounds orally before being circulated in writing) isn't told so explicitly. Spens and his sailors know that the journey will very likely end in disaster, but there is no talk of disobeying the king's orders.

A second difference is that Shakespeare typically puts a twist on the inversion of social roles during a time of natural disturbance. While the Scottish lords in "Sir Patrick Spens" learn (too late) that they, like the commoners, are subject to the elements, the elements are not really in control in *The Tempest*: the play's second scene reveals that the magician Prospero (who is not only a magician but the *rightful* ruler) is actually in command of the storm. A useful question for discussion is how "Sir Patrick Spens" would be changed if it were revealed that the rightful king of Scotland were a magician who had arranged the storm.

Perhaps the crucial difference between the poem and the play is that the central event on which both turn—the storm—is never depicted in the poem. The key structural device in "Sir Patrick Spens" is a sort of dramatic elision: the reader is presented with scenes before and after the storm but not the storm itself. How is it that the poem's haunting effect arises from the strategy of leaving something out?

Questions for Discussion

1. In what ways does the king's "Drinking the blude-reid wine" help to set the tone of the ballad?

2. Like the sailors, the Scots lords are reluctant to set sail—but for different reasons. What does the difference reveal?

3. What is the significance of the last line?

T. S. ELIOT

Journey of the Magi

Many of the thoughts and images in this poem are connected by the words "and" and "but." What does this tell us about how the speaker's mind is working? Is this a carefully constructed account of the journey or a spontaneous one? What happens to the narrative in lines 32–35? What does the speaker mean by "set down?" The first two stanzas describe an event in the past, and the last stanza interprets it. How has the speaker's state of mind been changed by the journey? Why are the magi "no longer at ease"?

KARL SHAPIRO

Auto Wreck

1. At what points does the poem violate strict chronology? For what purpose?

2. What is the speaker's relationship to the main action?

3. What kind of expectation is created by the short, terse title? Why does the poem not contain the usual word for such an event, "accident"? Which words, phrases, and images seem especially intended to shock or create revulsion? What evidence is there in the poem that the poet is consciously working against the common assumption that only certain subjects are poetic?

4. Describe and compare the psychological effects of the similes in lines 3

("artery"), 22 ("tourniquets"), and 35 ("flower"), and the metaphors in lines 4 ("floating"), 6 ("wings"), 21 ("husks"), and 29 ("wound").

5. How many details are given about the wreck itself? List all of the details given about the scene. What do the details emphasize? Why does the poem begin after the fact, with the coming of the ambulance instead of with the crash itself? Why are we told so little about the victims?

6. What is the poem "about"? What philosophical question does it ask? How does the poem make its shift from the details of the scene to issues of cause, responsibility, fate, and the selection of victims? How are we prepared for the terms "expedient" and "wicked" in the last line?

DENISE LEVERTOV

What Were They Like?

How would you characterize the language in each part of the poem? What does it tell us about the individual speakers and about the differences between them? Who might the speakers be? How are the answers the first speaker receives different from what he or she expected? What is the effect of presenting all the questions first, then following them with all the answers? How would the effect differ if the questions and answers alternated?

WILLIAM CARLOS WILLIAMS

The Dance

Does your understanding of this poem depend upon your having seen Brueghel's painting? Is this just a description of a painting? How is the poem like a song? Like a dance? How would you describe the structure of the poem?

PERCY BYSSHE SHELLEY

Ode to the West Wind

Just as Williams's "The Dance" creates the music and movement of the dance, this poem creates within itself the sound and movement of the wind. It is written in *terza rima*, a form that links each three-line stanza with end rhymes (aba, bcb, cdc, etc). This creates a sense of connectedness that is then interrupted by the section break. The effect is something like that of a wind blowing, dying down, and blowing again.

Writing Assignments for Chapter 6

1. Some might argue that a ballad like "Sir Patrick Spens" is politically subversive, exposing as it does the folly of the ruling class. Others could point out that the hierarchical structure of medieval Scottish society is never called into question—that Sir Patrick Spens and his sailors dutifully follow orders. Which view, if either, does the poem support?

2. Write a poem based on a work of visual art that you find appealing or evocative.

3. Trace the imagery of dead leaves through "Ode to the West Wind." How many different ways is this image used and with what figurative devices? How does this one image unify the poem?

7 EXTERNAL FORM

While this chapter contains specimens of several poetic forms—the villanelle, the sestina, and the concrete poem, for example—the editor has chosen to illustrate in detail one form—the sonnet—so that students can get to know it well and see not only its basic form but also what variations can be played upon it. This way, too, students can begin to see what the form is good for: what can be done within its limits and challenges, and why poets are attracted to a particular form for particular tasks and ideas.

Planning Ideas

• Years ago I decided that the best way to teach the sonnet was to have students write their own. Some of the early results were so charmingly innocent of poetic convention that I combined a few of the more egregious qualities in a parody that I now use in an exercise called "How to Write a Lousy Sonnet." I hand out copies of the following compilation, which I gladly bequeath to you:

> My loneliness is lonesome. Woe is me!
> My heart is full of feelings that I feel.
> These feelings come from one that I'll call "Thee."
> Thou closed thy heart, and over I did keel.
> At first thou gave me hopefulness to hope,
> Then stripped my heart as one would peel an orange.
> Thou made me feel the feelings of a dope;
> My heart is opened as is door on door hinge.
> And only sorriness is left to me,
> The sorriness of sorrow without end:
> Thou left me as a beached whale leaves the sea,
> And landed in the arms of my best friend.
> > Now all that's left is chewed-up orange rind,
> > Unless immortal verse can change thy mind.

Since I tell the class that this is a student-written piece, it gives even first-time sonneteers great confidence: "Nothing I write," each one thinks, "can be *that* bad." And it actually works, helping students avoid some common problems: lack of enjambment, reliance on abstraction (all those "*feelings*") rather than concrete imagery, padding ("*hopefulness to hope*"), cliché ("*Woe is me!*"), stretched metaphor or simile (that "*whale*"), mixed diction ("*Thou*" and "*dope*" in the same poem—even the same line), too-easy rhyme (*me / thee*), and strained rhyme (*orange / door hinge*).

164

- If the above exercise doesn't do the trick, try the passage in *The Adventures of Huckleberry Finn* in which Huck is stricken by the beauty of the fourteen-year-old Emmeline Grangerford's elegy for Stephen Dowling Bots, who drowned in a well. Representative lines:

> They got him out and emptied him;
>   Alas it was too late;
> His spirit was gone for to sport aloft
>   In the realms of the good and great.

- The following pairs of poems play off each other well: Constable's **"My lady's presence makes the roses red"** and Shakespeare's **"My mistress' eyes are nothing like the sun"**; Wordsworth's **"Nuns Fret Not"** and Keats's **"On the Sonnet"**; Johnson's **"Sonnet to a Negro in Harlem"** and McKay's **"The Harlem Dancer"**; Milton's **"When I Consider How My Light Is Spent"** and Thomas's **"Do Not Go Gentle into That Good Night"**; Lampman's **"Winter Evening"** * and Roberts's **"Potato Harvest."**
- Wordsworth's mention of "altar, sword, and pen, / Fireside . . ." in **"London, 1802"** provides a good way of introducing *metonymy*.

The Sonnet

JOHN KEATS

On the Sonnet

The speaker's implicit claim here is that while formal constraints may be necessary for poetry, the form should be adapted to embody in an appropriate way the individual poem's content.

Questions for Discussion

1. The speaker seems frustrated that the sonnet "must" be fettered by "dull rhymes" despite its "painéd loveliness" (lines 1, 3). If the speaker really thinks the sonnet has no need of rhyme, why doesn't the sonnet employ blank verse?

2. What are the "dead leaves" (line 12)? Does Pope's "Sound and Sense" (p. 815) offer examples of such dead leaves? Does Constable's "My lady's presence . . . ," unlike Keats's sonnet, contain an example of one of Pope's "expletives" ("Sound and Sense", line 346)?

WILLIAM WORDSWORTH

The world is too much with us

It has been said that Wordsworth longed to see Proteus and hear Triton only because he was secure in the knowledge that he never would. Nevertheless, lines like "Great God! I'd rather be / A Pagan suckled in a creed outworn" were calculated to seem shocking in nineteenth-century England—and can still seem bold. Part of the reason is a function of form. The poem follows a standard rhyme scheme for the Italian sonnet, but Wordsworth deviates from the standard shift in content between the octave and the sestet. Instead, the octave "invades" the sestet; the first part of line 9 concludes the sentiment expressed in the first eight lines—as though the world really *were* too much with us. On the heels of "It moves us not," then, "Great God!" seems to explode with all the force of repressed desire.

Questions for Discussion

1. Since part of the speaker's complaint is that we *aren't* moved by the world around us, in what sense is the world "too much with us"?

2. Does the poem's tight structure complement or conflict with the poet's desire for the wildness of pagan belief?

PERCY BYSSHE SHELLEY

Ozymandias

This poem is structured by three levels of address: that of the speaker, the traveler, and the statue itself. How does this narrative structure fit with the image of the ruins? What qualities are attributed to the sculptor? Is there an implied parallel between sculptor and poet? If so, how might the writing of the sonnet compare to the sculpting of statue? What implications for the historical place of art do the words on the statue have?

WILLIAM WORDSWORTH

London, 1802

What aspects of English life and institutions are portrayed as stagnant? What evidence does the poem offer? What strategies does the poem use to persuade us that England needs renewal? Why is a poet called on for the solution? Why Milton?

GWENDOLYN BROOKS

First Fight. Then Fiddle

What is the major opposition at work in the poem? Does the poem really believe that fighting and fiddling can live in two separate spaces? Describe the tone of the poem.

DIANE ACKERMAN

Sweep Me Through Your Many-Chambered Heart

What techniques does the poet use to make the poem seem off balance? How is this appropriate to the speaker's state of mind? Compare this poem to another sonnet, Donne's [Batter my heart, three-personed God . . .] (p. 791). Do you see any thematic or formal similarities between the two?

More Sonnets: A List

Other sonnets in the following that might be used to supplement this unit include:

Browning	How Do I Love Thee
Donne	[Batter my heart, three-personed God . . .]
	[Death be not proud, though some have callèd thee]
Frost	Design
	Range-Finding
Gilbert	Sonnet: The Ladies' Home Journal
Keats	Bright Star
	On First Looking into Chapman's Homer
	On the Grasshopper and the Cricket
	When I Have Fears
McKay	America
Millay	[I, being born a woman and distressed]
	[What lips my lips have kissed, and where, and why]
Yeats	Leda and the Swan

Other Stanza Forms

DYLAN THOMAS

Do Not Go Gentle into That Good Night

At first it might seem strange that Thomas chose as exacting a form as the villanelle for a poem that seems an outburst of passion. But the passion is highly constrained, presumably by the speaker's sense of frustration that his relationship with his father has somehow remained unfulfilled. Just as the wise, good, wild, and grave men rage against the dying of the light not because they are fearful but because somehow all their wisdom, goodness, wildness, and gravity have not been enough in this world, the speaker asks his father to "Curse, bless" him as an appropriate response to human vulnerability—as though it wouldn't matter whether his father cursed or blessed him, as long as the tears were fierce. The villanelle lends itself to this kind of sentiment: for one thing, the repetition of the first and third lines lends the poem a sense of urgency. For another, the four-line sixth stanza, with its inclusion of the two catch lines at the end, both provides a sense of closure and strains against closure: the final line could as well be the beginning of a new tercet as the end of a quatrain (or it could be the *last* line of a new tercet—that's where the ear expects the repetition of "Rage, rage . . . ," and so the first two lines of that tercet seem to have been left out).

Questions for Discussion

1. What do the wise, good, wild, and grave men have in common? What do they have to do with the speaker's father?

2. Who are the wild men?

3. Trace the variations on imagery of light and darkness in the poem. How do we know that light represents life and darkness death (rather than, say, sight and blindness)?

MARIANNE MOORE

Poetry

Is the speaker more concerned with reading or writing poetry? What is her idea of "the genuine"? (line 3) What does she dislike about poetry?

ARCHIBALD MacLEISH

Ars Poetica

How is this poem structured? What is the effect of juxtaposing statements about poetry with poetic images? Can you summarize the poem's ideas about what poetry should be?

The Way a Poem Looks

E. E. CUMMINGS

[Buffalo Bill 's]

1. What accounts for the sense of time's having passed? What evidence is there of contrast between present and past? How is each viewed by the speaker? How is the speaker characterized?

2. Does the poem seem to be mostly about Buffalo Bill as a person? Buffalo Bill as a performer? Buffalo Bill as an act? About death? About youth and vitality? About memory? What parts of the poem would you emphasize to defend your answer? Are there parts you would have to ignore?

3. How does the personification of "Mister Death" (line 11) differ from the personification in Donne's "[Death, be not proud, though some have calléd thee]" (p. 1088)? How much of the difference depends on Cummings's withholding of it until the last line?

Writing Assignments for Chapter 7

1. See the first of the Planning Ideas above. An alternative is to write a parody of one of the poems in this chapter.

2. Poetry was originally oral, and poets and critics since the seventeenth century have complained that the printing press is destroying poetry as an art. In recent years worries have become especially intense and articulate; some critics insist that linear form radically distorts sequential experience by forcing the eyes to translate through a sign language that is more artificial and less natural than the aural symbols. Pick one or more poems from this chapter that seem(s) to respond to that criticism, and write an essay addressing the relation between the visual and the aural in the poem(s).

8 THE WHOLE TEXT

This chapter includes several very short poems, poems brief enough to discuss fairly exhaustively in terms of all the poetic elements we have explored thus far in the text. When you take up this chapter, it may be helpful to provide students with a list of these elements to serve as a reminder and checklist for future analyses of poems. Of course no poetry analysis should be a mere exploration of one isolated element after another, and this is a point well worth emphasizing and reemphasizing. Like the Dacca gauzes described in Ali's poem (p. 790), any work of literature is made up of interwoven parts. The real task is to understand how the parts combine and interrelate to create the whole.

Planning Ideas

- In preparing your syllabus, you might consider using this unit as an opportunity to "revisit" poems explored more narrowly in previous chapters and to study some favorite selections from the *Reading More Poetry* section at the end of the text.
- Ask students to choose a poem discussed earlier in the term principally in regard to one element. Before class, have each write a paragraph describing the other aspects of the poem that contribute to the work as a whole and their interrelations. Spend one class period discussing the poems the students have chosen to write about.
- Bring to class a short poem (sonnet length or briefer) that the class has not studied before, making the poem available through use of photocopies or an overhead projector. Give the class several minutes to come up privately with as many critical observations about various elements of the poem as they can. When you discuss the poem as a whole, supplement student observations as necessary, encouraging students to see the interrelatedness of the various elements they observe.

W. H. AUDEN

Musée des Beaux Arts

This poem offers a layered perspective on the Greek myth of Icarus. The myth of Icarus can be read as a moral tale about excessive ambition and its consequences. Brueghel, an "Old Master," interpreted the myth in painting by changing the setting to a sixteenth-century Dutch peasant society. The speaker in the poem, looking at the painting, gives his own gloss on the painting and myth.

Questions for Discussion

1. Describe the speaker's views about suffering.

2. Does your understanding of the poem depend on seeing the Brueghel painting?

ANNE SEXTON

With Mercy for the Greedy

To open discussion of this thought-provoking poem, I like to ask students to look closely at the way the speaker describes the cross her friend has sent her. Some of the description is quite conventional: "no larger than a thumb, / small and wooden." Other aspects of her description are joltingly *un*conventional: "He [Jesus] is frozen to his bones like a chunk of beef." Exploration of such lines will quickly reveal how subtly and powerfully the speaker's relationship to Christianity and the problems of belief are conveyed in her reactions to the gift.

Some attention to the first and last stanzas may also prove fruitful. The friend's request in the first stanza (that the speaker attend confession as well as wear the cross) and the speaker's response to this request in the last stanza reveal that the speaker thinks her life work has been one long confession. Her poetry holds the catalogue of sins she has to confess. (Note the biblical echo from Genesis 25:29ff, in the reference to "pottage.")

Questions for Discussion

1. What is the speaker's reaction to her friend's request and gift? Is she offended? pleased? touched?

2. Why does the speaker suggest that poems offer "mercy for the greedy"?

3. What sense do you make of the metaphors for her poetry that the speaker offers in the last two lines of the poem?

EMILY DICKINSON

[My Life had stood—a Loaded Gun—]

What are the implications of describing one's life as a loaded gun? As a gun, the speaker is owned, possessed, and carried away, but she is also powerful, lethal. How is this contradiction summed up in the last stanza? Analyze the use and meaning of "power" in this stanza and in the poem as a whole.

ROBERT FROST

Design

Since Frost's poem confounds our usual associations for "whiteness," I like to open discussion by asking students to list the conventional associations of the "color" white on the board. After we have a list—probably including notions of purity, innocence, goodness, absence (of color), marriage—I turn our attention to the poem and to Frost's creepy tableau of albino spider, moth, and flower. Frost's choice of words in the poem forces us to see this whiteness as unsettling, with his references to "witches' broth" and "death and blight" in the descriptive octave of the sonnet. In the sestet, he proffers the questions such an eery confluence of elements prompts.

Questions for Discussion

1. What parallels do you see between the existence of this scene in nature and its crafting as an image in the poem? How appropriate to his theme is Frost's choice of the sonnet form?

2. What philosophical questions are raised in the final couplet of the poem? In what sense might the "design of darkness" be appalled by the scene Frost describes?

Writing Assignments for Chapter 8

1. Read several of Sexton's poems from the volume *The Awful Rowing Toward God*. Write an analysis of "With Mercy for the Greedy," based on your understanding of Sexton's response to Christianity.

2. (An alternative to writing assignment 1 in the text): Look up Ovid's story of Icarus and his father Daedalus and read it carefully. Then study a reproduction of Brueghel's *Icarus*, giving attention to the details Auden "borrows" for his poem. Write an essay discussing Auden's use of story and picture in "Musée des Beaux Arts." Are story and poem equally important to the poem's message(s) and effects?

3. Compare Frost's "Design" in form and content to Hopkins's "Pied Beauty" (p. 772), which is also about design, or the lack of design, in nature. Compare the last lines of each poem. How do their conclusions differ?

▼ ▼ ▼

Exploring Contexts

Poems treated in isolation, as if art belonged to a separate world having nothing to do with the real world, can very quickly come to seem irrelevant, effete, and boring; this section suggests how the concerns of poems relate to ordinary reality. The connections are not always easy, but they are rewarding and exciting. Even if your course does not allow you time to consider fully all of the issues raised in this section, you can point outward from the poems by assigning the poems in at least one or two chapters and thus at least suggesting to your students that poetry is vitally connected to the world at large, not an insulated and purely academic exercise. I have found the kind of issues suggested here to provide the most exciting teaching experiences of any I have had; among other things, attention to these groups of poems can minister to the students' need to connect things, rather than seeing them in neat little course-size blocks, and to see their subject matter in an interdisciplinary way.

Success in these chapters can be pretty much guaranteed by proper preparation during the earlier class meetings. If, for example, you have at least tentatively or suggestively raised questions along the way about what poems by the same author have in common, or whether knowing about the historical context affects one's interpretation of a poem, you will find students ready for the greater depth such questions can take on here. Along the way in this Guide, I have tried to raise such issues fairly often, and if you have broached such questions at all, you are well set up to investigate them in more detail through the groups here.

9 THE AUTHOR'S WORK AS CONTEXT: JOHN KEATS

Studying Keats's poetry works well in part because of its sensuous appeal and in part because the poems included here were written over a relatively short period of time and thus are fairly homogeneous (although one can certainly see an increasing confidence and an acceptance of the world's pain). The poems Keats wrote after "To Autumn"—none of which are included in our text—are generally thought vastly inferior to, say, the ones written during the great creative outburst of May 1819. An interesting exercise, especially for advanced students, is to compare the poems written after September 1819 to the ones written earlier (see Writing Assignment 3 below).

Planning Ideas

- If you are going to spend three or four days on Keats, I suggest using the letters near the beginning—on the first or second day—so that the poet's own ideas about his work can become an integral part of the continuing discussion. Poems especially illuminated by the prose include **"To Sleep,"** **"Ode to a Nightingale," "Ode on a Grecian Urn," "Ode on Melancholy,"** and **"To Autumn."**
- It is useful to review Keats's **"On the Sonnet"** (p. 873) before reading the sonnets in this chapter.
- A slide of Albrecht Dürer's *Melencolia I* works well with Keats's **"Ode on Melancholy."**
- As the index indicates, quite a number of poets are represented by several poems, and you may want to teach in a unit groups of poems by one or more additional authors. Or you may want to vary which authors you teach intensively, sometimes teaching someone other than Keats and Rich. Emily Dickinson and Sharon Olds, generously represented in the text, are other authors whose poems teach especially well as a group, and in this edition the editor has included quite a number of poems that are seldom anthologized. The ranges of tone and subject are more varied in Dickinson than teachers working from standard anthologies may have been led to expect, and the Olds poems play very subtle variations on recurrent situations and relationships. John Donne is another good poet to teach in such a unit. It works well to have the students work in groups of four to seek out information for in-class presentations. Each student is responsible for one of the following: 1) relevant biographical details; 2) relevant cultural context; 3) typical poetic techniques; 4) poetic development.

On First Looking into Chapman's Homer

The Italian sonnet offers a variety of options for the rhyme scheme of the sestet. Here Keats chooses to follow the *a-b-b-a-a-b-b-a* of the octave with *c-d-c-d-c-d*. This is an open-ended pattern; the ear half-expects another line, one with a *c* rhyme, after the fourteenth. This openness, combined with the lack of a full stop in in the exotic-sounding *"Darien"* (compare the *"gold" / "hold" / "told" / "bold"* of lines 1, 4, 5, and 8), partly accounts for the tone of awed discovery of something mysteriously grand.

Questions for Discussion

1. Why does the speaker choose to associate his experience of reading a book with the night sky and the Pacific Ocean?

2. Would a poet writing today be likely to refer to Cortez in the way Keats does? What does the poet's choice of words tell us about cultural assumptions in early nineteenth-century England?

On the Grasshopper and the Cricket

1. What qualities and values are associated with drowsiness?

2. In what sense is the grasshopper's song "poetry of earth"? In what different sense is the term appropriate for the cricket's song?

3. Why is it appropriate that line 9 contains eleven syllables (the technical term is *hendecasyllabic*) instead of ten?

When I Have Fears

What does the imagery of lines 1–4 imply about the nature of the imagination? The imagery of lines 5–8?

Ode to a Nightingale

1. What qualities of the "lot" of the nightingale does the speaker find attractive in stanza I? If not envy, what feeling about the nightingale's happiness

does the speaker have? What different ways of joining the nightingale does he propose in stanzas I–III? In stanza IV? How does stanza VIII modify the solutions of the early stanzas?

2. What characteristics are associated with the world "where men sit and hear each other groan" (line 24)? What are the attractions of "numbness" (line 1) and "easeful Death" (line 52)?

Ode on a Grecian Urn

What details does the poem provide about the "tale" told by the urn? Why can the urn as "sylvan historian" (line 3) express the tale "more sweetly" than a poem can? Why does the poem place so much emphasis on uncompleted actions? What is the tone of the final two lines? How heavily does a tonal description of these lines depend upon whether all, or just part, of the lines are presumed to be inscribed on the urn (see footnote 6)?

Ode on Melancholy

Although the opening stanza ostensibly tells the reader to *avoid* the sources of melancholy, the long vowels establish a melancholic tone, qualifying the *kind* of melancholy the speaker wishes to consider: the kind whose onset is "Sudden" (line 11; note the effectiveness of the trochee in this position). The speaker's claim is that only an elite company characterized by the one "whose strenuous tongue / Can burst Joy's grape upon his palate fine" (lines 27–28) can experience melancholy. If the poem in effect invites the reader to become a part of that company by participating in the speaker's sorrow (if we didn't do that, we couldn't appreciate the poem), the speaker also claims that such participation has a cost: consorting with Melancholy leaves one's soul "among her cloudy trophies hung" (line 30).

Questions for Discussion

1. What do the ninth and tenth lines mean?

2. Is the mistress of line 18 a human being or the "She" of line 21—that is, Melancholy personified?

3. Why does the speaker claim that someone like Melancholy lives with Beauty, Joy, and Pleasure?

To Autumn

What stage of autumn is implied by each stanza? What images are associated with each stage? What qualities described here are associated in other Keats poems with the world of imagination? Compare the four preceding odes. How would you describe the tone of each?

Questions on the poetry and prose of Keats

1. Bowers recur often in Keats. How are they characterized? What kind of emotional reactions do they generate? What other images does Keats associate with them?

2. How frequently is Keats concerned with the external world of pain and fretfulness? What alternative escapes from the external world or solutions to its problems does he suggest or portray? How do the alternatives vary from the early poetry to the late? Is there any pattern of tonal differences from the early to the late poetry?

3. What themes recur most often in the poems here? What images? What kinds of images? What metrical pattern does Keats seem most fond of? What stanza forms? Does Keats seem more successful in exploiting the potential of the sonnet or the ode? What tendencies of each form seem to attract him? What changes in Keats help to explain his preference for the ode in later poems?

4. Which poems are most illuminated by knowledge of Keats's life? By familiarity with his letters? What kind of contribution to a poem's effect is made by biographical information? Are any of the poems completely inaccessible without biographical knowledge?

Writing Assignments for Chapter 9

1. Reread the passages from Keats's letters of November 22 and December 21, 1817 (pp. 933–34), especially the description of "Negative Capability" and the analogy of the flower. (In the latter passage Keats puts a new twist on the old argument about whether it is better to be a spider [to spin out one's own creations] or a bee [to transform what has been gathered from others into some-

thing new].) Then reread the poems. What evidence do the poems contain that Keats's artistry is consistent with the ideas he endorses in his letters?

2. Suppose Keats were the only poet identified with the Romantic sensibility. Basing your ideas solely on the poems and prose contained in the text, write an essay that outlines the main characteristics of Romanticism.

3. Find, in a complete edition of Keats's poetry, the poems he wrote during the last seventeen months of his life. Write an essay that describes how these poems differ from the ones in our text.

10 THE AUTHOR'S WORK IN CONTEXT: ADRIENNE RICH

While Keats's poetic career lasted only a few years, Adrienne Rich's poetry has developed over several decades, changing remarkably in the process. Despite these changes, and despite the complexity of her work, the poems remain fairly accessible. And what W. H. Auden said of her first volume of poetry (*A Change of World*, 1951, published when Rich was twenty-one) remains true of her most recent work: "[T]he poems a reader will encounter in this book are neatly and modestly dressed, speak quietly but do not mumble, respect the elders but are not cowed by them, and do not tell fibs: that, for a first volume, is a good deal." While retaining the "good deal" of understatement, deference, and polish of her early poetry, Rich's more recent work speaks in a voice very much her own. Rich talks openly about the development of her poetry in "Talking with Adrienne Rich," (p. 960).

Planning Ideas

- As with Keats, it makes sense to introduce Rich's prose before discussing much of the poetry.
- Poems by Rich that are not included in this chapter are listed in the text on page 941. "**Aunt Jennifer's Tigers**" (p. 685) pairs usefully with "**Orion,**" and "**Letters in the Family**" (p. 705) with "**For the Record.**"
- The speaker in "**Leaflets**"* desires her poems to become forgotten scraps of paper, but only after the man to whom she has sent them has taken the poems to heart, has made them his own. Because "the imagination crouches in them" (line 120), the poems are worth passing on. But the speaker hints at a situation that continually confronts teachers of poetry: half the battle is lost if the words on the page are approached in the wrong spirit—especially if the student is "doing" poetry as a chore, as mundane homework. Try a sort of "thought experiment" with the class. Ask them to imagine themselves in the situation dramatized in lines 100–102 of "**Leaflets.**" Something like this: "You are a doing dangerous undercover work to help free an oppressed people. If you are caught you will be tortured and killed. As you pass a barricade, your heart pounding, one of the guards (a member, like you, of the underground?) presses a crumpled piece of paper into your hand." Or, to borrow an idea from Walker Percy, "You are on a desert island. After months without anything to read, you see in the shallow surf a bottle holding a message." Or, "You are in the

attic of your ancestral family home. Under the false bottom of a trunk you find a yellowed, sealed envelope. On it are the words, *To the One who Discovers my Secret.*" Do what you can to encourage students to approach Rich's poems (or anyone else's) in the spirit in which they would approach the messages in the thought experiments.
- Other poets, especially Donne, Dickinson, and Olds, can be studied intensively. See the last of the Planning Ideas in the previous chapter for details.

At a Bach Concert

Where is the "here" of line 3? What is "this antique discipline"? What claims is the poem making about art? How does the structure of the poem reinforce these claims?

Storm Warnings

This poem develops a complex metaphor of changing weather to describe human emotions and psychology. Rich has recently said of it, " 'Storm Warnings' is a poem about powerlessness—about a force so much greater than our human powers that while it can be measured and even predicted, it is beyond human control. All 'we' can do is create an interior space against the storm, an enclave of self-protection, though the winds of change still penetrate the keyholes and 'unsealed apertures.' "

Questions for Discussion

1. What is the speaker's relationship to her internal weather, especially in lines 15–21 and 26–28?

2. The poem was written in the same year as "At a Bach Concert" and "Aunt Jennifer's Tigers" (p. 685). What similarities of form and theme can you identify in these three poems? How might the metaphor of an internal storm apply to the other two poems?

Snapshots of a Daughter-in-Law

The speaker refers to an Emily Dickinson poem that you have read, "My Life had stood—a Loaded Gun" (p. 906). How is that poem relevant to the situation in this poem? How does the poet Emily Dickinson figure for the woman in this poem? How does this poem differ in form and content from earlier Rich poems?

Orion

This poem provides an interesting contrast to the indoor / outdoor dichotomy developed in "Storm Warnings." In "Orion," instead of carving out a relatively safe place against the storm, the speaker invokes a "genius" (which originally meant an attendant spirit) who dwells about as far outdoors as one can get: in the night sky (line 3). Orion is a hunter, quintessentially male, fierce, egotistical. The female speaker, in contrast, fails to appropriate such stellar qualities: "Indoors I bruise and blunder, / break faith, leave ill enough / alone, a dead child born in the dark" (lines 19–21). In the end, though, the speaker shoots a "cold and egotistical" gaze back at the constellation.

Questions for Discussion

1. Why does the speaker refer to Orion as a "half-brother" (line 7)?
2. Why are "pieces of time" referred to as "frozen geodes" (line 23)?

Leaflets

Like "Orion," this poem involves a confrontation with a male counterpart— in this case a young political activist. He has told the speaker that "poetry is nothing sacred" (line 104); presumably he feels that one makes a difference in the world by directly taking part in revolutionary actions—not by writing poems. The speaker's reply is that in a perfect world (if life were "uncorrupted"), there would indeed be no need for poetry (line 107). But clearly we do not live in such a world.

Questions for Discussion

1. Note the effectiveness of the placement on the page of the simile at the beginning of section two. Also, after the word "*stretched*," one reads the verb "*tear*" (meaning "*rip*"). But a few lines later the ripping gives way to weeping: the male cries "the tears of Telemachus" (the son of Odysseus and Penelope). Why does the speaker associate her friend with Telemachus?
2. Paraphrase lines 52–53. Does Rich's noting the Simone Weil quotation help?

Planetarium

As with the implicit connection between speaker and constellation in "Orion," the speaker's bombardment by signals and pulsations in "Planetarium" (lines 35–45) presents a very different image from that of the speaker in "Storm Warnings," who closes the shutters against the elements. This woman is more active than those in the preceding Rich poems; the speaker here sees herself as not only the passive receiver of signals but the translator of them. Considering Rich's comment in "When We Dead Awaken" that the woman in the poem and the woman writing the poem become the same helps us understand the role of Caroline Herschel as an inspiration for the poem. She was a woman who, unlike the speaker in "Orion," did more than gaze at the stars, more than return Orion's icy stare. She used her intelligence and imagination to make a contribution, although she went unrecognized for it.

Questions for Discussion

1. How does this poem challenge the dichotomy of maternal love versus egotism that Rich names in "When We Dead Awaken"?

2. Why is it important for Rich to write to and about historical women? How is this different from writing about mythic women? About herself? How is Rich's treatment of Caroline Herschel similar to that of Marie Curie in "Power"? How is it different?

3. Despite the fact that the poem's speaker receives the "most / untranslatable language in the universe," she is "trying to translate pulsations into images" (lines 38, 43–44). What figurative resources does the poet employ to translate the (nearly) untranslatable? Can you generalize about why poetry must always use figurative devices rather than more immediately transparent language?

Diving into the Wreck

Compare this wreck to the ruins in Shelley's "Ozymandias" (p. 875). The diver in this poem says that she came for "the wreck and not the story of the wreck / the thing itself and not the myth" (lines 63–64). The speaker in Shelley's poem seems to be interested not in the ruins themselves but in the story of the ruins.

Questions for Discussion

1. Why isn't Rich's diver interested in the story of the wreck?

2. What is the wreck? What is the diver's relationship to the sea (lines 39–40)?

Origins and History of Consciousness

Rich's work, taken as a whole, chronicles a "history of consciousness" among women, a history she continues to make and to write. Two later poems, "Letters in the Family" (p. 705) and "Walking Down the Road" (p. 742) were written in 1989. They represent a very different state of consciousness from that of the women in the earlier poems, including this one.

Questions for Discussion

1. In what ways is the "dream of a common language" (lines 12, 33) similar to the project of the diver in "Diving into the Wreck"?

2. What physical "origins" unite the lovers in this poem? What psychological bonds unite them? Contrast the description of life in part III to that in "Living in Sin" (p. 907).

Writing Assignments for Chapter 10

1. In her comment on "Orion" in "When We Dead Awaken" (p. 964), Rich says that "the word 'love' is itself in need of revision." Write an essay based on one or more of Rich's poems in which you discuss the terms of love's redefinition.

2. Rich recently said of her college days in the late 1940s, "I had no political ideas of my own, only the era's vague and hallucinatory anti-Communism and the encroaching privatism of the 1950s. Drenched in invisible assumptions of my class and race, unable to fathom the pervasive ideology of gender, I felt 'politics' as distant, vaguely sinister, the province of powerful older men or of people I saw as fanatics. It was in poetry that I sought a grasp on the world and on interior events, 'ideas of order,' even power." Using the poems col-

lected in the text as well as other poems by Rich, write an essay that charts the development of the poet's political consciousness. Address the question of what is gained and what is lost in the movement from the early poems to the more overtly political ones. Do certain poems contain the best of both worlds?

11 LITERARY TRADITION AS CONTEXT

J. V. Cunningham's two-line poem "History of Ideas" not only provides a well-turned example of the epigram, one that admirably fulfills Coleridge's criteria in "What Is an Epigram"? but also strings together the first section of this chapter (Echo and Allusion) and the last (Mythology and Myth). The nod to the New Testament claim that "God is love" (I John 4:8) is abruptly inverted: in the modern world, "Love is God." As the poem's title hints, this idea arguably encapsulates a prevailing myth of the twentieth century. The point is worth making early on; students often assume that myths belong to other cultures and not to their own. Part of the problem is slippage in the usage of the word *myth*. To a good many it means simply "that which is not true." But we are using it to mean something like, "the kind of story or idea that we accept without thinking, the kind that gives us a sense of our place in the world." It is worthwhile to spend a little class time generating ideas about the myths of our culture. For example, do the stories we hear and see in movies and on TV (including the commercials) bear out Cunningham's claim about the point we have reached in the history of ideas? By what other myths do we orient ourselves?

Characteristic of poets who take on mythic subjects from ancient cultures is the desire to supply something that the myth is lacking, to claim the myth and make it relevant for readers today. Choosing a character or incident from a mythological tradition places the poet within that tradition, in dialogue with other poets. Hence the concern in this chapter with allusion, traditional poetic genres, and parodies of well-known poems. The authors here frequently draw on and challenge popular conceptions and misconceptions of mythic stories. Some poems take off from a textual source for the myth, others on imprecise recollections reinforced by popular symbolism in our culture. In class, I find it useful to try with students to determine what a poet's point of departure is. I ask them to read a poem and to see if they can identify the myth from memory. Next, we try to find one or several textual sources for the myth, look for other poems that retell the same myth, and finally, discuss how the accumulated information changes our understanding of the poem. I also get students to consider the difference between reworking an important myth in the culture and making up a new story, including the poet's advantages and disadvantages in using a story toward which his or her readers may already have strong feelings or opinions.

188 ▼ Literary Tradition as Context

Planning Ideas

• As most of our students have inherited their ideas about poetry from the
Romantics, they need to be shown that a good poem need not be a spontaneous outpouring of emotion, that it does not necessarily come directly
"from the heart." Marlowe's **"The Passionate Shepherd to His Love"** provides a good starting point. Exposure to even the sketchiest account of
Marlowe's life—his generally rebellious spirit, his undercover work for
Queen Elizabeth, his reputed atheism and association with the "School of
Night," his violent death in a tavern brawl—may make him seem an
unlikely author of a poem like **"The Passionate Shepherd."** Try asking
students who know nothing of Marlowe's life to speculate, on the basis of
the poem, about what sort of person he must have been. The result can
bring home the idea that poets sometimes write as an intellectual exercise—an experiment in creating an interesting specimen of a particular
"kind"—not as an expression of their innermost feelings.

• A good companion piece (in addition to Ralegh's **"The Nymph's Reply to
the Shepherd"** and Williams's **"Raleigh Was Right"**) for Marlowe's poem
is Marvell's **"The Garden"** (p. 1108), since it comments humorously on
the pastoral tradition. As it also touches on the biblical account of Adam
and Eve in the Garden of Eden, it can lead nicely to a discussion of
"Adam's Task," "Eve Names the Animals," and **"Eve."** These poems in
turn can be followed by **"Another Christmas Poem,"*** which pairs well
with Jiles's **"Paper Matches"*** (p. 1043).

• Be sure to have your students read the Williams ("This is Just to Say," p.
1138) and Arnold (**"Dover Beach,"** p. 741) poems (and the originals for the
other parodies and replies) at least a few days before they read the Koch
and Hecht parodies so that they will get the full effect from a first reading.
Looking at a parody first and then an original makes for an artificial recon-
struction of effect.

Echo and Allusion

ANDREW MARVELL

To His Coy Mistress

See sample analysis (Guide, p. 213)

Poetic "Kinds"

As with stanza forms, we have chosen to exemplify one kind in detail rather than give single examples of many different kinds; this intensive method can provide your students with a full sense not only of what an epigram is but of what the notion of poetic kinds is good for.

I prefer to assign a large number of the poems in this group before even suggesting any kinds of definition; that way students can put together a kind of empirical definition of their own, helped perhaps by poems that explicitly ("What Is an Epigram?") or implicitly ("Epitaph on Elizabeth, L.H.") describe characteristics of the kind.

Originally, epigrams were poems inscribed on something: a temple, grave marker, shrine, monument, or triumphal arch. But very early poets developed imitative poems that, like such inscriptions, pretended to be designed to attract the attention of "passers-by." The origin suggests the reason for the tendency toward brevity (and demonstrates how conventions develop in a poetic kind), although some poems that have passed as epigrams are pretty long. The epitaph, although not so popular as it once was as an actual inscription for tombstones, is probably the most common modern variety of epigram that still bears a recognizable relationship to its origins.

Most English epigrams are more or less based upon the model of Martial, the witty and sophisticated poet of first-century Rome who brought the kind to its most accomplished level in Latin. In Martial's hand the epigram was usually short, pointed, and often satiric. But some English poems draw from an alternate (and earlier) version of the tradition exemplified and preserved in the *Greek Anthology*, a collection of poems written over many centuries, some of them dating from as early as the sixth century BC. Some of these Greek epigrams fit the description of Martial's epigrams, but some lack the "turn" at the end, and many are neither comic in tone nor satirical in intention. Some poems have plaintive or sensuous or even sublime tones and some have substantial philosophical intentions, despite their brevity.

Epigrams were especially popular in the early seventeenth century, and they have had several vogues since, most notably in the nineteenth century. Eighteenth-century poets wrote surprisingly few epigrams, perhaps because preference for the couplet did not mean the absolute independence of each couplet. Pope, for example, made most of his couplets seem complete in themselves, and their witty turns would allow many of them to pass as epigrams, but their full effect usually depends upon connections, imagistic or otherwise, with the surrounding context. An interesting exercise might be made of comparing some two-line epigrams with Pope's couplets in "Sound and Sense" on page 815.

BEN JONSON

Epitaph on Elizabeth, L.H.

It was customary to abbreviate titles and last names on tombstones in Jonson's time, and it has been suggested that Elizabeth was titled (L = Lady), a small child, and the last in her family line (see line 10). In any case, Jonson uses the epitaph as a metaphor for talking about poetry and the demands of the epigram in particular.

Questions for Discussion

1. What details suggest the poem's self-consciousness about the tradition of the epigram? What dramatic situation is implied by "Reader, stay" (line 2)? What different meanings are implied in "a little" (line 2)?

2. Is line 4 simply a courtly compliment or does it make a serious philosophical statement? Line 6? How can you tell in each case? What attitudes does the poem take toward death? Toward the ongoing world? Toward the life of *noblesse oblige*?

3. Is the poem witty? Is it funny? Does it contain a "sting"? Describe the poem's tone.

Imitating and Answering

SIR WALTER RALEGH

The Nymph's Reply to the Shepherd

WILLIAM CARLOS WILLIAMS

Raleigh Was Right

1. What (besides "if") are the key words in Ralegh's answer?
2. According to Ralegh, what does the pastoral vision ignore?
3. After you have read Ralegh's parody of "The Passionate Shepherd" and Williams's response to both poems, do you find Marlowe's poem less effective?

More effective? Does Marlowe seem conscious of the kinds of questions that the parodists raise? What indications are there in the poem that he ignores the questions on purpose? Does such a refusal to raise questions make the poem more simple? More complex?

E. E. CUMMINGS

[(ponder,darling,these busted statues]

1. In what ways is this poem easier to read after having analyzed "To His Coy Mistress"? What specific evidence can you find that the author of "(ponder,darling" had "Coy Mistress" in mind?

2. Why are the first and last parts of the poem in parentheses? In what way does the nonparenthesized section differ from the parenthesized sections? What other devices of contrast do you find?

3. Why are such formal and archaic words as "*ponder*" and "*yon*" juxtaposed with slang such as "*busted*" and "*motheaten*"?

4. How do the ravages of time in this poem differ from those in "To His Coy Mistress"?

5. How does this poem vary from the basic *carpe diem* pattern? Could you tell, from the language of the poem itself, that it was not written in the seventeenth century, when the *carpe diem* motif flourished?

6. What is the setting of the poem? How is the setting important? How does the aqueduct unite the setting with the theme of the poem? Try to explain the speaker's habit of associating what he looks at with the argument he is trying to construct.

7. How do you explain the stanza divisions?

KENNETH KOCH

Variations on a Theme of William Carlos Williams

ANTHONY HECHT

The Dover Bitch

How closely is each poem based on its model? (See Arnold's "Dover Beach" [p. 741] and Williams's "This Is Just to Say" [p. 1138].) How much knowledge of the original does each depend on? Is the relationship between model and parody strictly structural? In what way does the original help the imitation toward a particular organization? Does the problem of organization seem easier when there is "a poem behind the poem"?

Mythology and Myth

JOHN HOLLANDER

Adam's Task

SUSAN DONNELLY

Eve Names the Animals
[see chapter introduction]

Both of these poems expand upon the role of naming in the biblical creation myth from Genesis 2–3, and so it is not surprising that both focus on language. But the two are quite different in tone. Which poem revels more in the sounds of words? Which more clearly makes a point?

CHRISTINA ROSSETTI

Eve
[see chapter introduction]

This poem tells the story of Genesis from Eve's perspective. According to the poem, who is to blame for the expulsion from the garden? What was Adam's role? The serpent's? What does this poem take from the biblical account and what does it add? Is there a difference between Eve's account of herself and the account of the narrator?

Questions for Discusion

1. How many of the poems in the group are "religious"—that is, how many of them have specific doctrinal aims? Chart the themes and rhetorical aims of the poems in the group. What patterns do you find?

2. Which poems draw upon highly detailed biblical information? How much knowledge of the Bible do different poets assume? Are there any patterns in this assumption (for instance, do twentieth-century poems seem to assume less specific knowledge)?

3. Which poems draw specifically upon a sense of appropriateness associated with certain events, seasons, or traditions? Are the poems in the group more solemn than average? Less solemn? What generalizations can be made about the tones of poems which draw heavily upon knowledge of the Judeo-Christian tradition? Sample some poems elsewhere in the anthology in which footnotes point you to Biblical allusions. How many different kinds of purposes can you find for the allusions? Poems worth considering include Plath's "Lady Lazarus" (p. 1117), Betjeman's "In Westminster Abbey" (p. 719), Stevens's "Sunday Morning" (p. 1127), Donne's "Batter my heart, three-personed God . . ." (p. 791), Larkin's "Church Going" (p. 843), Herbert's "Easter Wings" (p. 890), Yeats's "The Second Coming" (p. 1145), and the passage from Milton's *Paradise Lost* (p. 775).

4. Do you notice any pattern to your expectations as you approach a poem on a specific religious topic? Are you more than usually dependent on footnotes here? Describe the difference between your emotional response to allusions you immediately recognize and those that you understand only after you have read a footnote or done research. Is your response even more complex after doing research or reading a biblical passage alluded to in a poem?

ALFRED, LORD TENNYSON

Ulysses

JAMES HARRISON

Penelope

MIRIAM WADDINGTON

Ulysses Embroidered

EDNA ST. VINCENT MILLAY

An Ancient Gesture

All four of these poems not only provide interesting perspectives on the myth of Ulysses (or Odysseus); they all, implicitly or explicitly, address the topic of gender roles in the ancient and modern worlds.

Questions for Discussion

1. What is the significance of Tennyson's referring to Penelope simply as "an agéd wife"?

2. Do "Penelope," "Ulysses Embroidered," and "An Ancient Gesture" have any ideas in common? How do the three provide different views of the woman's side of the relationship?

3. What do the speaker's reasons for rebuffing the suitors in "Penelope" tell us about her? About her relationship with Ulysses?

4. What are some of the implications of the title "Ulysses Embroidered"?

5. Why does the speaker in Millay's poem call the gesture of wiping her tears with her apron "authentic, antique, / In the very best tradition, classic, Greek" (lines 11–12)?

LANGSTON HUGHES

The Negro Speaks of Rivers

MAYA ANGELOU

Africa

Both of these poems deal with the dual heritage of African Americans. How does the speaker in "The Negro Speaks of Rivers" see the relationship between his various myths he inherits as an African American? How does the use of river imagery differ in the two poems? How does describing Africa as a woman determine the images of violence in "Africa"?

DEREK WALCOTT

A Far Cry from Africa

The title is deliberately ambiguous: just as the speaker is both responsive to the cries reaching far from their origin in Africa, he is "a far cry" from being a native African. He is of mixed ancestry, and the claims placed upon him by both sides have him "divided to the vein" (line 27).

Questions for Discussion

1. How do lines 9–10 reflect the larger dilemma of the poem?

2. What does the speaker mean by the claim that "upright man / Seeks his divinity by inflicting pain" (lines 16–17)?

Writing Assignments for Chapter 11

1. Compare the role of woe in Susan Donnelly's "Eve Names the Animals" and Christina Rosetti's "Eve." (See especially line 22 in Donnelly's poem.)

2. Either support or refute the claim that "all my verse is rotten" in the last line of Wendy Cope's "Not only marble, but the plastic toys." It might be helpful to consider the poem's model, Shakespeare's "Not marble nor the gilded monuments." Does Cope's poem in fact fall far short of Shakespeare's? If so, can you be specific about why? If not, what makes it such an effective parody?

3. Regardless of your ethnic heritage, you know something of the universal human dilemma of divided allegiances: various groups make their claims on you, and sometimes those claims conflict. Using Walcott's "A Far Cry from Africa" as a reference point, write an essay describing your experience of being pulled in two directions. Use the library to find out something about Walcott, and read as many of his poems as you can. Are there parallels between his experiences and yours?

4. It would be easy to "explode" the myth described in Judith Oritz Cofer's "How to Get a Baby": the system for receiving a *waiwaia* involves frequent sex, which of course would increase the woman's chance of becoming pregnant. Or the myth of the scorpions in Ríos's "Advice to a First Cousin": scorpions do not really reason, as the speaker's grandmother claims they do. Write an essay on either or both of these poems, explaining what would be lost by exploding the myth.

12 HISTORY AND CULTURE AS CONTEXT

This chapter offers the opportunity to read and analyze poetry within the specific historical and cultural contexts of each poem. While you will want to make students sensitive to their lack of knowledge about some contexts (so that they will seek out the knowledge they need instead of blithely analyzing poetry with no sense of the background), it can be counterproductive to make them feel ignorant. That is why I like to begin with a poem for which many students will understand the contexts immediately. Ai's "Riot Act, April 29, 1992" works well for my purposes, since most students will know about the series of trials associated with the Rodney King beating and the riots in South Central Los Angeles that were the aftermath of the acquittal of the officers involved. Once students realize how their special knowledge of the L.A. riot gives them useful expertise as readers and critics of this poem, they move more readily and enthusiastically toward *becoming* experts on the contexts of other poems that treat subjects remote from their experience.

Planning Ideas

- Before the first class day on this chapter, give the students a photocopy of Ai's **"Riot Act, April 29, 1992,"** without footnotes. Ask them to supply the footnotes they believe future generations might find helpful in understanding the poem and to bring these to class.
- Well before class, assign several groups of students to do background research on a number of the poems in this chapter and to share their findings at the appropriate time (e.g., research methods of warfare used in World War I as background to Owen's **"Dulce et Decorum Est"**).
- Create a unit to study and discuss issues of African American identity and racial equality using such poems as Claude McKay's **"America,"*** Langston Hughes's **"Harlem (A Dream Deferred),"** Robert Hayden's **"Frederick Douglass,"** and Ai's **"Riot Act, April 29, 1992."** Ask different students to research the context of each poem before class, paying particular attention to the social and legal situation of African Americans at the time each poem was written.
- If you assign the poem **"Sonnet: The Ladies' Home Journal,"** ask each student to choose and bring to class a magazine article that portrays what they consider a false picture of some aspect of American life. Use these as the basis for a discussion of the poem's message and its continued relevance.

• Assign Elizabeth's poem, **"When I Was Fair and Young"** along with Herrick's **"To the Virgins, to Make Much of Time,"** Lovelace's **"To Amarantha, that She Would Dishevel Her Hair,"** and Marvell's **"To His Coy Mistress,"** and create a unit in which you talk about relations between men and women in the sixteenth and seventeenth centuries and how these relations are reflected in poems about love written at that time.

Times, Places, and Events

CLAUDE McKAY

America

1. How does the poem manipulate the opposing forces of energy and stability into qualities both positive and negative for the speaker?

2. Could you prove, from the poem itself, that the poet was an African American? Which details in the poem take on a new dimension when you keep this fact in mind?

LANGSTON HUGHES

Harlem (A Dream Deferred)

This poem was written in 1951, before the explosion of the civil rights movement in the 1960s. The dream in the poem may refer to the aspirations of African Americans to move out of the poverty-stricken conditions of the urban ghetto in Harlem and elsewhere and to participate in the "American Dream." More generally, it refers to any frustrated plan of self-fulfillment. None of the alternative similes describing what happens to a dream deferred is hopeful. How does the bleakness of this poem compare with the poems written by Adrienne Rich in 1951?

ROBERT HAYDEN

Frederick Douglass

This poem has something to say about what it means for a person or a group of people to remember and claim a hero, what it means to pursue the dream of a great leader. You might use discussion of this poem as an opportunity to explore the issues of leadership and hero worship in contemporary terms. For whom is Bill Clinton a hero? O. J. Simpson? For whom is Hillary Clinton a leader? Anita Hill?

Questions for Discussion

1. Which lines of the poem do *not* deal with remembering?

2. In what repute or esteem is Frederick Douglass held today? To what degree does the answer to that question depend on whom you consult, according to age, race, political affliation, etc?

WILFRED OWEN

Dulce et Decorum Est

Horace's poem on which the title is based can make an interesting comparison; it is the second ode in his third book of *Odes*. Some questions for discussion: Which physical details in the first stanza are the most dramatic? What is implied by the comparison to "beggars" (line 1)? to "hags" (line 2)? Why are the shells said to "hoot" (line 7)? to be "disappointed" (line 8)? What is accomplished by giving human attributes to inanimate objects?

(*Note:* Owen was killed in November 1918, barely a week before the Armistice. Only four of his poems had been published at the time of his death.)

DUDLEY RANDALL

Ballad of Birmingham

Like "Harlem," this poem offers a despairing picture of the lives of African Americans, this time at the height of the racial violence of the 1960s. Rather than similes, however, this poem uses realistic details. Describing an historical event, it focuses on a particular story to show that no one, no matter how innocent, can escape the violence of the struggle. The irony is that a child is killed as a result of her mother's attempts to protect her from harm.

Questions for Discussion

1. What devices make this account more than a detached description of an event?

2. How do the dialogue, repetition and symbolism contribute to the poem's power to go beyond the specificity of the particular incident?

AI

Riot Act, April 29, 1992

Either through student reports (see Planning Ideas above) or through general discussion, review the events preceding the April 29th riots: the repeated TV screenings of the Rodney King beating, the much-publicized venue change for the police officers' trial to mostly white Sonoma County, and the trial verdict. Students will readily see how important knowledge of this background is to understanding Ai's poem. After establishing the trial context, I like to ask students what additional elements of the poem they believe should be annotated to help future generations understand Ai's work (see Planning Ideas). Their list will probably include the brand names "Reebok" and "Nike" and references to sports and entertainment personalities Michael Jordon, Magic Johnson, and Spike Lee. It might also include the street slang appellation "homey," references to movies *(The Night of the Living Dead, Mo' Money)*, and the "trickle down" theory of economics current during the Reagan and Bush administrations. A century from now, readers might also need to know something about the social and economic situation of African Americans living in South Central Los Angeles at this time.

Questions for Discussion

1. Characterize the speaker. How does he view his day-to-day life?

2. What is the speaker's view of what's "out there" (line 4)—the things that are *not* part of his daily existence?

3. Who are the "zombies" the speaker refers to in line 26? What is the speaker's view of white America? How does the speaker imagine that white America views him?

4. How, in the course of the poem, does the speaker justify his actions? What do you make of his references to self-destruction?

5. Does it matter whether the poet is African-American, Asian, or "white"?

Ideas and Consciousness

ELIZABETH

When I Was Fair and Young

This poem is a response to the spirit of *carpe diem,* but this time from the woman's perspective. The speaker clearly sees her refusals of male advances as a kind of power, but that power is bound to her youth and beauty. When the youth and beauty have faded, the speaker no longer feels the power of refusal. If you read this poem in conjunction with Herrick's "To the Virgins, to Make Much of Time," Lovelace's "To Amarantha, that She Would Dishevel Her Hair," and Marvell's "To His Coy Mistress," you might use the questions below as prompts for discussion.

Questions for Discussion

1. What kind of power do the women in these poems possess?
2. What are the grounds for the arguments of the men?
3. What fears do the men play on, and how is that fear borne out in this poem?

EDNA ST. VINCENT MILLAY

[Women have loved before as I love now]

Taking up this poem for discussion provides a good occasion to talk about how context can affect tone. Millay here chooses two grand stories of illicit love—two among the most dramatic and tragic in the annals of literature—to serve as the bases of her speaker's comparison. Provided with a little information about the place of Tristan and Isolde and Helen and Paris in the literary history of lovers, students will quickly recognize the *hubris* of the speaker's claims.

Questions for Discussion

1. How do the allusions to Tristan and Isolde and Helen and Paris help to characterize the speaker's style of loving? By implication, how does the speaker characterize the love affairs in which she is likely to be involved? How would *you* characterize them?

2. Would you like to be the speaker's roommate? Have you ever been tempted to describe one of your own romantic relationships in dramatic and absolute terms?

3. How, by implication, does the speaker view modern romance?

LIZ ROSENBERG

Married Love

What sacrifice does the speaker make to marriage? What does she gain from being married? Why does she address her husband as "Oh, husband," rather than calling him by his name? How does the poem create the sense of the woman's isolation? How do the "As ifs" function in the last stanza? Compare this poem to Rich's "Living in Sin" (p. 907).

ADRIENNE RICH

Delta

Compare the rubble and water imagery in this poem to Rich's "Diving into the Wreck" (p. 955). To what is the rubble contrasted? What does this poem gain from its greater economy?

JUDITH ORITZ COFER

Unspoken

Cofer sets up a delicate contrast between the uncertainty, pain, and inexperience of adolescence and the pleasures and relative confidence of experienced adulthood. The speaker's reference to Michelangelo's belief that the nascent form of every sculpture awaits the sculptor in the marble is not only reassuring—in the sense that it suggests the awkward child-woman will someday find completion and maturity—but also in that it implies that the speaker, at least, believes the adolescent will someday become a woman of beauty. My students are near enough in time to the pangs of adolescence to remember what a difficult stage it can be. Older students may relate more closely to the speaker's (parental?) voice. Whatever the composition of the class, it may be useful to raise the question of *audience* in this poem. Could an adolescent read this poem with real comprehension? Could a man, whether adult or adolescent?

Questions for Discussion

1. Given the speaker's understanding of so much that is painful and / or mysterious to the girl she mentally addresses, why does the speaker remain silent? Why doesn't the speaker tell the girl (her daughter?) what she is thinking? What is the "covenant of silence"? Who made the "covenant" and why?

2. Are there topics that would be useful for you to discuss with your parents that you, nevertheless, do not ever discuss? Why, or why not?

SHARON OLDS

The Elder Sister

This poem describes the relationship between women's bodies. The speaker describes her attitude toward her sister in physical terms. She uses metaphors to describe her sister's body and her own. Are the relationships between women's bodies in this poem metaphors for the emotional and psychological relationships between them? What are the implications of the final metaphor of the hostage?

Writing Assignments for Chapter 12

1. Compare Claude McKay's "America" to Shelley's "Ozymandias." Which poem is the more specific? Which do you find the most effective in conveying its message?

2. Research the aftermath of the Rodney King trial in the library, looking at a minimum of three magazine and three newspaper articles from *different* magazines and newspapers. Write an assessment of the accuracy of Ai's poem, based on your research.

3. Taking Ai's poem "Riot Act, April 29, 1994" as a model, write your own poem on the riot of April 29th, from the point of view of an Asian shopkeeper

in South Central Los Angeles or from the perspective of a white member of the trial jury.

4. Read the article on the candidacy of Marion Barry for mayor of Washington, D.C., in the September 5, 1994, issue of *The New Yorker* magazine. Write a sonnet similar to Robert Hayden's *or* a campaign song in which you either praise Barry and support him as a mayoral candidate or judge him and assert that he could not serve his city well.

13 THE PROCESS OF CREATION

Some of your students will be closet poets, and among them will be a few who not only write poems but also actually labor at and revise their work. These amateur poets will have some sense of the effort behind the vision and revision of a poem. Most students, however, have thought little about the process of poetic creation and may think of poems (when they think of poems at all) as literary artifacts that fall complete from poets' minds onto paper. This chapter offers examples suggesting the process by which the pretty good poems of excellent poets become much better, even great poems. Some of the Planning Ideas below offer a way to let students experiment themselves with the same process.

Planning Ideas

• Supply students with a draft of a short, amateur poem. (I have provided one sample below.) Using an overhead projector, revise the poem as a class, sharpening images, polishing language, and strengthening the overall effect of the work. (When there is disagreement about a revision that cannot be worked out through discussion, resolve the disagreement with a class vote.)

Sample Poem:

"A Missing Table Leg"

How can you say that?
Feelings and emotions can't be spoken
like the 7 o'clock weather report.
Gentle hands and soft, wet lips
are the only way to talk with someone
that you loved.
It only takes a little of that once
abundant love
to stop a person from turning into
a crushed tomato soup can that lies next to
the egg shells and coffee grounds.

• Divide students into groups of three or four. Give each group the same early version of a poem by a major poet—a poem *not* represented in this text. Ask each group to revise the poem, improving it in as many ways as possible. Have a spokesperson from each group share the results with the class, briefly explaining their choices. Then supply the final version of the poem—the poet's ultimate revision—so that the groups can compare their efforts with the poet's.

- Photocopy the "final" versions of the poems you assign, and provide copies for each student so that it will be easier for them to place the versions side by side and make comparisons.

JOHN KEATS

Bright Star

To begin, you might ask two students to compile a list of "variants" on the blackboard so that the class can focus easily on the specific changes Keats made between the earlier and later versions of his poem. Remind the class that even changes in punctuation and spacing can make a difference in the poem's effect. For example, in the later version of this sonnet, Keats changes the emphatic exclamation point at the end of line 1 to a dash. In the earlier version, the exclamation point brings the first line to a full stop. The dash that replaces it in the later version helps create continuity between the first line and those that follow, but it also sets off lines 2–8, which clarify what the speaker does *not* want to imitate about the star's situation: "*Not* in lone splendor . . ." (my emphasis). This bracketing also helps to clarify the contrast between lines 2–8 and lines 9–14, in which the poet describes the aspects of the star's situation that he *would* like to share.

The first revision of wording that occurs in the later version is the substitution of "aloft" for "amid" (line 2). This, for me, is an example of revision toward greater clarity and away from the expected. The word "aloft" not only conveys a sharper visual picture of the star high in the sky, but it is the more original, less-expected word choice. The second word substitution—"patient" for "devout"—seems in some ways a more significant revision, since a lover would *want* to portray himself as being devout, but in the earlier version the word "devout" appears in the section listing the things the poet does *not* want to imitate. Other kinds of revisions include: (1) revision to create ambiguity, (2) revision for greater metrical regularity, (3) revision toward greater euphony, (4) revision to create or reinforce image patterns, and (5) revision to alter the poem's meaning.

Questions for Discussion

1. Why do you think "morning" waters become "moving" waters in the later version? What is gained through this change?

2. How is the rhythm or meter of line 8 altered by the addition of the word "the"?

3. Why do you think Keats gets rid of the construction "Cheek-pillowed" (line 10)? Why does he substitute "to feel" for "to touch" (line 11)?

4. How do the changes in the final couplet of the poem alter its meaning and effect?

JOHN KEATS

La Belle Dame Sans Merci

The major change in this poem from the early to the late version is the addition of three final stanzas that provide details about the dream with which the earlier version ends. Stanzas X and XI recount the details of the knight's dream, in which bloodless, emaciated kings, princes, and warriors warn the dreamer that the woman he has fallen in love with is the beautiful woman without mercy, or the beautiful, pitiless woman. The addition of the more detailed dream contributes to the dark fairy-tale quality of the poem and enhances its mythic resonance. The testimony of the men in the dream creates the sense that the knight's experience is not unique—that this mystical woman is the *femme fatale*, or at least *femme malade*, that men are said to fear.

Questions for Discussion

1. What is the effect of reprising most of the first stanza in the final stanza of the later version? How does it effect our sense of closure?

2. Modern poets sometimes create poems that lack closure to provoke thought. If you find the repetition of lines satisfying in the later version, could it have anything to do with the type of poem Keats is striving to imitate? (How do you expect a ballad to end?)

EMILY DICKINSON

[Safe in their Alabaster Chambers—]

Dickinson's 1861 version of her 1859 poem, with its completely different second stanza, shows us poetic genius at work. The earlier version is a neat, fairly conventional poem about the great divide between life and death and the uselessness of human wisdom in the face of mortality. In the later version, the theme alters slightly: the later version is perhaps more about the insignificance of human activity from the perspective of death. Yet the change in theme is not

Dickinson's triumph. The triumph is that she took an undistinguished poem treating a common poetic theme and revised it to make it something wholly original.

The revised stanza forces us to share the perspective of the coffin's inhabitants. Instead of standing outside the picture, as we do in the 1859 version, in the 1861 version, we *feel* the world rotate above those who are buried and sense movement from their perspective. Almost simultaneously, we are brought to realize that these same great movements have no noise, no effect, for the inhabitants of the alabaster chambers themselves.

Questions for Discussion

1. The words and images of the revised second stanza have a grandeur and a sweep of which the original version has not the slightest hint or whisper. Where does the power of the second stanza come from?

2. What is the effect of the greater number of dashes in the later version of the second stanza?

3. What sense do you make of the last line of the 1861 version?

Writing Assignments for Chapter 13

1. Write an essay in which you argue that one version of the "Ballad of Lord Randall" should be preferred over the other. Provide detailed support for your assertions.

2. If you have written a poem for this or another class, do a careful revision of it, taking several days to think and rethink your choice of words, images, meter, and form. Then write an essay justifying the changes you have made.

∨ ∨ ∨

Evaluating Poetry

One of the most vexed questions in literary-critical circles is whether our judgments about literature are so implicated in a limited, even oppressive world view that it would be better to abandon the whole enterprise of literary evaluation. Even the term *evaluation* can be seen as unduly emphasizing a poem's *value*, which in Western industrialized culture has a primarily monetary connotation—as if a poem would need to sell well in order to be good.

But while there is certainly some danger of being overly proscriptive about literature, particularly in an increasingly pluralistic society, one can just as easily (perhaps even more easily in the current climate) err on the other side by assuming that all literature is equally good. Our students know better. In my experience the great majority are uneasy with shilly-shallying about the quality of a poem: they want to know whether it is good and how they can tell. The best course is to be as clear as possible about criteria for evaluation, all the while trying to remain aware of the cultural limitations that make us see the world the way we do.

Planning Ideas

- The chapters above include three planning ideas or writing topics that ask students to write their own poems. (See the second planning idea in Chapter 1, the second writing assignment in Chapter 6, and the first writing assignment in Chapter 7.) While I tend not to have students evaluate their peers' poetry (not only because many of the students are fledgling poets who regard their creations as personal, but also because some of the evaluators are fledgling critics), having students evaluate their own poems can be fruitful. Such evaluation can be done in an analytical essay or fairly informally in a journal. Either way, it helps to get students thinking about why some things worked well and some didn't, especially if they can find examples of similar moments of success and failure in the poems in the text.

- Irving Layton's **"Street Funeral"** pairs well with Shakespeare's **"Th' expense of spirit is a waste of shame."** Both poems depict sensory pleasures as ultimately illusory, but of course both make their cases by employing imagery that strongly appeals to the senses.

- Have students read all the short Emily Dickinson poems in the Reading More Poetry section along with **"The Brain—is wider than the Sky—."** Many of these poems are not usually anthologized, and they suggest a poet more playful, more comic, more fanciful, and more flirtatious than the somewhat somber Emily Dickinson that emerges from some of the more familiar lyrics. Dickinson—as represented in this book—is a good poet to study in combination with Adrienne Rich, not only because Rich remembers and consciously departs from her mode of seeing and telling (see **"Snapshots of a Daughter-in-law,"** lines 43–46), but also because Dickinson's quiet but resolute bursting of formal bonds resembles so closely that of Rich in an early poem like **"Aunt Jennifer's Tigers"** (p. 685).

- See the "How to Write a Lousy Sonnet" exercise, detailed in the first of the Planning Ideas in Chapter 7 above.

IRVING LAYTON

Street Funeral

Ostensibly this poem makes a fairly straightforward statement: "We're better off dead." Several things, though, call that idea into question. First, the speaker doesn't really state that the unnamed subject of the poem is glad to be turning slowly into grass instead of putting up with life's troubles; the last sentence is a *question*. Not only does the speaker's use of a question instead of a statement imply that one might disagree with the dead man's opinion, it would of course be impossible for a dead man to have an opinion if consciousness had really ended with his biological life. The only ones who can conceivably be glad—about anything—are those who are alive on earth now and those whose consciousness extends beyond earthly life. The poem, then, centers on a paradox: the suggestion of an unthinking being's thoughts. Perhaps the real focus is on the *speaker's* thoughts as those of the dead man are contemplated.

The phrase *"long adultery / with illusion"* might seem despairing, but the metaphor of adultery implies that the possibility exists for a *legitimate* relationship with the world—a relationship that would not be illusory. Note that while the speaker seems fully aware of the degrading, deluded, unfulfilling life we ordinarily live, the speaker is quite clearly capable of appreciating beauty; degradation isn't the *whole* picture.

The glimpses of beauty in the poem are all confined to the areas traditionally thought to be not only subrational but also subanimal: the vegetable world and the weather. It is the *"frosty morning"* that makes the *"coffin wood"* burst into *"brilliant flowers."* It is the *"clean grass"* that will provide a preferable alternative to our animalistic existence.

Questions for Discussion

1. Why is it significant that the dead man has no name?

2. What does the phrase *"other animals"* imply about the speaker's view of the human condition?

3. The poem's first three lines make eating meat seem disgusting. How, though, does the poem differ from a simple vegetarian manifesto?

4. Are the *"child"* and the *"sly man"* whose conscience bothers him different people? The same person? Which reading makes more sense?

5. How is it that the speaker manages, in the last three lines of the first stanza, to make erotic love seem like a disease?

GALWAY KINNELL

Blackberry Eating

This poem bears some resemblance to Andrew Marvell's The Garden (p. 1108), especially to passages like, "The luscious clusters of the vine / Upon my mouth do crush their wine . . . ." Like Marvell, Kinnell uses onomatopoetic words to give the reader the sensory impression of actually eating fruit. Note that fruit-to-mouth exchange is immediate; the speaker's hands do not touch the berries directly: ". . . as I stand among them / lifting the stalks to my mouth, the ripest berries / fall almost unbidden to my tongue, / as words sometimes do. . . ." The connection between the sensory experience of eating and the choice of words is explicit. Kinnell provides a clue about what it is about words like *"strengths," "squinched," "squeeze,"* and *"splurge"* that makes them appropriate: they are "many-lettered, one-syllable lumps"—and so they resemble blackberries, with their clustered surfaces, more than they would, say, blueberries or cherries.

Questions for Discussion

1. How does the sound echo the sense in a line like, ". . . among the fat, overripe, icy, black blackberries . . ."? in a passage like, ". . . the stalks very prickly, a penalty / they earn . . ."?

2. Why does the speaker claim that blackberry-making is a "black art" and blackberry-eating a "black language"?

EMILY DICKINSON

[The Brain—is wider than the Sky—]

In this poem, as in "I Reckon—when I count at all—," the speaker values the brain—and, implicitly, at least, the poet—above all else. What other similarities do you see between these two poems, which were probably written around the same time? How do they differ from other Dickinson poems you have read? In "The Brain . . . ," what is the implication of the "*and You*" of line 4? How do "*Syllable*" and "*Sound*" differ? What does the difference imply about the relation between the brain and God?

Writing Assignments for
Evaluating Poetry

1. "Street Funeral," like Andrew Marvell's "To His Coy Mistress," incorporates all three of the "souls" that the psychology of Marvell's day attributed to human beings: the vegetable, the animal, and the rational. Whereas the speaker in "Coy Mistress" ostensibly opts for the animal soul over the vegetable, that situation is reversed in "Street Funeral." In both poems, though, the rational part of us plays a much greater role than a first reading might imply. Using details from both poems, write a four- or five-page essay developing this idea. Devote the last page or so to an explanation of which poem is more effective in its handling of our complex make-up.

2. Imagine that you are the poetry editor of a good periodical, one that appeals to broad spectrum of well-educated readers (*The New Yorker*, say, or *The Atlantic*). You have space in the upcoming issue for only one poem, and you have narrowed the choices from a field of several dozen to two, both of which should be included in our text. Write a three-page rejection letter to the author of the runner-up. Explain in precise terms why you ultimately decided on the other poem. If you wish, spend a paragraph or two on the chosen poem's strengths, but the bulk of your letter should describe the weaknesses of the second-place finisher. Be careful here not to short-circuit your argument by deciding ahead of time which sorts of poems are appropriate and which are not. Don't say, for example, "Our readers like uplifting poems, and yours is

depressing" or "Your poem is unrhymed, and our readers prefer rhyme." Are *all* depressing poems artistically inferior to uplifting ones? Should *all* poems be rhymed? Assume that your readers would answer "No" to both questions; they enjoy all sorts of poetry, as long as it is carefully crafted and somehow compelling. Your rejection letter, then, should point out in as much detail as possible why the poem is not quite successful in fulfilling its goal, in doing its job.

A Sample Analysis

ANDREW MARVELL

ANDREW MARVELL

To His Coy Mistress

The title suggests the situation—a man is speaking to his beloved—and before we are far into the poem we recognize his familiar argument: let's not wait, let's make love now. But much more is going on in the poem than this simple "message."

Seduction is a promising subject, but it is nearly as easy to be dull on this subject as on less fascinating ones, and the subject has inspired some very dreary poetry. The interest and power of this poem depend on more than the choice of subject, however useful that subject is in whetting a reader's expectations. No reader is likely to use the poem as a guide for his or her own life, and few readers are likely to read it at a moment when their own lives precisely parallel the poem's situation. Its relevance is of a larger kind: it portrays vividly and forcefully a recognizable situation, saying something about that situation and, more importantly, making us react to the situation and feel something about it. Experiencing a poem involves not only knowing what it says but also feeling the pleasures provided by its clever management of our own ideas and emotions. All poems have a design on us—they try to make us feel certain things—and the full experience of a poem requires full recognition of the complexities of design so that we can feel specific emotions and pleasures—not only the general ones of contemplating seduction.

Let's begin at the beginning. What do you expect of a poem about a would-be seduction? One thing you can be almost certain of is that it will contain attractive images of physical enjoyment. The first verse-paragraph (lines 1–20) contains such images, and so does the third (especially lines 33–38). The first set of images suggest the languorous, lazy appeal of a timeless world where physical enjoyment seems to fill all time and all space. First are images of rich sensuousness; the leisurely contemplation of enjoyment, the timeless walks in exotic lands, the finding of precious stones, the luxury of delaying the supreme moment. Gradually sensuousness becomes sensuality, and the speaker imagines himself praising various parts of the young woman's body. In line 33, the poem returns to sexual contemplation but with much more intensity. Now the young woman seems to be not only a passive object of admiration but a live, breathing, perspiring, passionate respondent. And a moment later, the speaker projects the beauty and energy of the love act itself. He suggests something of his anticipation of supreme ecstasy by the vividness and intensity of the images and language he uses: from the languid, flowing, floating suggestions of the early lines through the breathless anticipation of lines 33–37 to the violence of lines 41–44 with their explicit visualization of the union, the rolling into one, of "strength" and "sweetness."

But not all the poem portrays glorious pleasure. The second verse-paragraph (lines 21–32) contains some pretty grim stuff. Instead of the endless languor of unhurried walks and exotic places in the early lines, we have anxiety and con-sciousness of time—a hurrying chariot moving up fast from behind. And instead of the centuries of body-worship, eternity consists of vast deserts. Grimmest of all is the image of a different kind of fall than the one the speaker desires—the carefully preserved virginity of the young woman, the speaker imagines, will be tested and destroyed in the grave by worms. The speaker summarizes with gross understatement and macabre humor in lines 31–32:

> The grave's a fine and private place,
> But none, I think, do there embrace.

The contrast with all that grimness of future dryness and death emphasizes both the unreal romanticism of the timeless world—which, according to the speaker, the young woman seems to want—and the vividly portrayed sensual pleasures of a potential moment right now. Such contrasts work for us as well as for the young woman; in fact, they are part of a carefully contrived argument that organizes the poem. We might well have expected, just from the title and the opening lines, that the poem would be organized as a formal argument. The first words of each paragraph clearly show the outlines: (1) "Had we . . ." (If we had no limits of time or space); (2) "But . . ." (But we do have such limits); (3) "Now, therefore . . ." The poem is cast as a long, detailed hypothetical syllogism; it uses the form of a standard argument, with vivid examples and carefully con-trived rhetoric, to suggest the urgency of enjoying the moment. It is a specious argument, of course, but real people have fallen for worse ones. But this isn't "real life"; the story doesn't even end. As in most other poems (and unlike most drama and fiction), the "plot" and its resolution have little to do with the final effect. Part of the point here is to notice the flaw in the argument. A good logician could show you that the speaker commits the fallacy of the "denied antecedent," that is, he proves what cannot happen but fails to prove what can. Of course seduction seldom gets worked out in purely logical terms, and so in one sense the logic of the argument doesn't matter—any more than whether the speaker finally seduces the young woman. But in another sense it matters a great deal and contributes to our complex experience of the poem. For if we spot the illogic and find it amusing (since the argument is obviously an effective one, logical or not), we not only feel the accuracy of the poem's observation about seduction but we experience something important about the way words work. Often their effect is more far-reaching than what they say on a literal level, just as this poem reaches much further than any literal statement of its "message" or "meaning." Poetry often exploits the fact that words work in such mysterious ways; in fact, most poems, in one way or another, are concerned with the fact that words may be used suggestively to open out on horizons beyond logical and syntactical categories.

Reading a poem about seduction is hardly the same thing as getting seduced, and only a very peculiar poet or reader would expect it to be, though some of the censorship controversies over the teaching of poems like this may sometimes imply that life and art are the same thing. Anyone who thinks they are is bound to be disappointed by a poem about seduction, or about anything else. One does not read a poem instead of being seduced, or as a sublimation, or as a guide. A poem about anything does not intend to be the thing itself, or even to re-create it precisely. Poetry, like other literature, is an ordered imitation of perceived reality expressed in words. By definition, by intention, and by practice, poetry modifies life to its own artistic ends, "ordering"—that is, making meaningful— what is only a version in any case. What poetry offers us is not life itself, naked and available, but a perspective (perceived reality) on some recognizable situations or ideas; not Truth with a capital T, but interpretations and stances; not passion itself, but words that evoke associations and memories and feelings. A poem can provide an angle of vision which in "real life" is often blurred through our closeness to experience. And just as the poet fictionalizes—whether he begins with a real event or not—we as readers end with his version, which exists in tension with other things we know, about words, about poetry, about arguments, about seduction, about everything. That tension tests not the "truth" of the poet's vision but the effects produced by the poem; the more we know, the richer these effects are likely to be.

Anyone with developed sensitivities and a modest amount of knowledge of the suggestiveness of words can find the crucial words that express and evoke the sensual appeal. The devices of contrast (the flowing Ganges flanked by rubies versus vast deserts; spacious wandering versus the confinement of a marble vault; eternal adoration vs. those traditional symbols of mortality, ashes and dust) may be readily seen by anyone willing to look at the poem carefully. In short, much of the poem is readily available to almost any reader who looks carefully; much of its power is right there on the page, and a reader need make only a minimal effort to experience it.

But a number of things in the poem require a special skill or knowledge. The poem's parody of a hypothetical syllogism is only available to those who can recognize a hypothetical syllogism and see the distortion in this one. Of course, not recognizing the syllogism is not too serious, as long as the reader "senses" the falsity of the argument and finds the incongruity in its effectiveness; he simply misses a joke which is part of the poem's complexity. But some other matters in the poem are more crucial, for lack of knowledge about them not only would drain the poem of some of its richness but might even force a misunderstanding of what the poem says on its most literal level.

Look, for instance, at the following words: "coy" (title) and "coyness" (line 2); "mistress" (title); "complain" (line 7); "vegetable" (line 11); "adore" (line 15). All of these words are common enough, but each offers a problem in interpretation because of changes in meaning. The poem was written more than three hundred years ago, in the mid-seventeenth century, and many words used then in a specific way have changed over the years. Words are, in a sense, alive and ever-changing; change is a part of the excitement of language as well as a potential frustration, and if we construe each of these words exactly as it is construed now we will be badly misled. The most obvious change in meaning is in the word "mistress," for to us it implies a specific sexual relationship, one that would make the elaborate seduction plea here seem a little late. The most common seventeenth-century meaning of "mistress" was simply "a woman who has command over a man's heart; a woman who is loved and courted by a man; a sweetheart, lady-love." This definition comes from the *Oxford English Dictionary*, a valuable reference guide that lists historical as well as modern meanings, with detailed examples of usages. The *OED* can also show us that the new meaning of "mistress" was coming into use when this poem was written, and perhaps the meanings are played off against each other, as a kind of false lead; such false leads are common in poetry, for poets often like to toy with our expectations and surprise us.

"Coy" and "coyness" offer a similar problem; in modern usage they usually suggest playful teasing, affectation, coquettishness. But originally they suggested shyness, modesty, reluctance, reserve, not simply the affectation of those things. Of course, we find out very little about the young woman herself in this poem (except what we can infer from the things the speaker says to her and the way he says them), but we are not led to think of her as sly and affected in her hesitancy to receive her lover's advances.

"Complain" and "adore" are more technical. The former indicates a lover going through the ritual of composing a "complaint"—a poem which bewails his misery because of a lady's disdain. Thus, the speaker here self-deprecatingly (but comically) imagines himself (in the unreal, timeless world of the first verse paragraph) as a pining swain, while his love is luxuriating half-way across the earth, oblivious to his pain. Obviously, the speaker wants no part of such sado-masochistic romantic nonsense; he prefers sexual pleasure to poetic posing. "Adore" technically means to worship as a deity; there is a certain irony in regarding the young woman's body as an object of religious worship, but this speaker carries through his version of the young woman's fantasy, modestly refusing to name those parts he wishes to devote thirty thousand years to, and regarding her "heart" (usually synonymous with soul in the Renaissance) as the ultimate conquest for the last age.

The term "vegetable" is even more complex, for it depends on a whole set of physiological / psychological doctrines in the Renaissance. According to those doctrines, the human soul was made up of three souls which corresponded to the different levels of living matter. The Vegetable Soul man possessed in common with plants and animals; the Sensible Soul he possessed in common with animals; the Rational Soul was possessed by man alone. The Vegetable Soul was the lowest and had only the powers of reproduction, nourishment, and growth. The senses, the passions, and the imagination were under the power of the Sensible Soul. A "vegetable love" would be without feeling or passion, appropriate to the lowest form of life. The speaker thus reduces the notion of timeless, romantic, non-physical love to what he considers its proper level—a subhuman, absurd one. He pictures love without physical involvement not as a higher spiritual attraction but rather as a lower, nonsentient one.

Several other parts of the poem similarly require historical knowledge. Lines

33–36 depend upon Renaissance love psychology which considered physiological reactions (the rosy skin, perspiration) to be stimulated by the release of "animal spirits" in the blood. This release happened when the emotions were heightened by sight of the beloved; phantasms from the eye descended to the soul and released the animal spirits. The soul was thus "present" in the physiological response (the animal spirits), and the speaker pictures it here as involved in the very moment of desire, trying to unite—through the body—with the soul of the beloved. This love psychology may seem somewhat naïve, but it is a humbling experience to try to explain our modern notions of how eyes and emotions relate to bodily processes.

The final two lines of the poem depend heavily upon specific knowledge. First there is an allusion to Greek mythology—an allusion which actually began several lines before the end with the reference to Time's slow-chapped (i.e., slow-jawed) power. According to the myth, Chronos (Time) ate all his children except Zeus (who had been hidden by Rhea), and Zeus afterward seized Chronos' power as chief of the gods. Zeus later made the sun stand still to lengthen his night of love with Alcmene. We cannot, the speaker says, make time stand still as Zeus did, but we can speed it up. His argument assumes the seventeenth-century belief that each sex act made a person's life one day shorter. The speaker keeps insisting that the coming of death—time's end—is easier to cope with if you have something interesting to do while you wait.

Up to now we have not even mentioned the man who wrote the poem, Andrew Marvell. Whether Marvell ever had such a coy friend as this poem implies is not very important to us (though it may have been very important to him). For us, the relevant point is the fiction of the poem—regardless of whether that fiction is based on actual fact. But some facts about authorship may be very useful to us as readers of the poem, as long as we use them to help us with the poem and do not simply engage in biographical speculation. In many cases, knowledge about the poet is likely to help us recognize his or her distinctive strategies, and reading other poems by the same poet often reveals his or her attitudes or devices so that we can read any one poem with more clarity, security, and depth; the index can guide you to other poems by Marvell. A reader may experience a poem in a satisfactory way without all of the special knowledge I have been describing, but additional knowledge and developed skill can heighten the experience of almost any poem. Poems do not "hide" their meaning, and good poets usually communicate rather quickly in some basic way. Rereadings, reconsiderations, and the application of additional knowledge allows us to hear resonances built into the poem, qualities that make it enjoyable to experience again and again. We have really only begun to look closely at this particular poem, and if you were to continue to reread it carefully, you would very likely discover riches which this brief discussion has not even suggested. The route to meaning is often clear on first reading a poem, but the full possibilities of experience may require more time, energy, and knowledge of the right questions to ask.

V V V

Teaching Drama

Many teachers find plays harder to teach than either stories or poems, perhaps because they are usually longer, and sometimes more complex structurally, and because some teachers consider plays out of place on a page instead of the stage. But these difficulties can be turned into virtues, for the features they represent all need to be discussed openly in class, especially the page / stage distinction. In the text we have tried to distinguish "drama" (that is, the play as literature, the work written down in letters) from "play" (the work performed on stage). We have, in deference to the function of the anthology as an introduction to literature, treated the plays as "drama," though we realize that it is difficult to make that distinction stick, and that this may not suit every teacher or every class. Many students have seen many plays or even acted in, directed, or otherwise assisted in play production. Not all students in an introductory literature course are literature majors, and some may even be theater majors or at least have a serious interest in the theater. So we have tried to redress the balance somewhat by emphasizing here, for you, the "play," and to lend some assistance to those who want to teach plays as works to be performed on stage (though we have not entirely abandoned those who want to teach drama as literature).

Your students will almost certainly need guidance and attention on issues of production and staging, and many may get involved rather more quickly in this kind of discussion than in the more literary discussions. Even students with no experience in play production or even in seeing plays often become fascinated with questions of how words on the page are fleshed out in speech and action.

The age-old custom of reading aloud in class, if not done too often (boredom, predictability, embarrassment) or with unrealistic expectations of how students will do at first (fear of failure, lack of confidence) can be especially effective in teaching plays. Usually it's best to do short scenes only, interrupting to ask questions about movement, or gesture, or intonation and (later) of interpretation. It is advisable to change parts often so that everyone gets involved. Diagrams on the board can help chart space and movement. Walk-throughs may be discouraging at first (students will unconsciously, or perhaps consciously, compare each other and themselves to actors on film or TV), but many will notice more readily than in reading how little things—a slight shift in tone, a small movement—make all the difference. The fact that your students have grown up on television and with movies is an immediate asset in teaching drama, though you may have to call attention to how the conventions of a stage are quite different from the "realism" of a camera. Participation can be a great asset in the drama part of your course, despite the well-known curse of the class ham. You may have to alter your strategy if there is a too-experienced actor who knows it all, or a class clown, or a born disrupter who takes advantage of the temptations of theatricality.

Several of the dramas in the text have been produced in excellent film versions. Although class time may be too precious to spend watching complete films, showing brief scenes on video works well to initiate discussion. And of course students can be assigned to watch videos outside of class. Written responses generally work well when they address some aspect of the differing demands of film and stage.

The discussions that follow suggest, in most cases, some things to emphasize that do not come up for much attention in the chapters themselves. Nothing is so boring to students as the rigidity of teaching one work as exclusively one thing—character, for example—and another as exclusively something else. We hope that the discussion will suggest to you some ways of varying, and complicating, the main emphases in the chapters. In addition to the commentary, we have included planning ideas, discussion questions, and paper topics.

∇ ∇ ∇

Drama: Reading, Responding, Writing

HAROLD PINTER

The Black and White

Unless they have been involved in dramatic productions in high school, students usually have little knowledge of staging, stage business, or the importance of physical gestures. *The Black and White*, because of its brevity and simplicity, offers a good opportunity to look at the importance of small gestures to dramatic effect.

Planning Ideas

• I find good way to introduce staging issues is to ask students to do a brief written exercise before class, or ask them to spend the first ten minutes of class writing a paragraph—with the text in front of them—on how they would dress one of the women and what facial expressions they would ask her to assume. One way to set up the discussion is to divide the class and have some write about one woman, some about the other, and then compare their decisions. If you use this strategy, have some students read their papers in class and ask them to defend their decisions by pointing to lines in the text. Get them to notice how the women repeat each other's phrases and how similar they are in age, in habits, even in their idiosyncrasies. Ask them to suggest how they would make the clothes and gestures of each reflect the other character without having them be identical. And why not identical?

- It may be useful to devote a few minutes of class discussion to looking at the way Pinter manages dialogue, devoting six or seven lines in the sketch to the women's discussion of the bread and tea—if one can call their exchange a discussion. I like to ask the class how much information about the bread and tea they can derive from the exchange. Then I ask how much information they can derive about the characters and their situation. What elements make the dialogue seem strange? Realistic? (This may be a good time, then, to discuss how conventions make things seem natural in a literary work that are not really natural at all, and how a transcription of actual speech, because it violates literary conventions, may seem strange or unreal.)

Commentary

Characters in drama have almost always spoken more clearly, pointedly, and logically than people do in real life, so you might point out the irony that in this sketch Pinter creates something like real conversation that, because it exists within a play, sounds strange. In real conversations people sometimes talk past each other instead of to each other. They may speak illogically or confusedly. They sometimes repeat their own or others' observations, and sometimes they talk just for the sake of talking.

Some students will notice that the women seem to be talking about the food, for example, just to pass the empty hours. It seems they've had nearly the same conversation many times before. The second woman doesn't even trouble to answer the first woman's query about her food, probably because both know what the answer will be: the same answer as the night before and the night before that. The pauses in the conversation suggest that neither has much to say. You might want to ask why the first woman pauses and then signals she hasn't heard the question—"eh?" Is she hard of hearing? Distracted with thinking about the bus lines? Attempting to gain some measure of control over the second woman?

These are the kinds of "gaps" in a text that allow, in reading or performance, room for interpretation. There is no definitively "right" answer to these questions, no clear-cut interpretation, but it is worth discussing the possibilities to demonstrate how you use the text—as well as your own experience or assumptions—to make interpretations. It may also be worthwhile because students may become aware, or be shown, how their assumptions, beliefs, and ideologies condition their choices or interpretations.

It seems likely that both women have very limited means. Both note that, while bread comes free with the soup they purchase, one must pay to have bread with tea. In these lines, as in others, the women echo each other. When the second woman repeats what the first has said about the bread, she does not seem to acknowledge new information. What does her repetition mean? Is it simply to fill time? To recognize shared experience?

As similar as the two women seem, I read their personalities as quite different. If the students have not already discussed the characters from an actor's perspective, I sometimes ask several women in the class how they would play each of the characters so as to distinguish between the two. The second, taller woman is clearly the more aggressive and confident of the pair. She procures the dinner, and she warns the first woman not to speak to strangers, as though she were more knowledgeable and experienced than her companion. The second woman appears to believe she is more attractive than the first. We realize this when she complains about the man who asked her to tell him the time. Her response turns his innocent query into a come-on. We end up feeling sorry for the poor fellow because the second woman was so nasty to him, but we also pity her for clinging to the notion that she's still an object of desire. Pity for the second woman melts away later in the sketch, however, when she insists the police who picked her up let her go because they "took a fancy" to her but replies to the first woman's question, "Do you think they'd take a fancy to me?" with "I wouldn't bank on it."

The women's situation is sad, but in the first part of the sketch they seem to take some consolation from their companionship and shared experience. However, the second woman's cruelty to the first dispels the earlier aura of friendship and makes the ending seem even bleaker than the rest of the play. So it is not surprising when, after the exchange about the policemen, the women plan to go in separate directions when they leave the milk-bar. One decides to go to Covent Gardens and the other to Waterloo Bridge. In both places—as in the nearly all-night milk bar—one would be likely to find lots of people gathered, even in the middle of the night. These will be places with "a bit of noise," "a bit of life."

Questions for Discussion

1. How would the blocking differ if you were doing the sketch as a film? Would you use "extras" in either case as a backdrop for the interaction between the two women? How important is timing in the conversation? How long would it take to play the scene appropriately? Where would the key pauses be? What would each woman's "body language" be like? How old do you imagine the women to be? What evidence does the play present about the previous meetings between the women? About their habits more generally? How important is the lighting? How much color would you include in the clothing, props, and background? Why?

2. Note that the exchange provides little information about why the two women have the habit of riding trains at night. Are they homeless? If so, how does that explanation affect your response to their situation? Why does the playwright choose not to make the exchange primarily "about" homelessness?

3. Could any of the byplay between the two old women be portrayed comi-

cally? What might be the advantage of playing one of the early exchanges for laughs? The disadvantages?

SUSAN GLASPELL

Trifles

Planning Ideas

- The first several hundred lines of this play belong almost exclusively to the male characters, even though most of the play is devoted to the conversation and activities of the two women. I often start class by asking what effect this opening might have on the reader or audience. In practical terms, why do the men speak first? Glaspell provides a fair amount stage direction at the beginning of the scene but little throughout the opening conversation between the men. You may want to ask the class to spend a few minutes blocking the movements of each character and suggesting appropriate gestures, expressions, etc. Should the men move, stand, or gesture differently from the women? The sheriff is described as taking off his overcoat and marking the beginning of "official business." Perhaps the class will want the men to move more expansively and authoritatively than the women. If so, what gestures might convey their sense of authority? What gestures, posture, etc., seem appropriate for the women? Does it seem more important to create actions that distinguish one male character from the others or to distinguish between the two female characters?
- If we were watching a production of *Trifles*, we would gradually piece together the information that Mrs. Peters is the Sheriff's wife. As a test of close reading, you might want to ask your students to identify the earliest lines of dialogue that would allow an audience to derive this information.
- Unsurprisingly, Mrs. Peters is more concerned than Mrs. Hale with the legalities of the case, and—at least in the first part of the play—she defends the men from Mrs. Hale's criticism by observing that what they are doing is "no more than their duty." Mrs. Hale, the Wrights' neighbor, appears more sympathetic to Mrs. Wright's situation and more aggressive in criticizing the men's behavior. Ask students why Glaspell makes the women different in these ways. How do their differences contribute to the conflict of the play? to its resolution?
- You might ask several pairs of "actors" from your class to enact one of the play's moments of discovery—perhaps the scene in which Mrs. Hale notices that the table is half-clean and that the "newly" baked bread has been left outside the breadbox. Include enough of Mrs. Peters's dialogue so that she is an integral part of the action. You might have three or four pairs of actors take a stab at performing this portion of the play, one right after the other. Ask those in the "audience" to take careful note of the

differences in interpretation from pair to pair. After each pair has performed, ask the class for a critique of each performance, emphasizing the directorial choices over the acting abilities of the students, and the ultimate indeterminacy of the written words.

Commentary

As the play unfolds and the two women begin to uncover the evidence that would provide a motive for the murder, the tension between their different perspectives is heightened. The women's gradual discovery of the "trifles" that could seal the case against Mrs. Wright offers several dramatic challenges. Because the clues are trifles, they need to receive enough dramatic emphasis so that the audience will register them, yet they must seem trivial enough to be missed by those trained to investigate crimes.

Gradually over the course of the play, the conflict between the women meliorates until, at the end, they are one in their determination to hide the evidence from the men. The class will readily observe that the men's condescending comments help to draw the women together, and you might lead them to note the many instances in which stage directions or whispered dialogue makes that happen—as though they are unconsciously driven to huddle near each other. Someone in the class may note that the women are also drawn together by their secret, shared discoveries about the murder and about the apparent desolation of Mrs. Wright's life. You may want to ask at what point the class believes Mrs. Peters begins to shift her loyalties from her husband and the law to Mrs. Wright. It seems to me that the real change begins when Mrs. Peters recalls the murder of her kitten and remembers the vehemence of her anger toward the boy who killed it. Mrs. Hale's implicit comparison between Mrs. Wright and the caged bird completes the sympathetic portrait. When the men return and renew their jokes about "the ladies," the decision is made.

Questions for Discussion

1. How broadly should Mrs. Hale mark her discovery in terms of vocal expression, gesture, facial expression? What should Mrs. Peters be doing at the time of the discovery? Should she be still? Upstage? Downstage? How distracting would it be to the audience if Mrs. Peters were moving busily downstage during Mrs. Hale's discovery? That is, how do you make sure the audience has its eyes on Mrs. Hale when she registers the significance of the half-dirty table and the misplaced bread? (Would this be good point at which to introduce what lighting can do?)

2. In this play it is notable that all the villains are male: the patronizing trio that investigates the murder, the lately murdered Mr. Wright, and the kitten-

killing boy. Has Glaspell stacked the deck in her play? Does it make any difference that the play was published in 1920? When were women granted the right to vote?

3. To what degree are the characters in the play "round" or well-developed? To what degree are they stereotypes?

Writing Assignments for Drama: Reading, Responding, Writing

1. I have had very good success with a writing format that can be applied to any of the plays in the text. The "staging paper" asks students to isolate twenty-five to thirty lines of dialogue and to think through a range of ways in which a director might handle the exchange. The student discusses these interpretive options in a two-page introduction that ultimately defends one option as particularly appropriate. The rest of the paper divides the text into what actors call "beats"—units of dialogue during which a character's motive for speaking (or remaining silent, or gesturing, or turning, or moving . . .) remains constant. When the character changes tack, even slightly (and the reason for the change might well be unconscious), a new beat begins. A beat is seldom more than a sentence long, and it can be as short as a word. The bulk of the staging paper consists of the student's comments after each beat. Each comment is written as though the director were explaining to the actor what caused the character to say what s/he said and move as s/he moved. In getting students to look closely at a short passage, the exercise gives them first-hand experience of drama's complexity—of the play's interpretive range and its collaborative requirements.

2. In a two- or three-page essay, explain what would change if the playwright had made his characters in **The Black and White** old men instead of old women.

▽ ▽ ▽

Understanding the Text

1 CHARACTERIZATION

Both dramas in this unit present studies of characters with pathological personalities, and a key question in both is how much the course of the pathology has been determined by societal strictures. In neither case does the playwright present a definitive answer to the nature / nurture question, but in both the question provides a useful point of entry.

In one sense *Getting Out* traces the process of Arlene's grieving the loss of her former self. (Late in the play Ruby consoles Arlene by saying, "You can still . . . you can still love people that's gone" [p. 1231]). But the audience's *experience* of the play is that Arlie is not gone at all: she is on the stage nearly all the time, as is Arlene. In beholding the two selves of a single character, one younger and one older, the audience occupies a point of privilege outside time's usual constraints. We're allowed not only to *theorize* about how personality develops through time but to *experience* the connectedness of past and present personality.

One reason Arlie's monologue about the frogs is so entertaining (after the play's premier, the speech almost instantly became a favored piece for acting auditions) is that we have already been introduced to the idea that this character has been "completely rehabilitated" (p. 1189). Regardless of whether at this early point in the play we entirely believe the Warden's claim, we soon come to experience Arlene as having matured: just after Arlie's story about the frogs, Arlene responds to Bennie's "You ain't as strong as you was" with "I ain't as mean as I was. I'm strong as ever." (p. 1190). We know, then, that the meanness of the frog-throwing Arlie is a thing of the past; we can laugh at it.

One way of appreciating this moment's complexity is to consider the way you would feel if you actually saw someone throwing your child's pets into the street. The theater offers a very different experience: rather than directly witnessing an act of cruelty, we are in a playhouse, where on some level we remain aware that frogs are not *really* flying through the air, no matter how caught up we are in the monologue. We are not even watching staged frog-throwing but hearing a character tell about a past action. Moreover, the character herself is an earlier version of the mature Arlene, who now has better things to do than throw frogs. Paradoxically, all this distancing does more than insulate us from an act of cruelty: it allows us the perspective to appreciate a side of Arlie that our emotions would prevent us from seeing if we watched a real person doing such a thing.

While Hedda Gabler's character is revealed through more traditional staging techniques, she too invites a complex emotional response. One early critic's bitter dismissal of Ibsen's play on the ground that Hedda is "crawling with the filthiest passions of the human race" seems as incomplete as the counter-claim that given the social conventions of her time, she can hardly help being the way she is. Both plays offer central characters who are compelling in part because there is more to them than first meets the eye.

MARSHA NORMAN

Getting Out

Planning Ideas

- *Getting Out* can serve to clarify—and in a way that students will immediately apprehend—the difference between the drama and the play. The experience of reading the drama can be frustrating because it is essential to know when it is Arlene saying or doing something and when it is Arlie, but the names are so similar that the reader can easily be mistaken. But watching the play involves no such difficulty: Arlene and Arlie are played by different actors. One way of overcoming the difficulty is simply to warn students ahead of time that they must read the names carefully. A way of reinforcing the drama / play distinction is to have students do staged readings of scenes in which both Arlene and Arlie are present.
- As one discusses ways of developing compelling characters, it is useful to focus on minor characters in *Getting Out*—especially Bennie and Carl—as well as on Arlene / Arlie. In some ways Bennie is the "good guy" and Carl the "bad guy," as dramatized by Arlene's literally choosing, and making the right choice, between Bennie's piece of paper and Carl's matchbook. But the two men are not the stereotypical hero and villain. To make the point, on the day before discussing Bennie and Carl, divide the class into two groups, each responsible for finding textual material on one of these characters. Each student's task is to find as many clues in the text as

possible that militate *against* seeing Bennie as purely heroic and Carl as purely despicable.

- Most members of Arlie's immediate family do not appear in **Getting Out,** but there are more than enough references to conclude that the family is nothing if not dysfunctional. The drama affords ample opportunity to broach the topics of incest, child abuse, violence, drug abuse, prostitution, and even eating disorders. The question of how much choice Arlene has in overcoming her destructive upbringing (as well as the implicit question of how much choice *any* of us has) is central to the drama.
- Two first-rate novels made into first-rate films explore some of the same issues as does **Getting Out:** Anthony Burgess's *A Clockwork Orange* (the film is by Stanley Kubrick) and Ken Kesey's *One Flew Over the Cuckoo's Nest* (film by Milos Forman). *A Clockwork Orange, Cuckoo's Nest,* and **Getting Out** all center on a violent rebel who is apprehended and "reformed." While all three provide thoughtful artistic presentations of the effects of behavior modification in the penal system, the three works are quite different in their impact on audiences—just as the Kubrick and Forman films affect audiences differently than do the novels on which the films are based. If you can use the novels or arrange screenings of the films, or even recommend reading and / or viewing, the comparison can be fruitful. (Note: *A Clockwork Orange* in particular—both the novel and the film—may contain material offensive to some, so you can perhaps get more students to read and / or watch by saying so.)

Commentary

The opening series of announcements, delivered in a droning tone before the houselights go down, helps the audience identify with the prison experience: the authority figure is there—or her voice is, anyway—subtly reminding all who hear or half-hear it that they're not in charge. Somebody else is, and one can't quite identify that Somebody. No doubt a good many members of the audience, like the prisoners who are used to the routine, aren't giving full attention to the content of the announcements. But if one chooses to attend carefully, one finds the details significant. While the message hints at wholesome, humane activities in which the prisoners may participate (reading in the library, eating outdoors at picnic tables, exercising), in each case the activity is mentioned only because it has been cancelled or postponed. The *promise* of a better life is there, but only the promise. Meanwhile, Frances Mills has a visitor at the gate—another promising sign. Then, oops; it's not Frances Mills, says the Voice. It's Frankie Hill. Too bad, Frances.

The slight disappointments that run through the opening monologue reflect in small measure the drama's larger concern with unmet expectations. The one thing that every prisoner thinks about, talks about, dreams about, is *getting out.* But when Arlene gets out, she finds life on the outside nearly impossible to negotiate. Whereas her alter-ego and former self Arlie used to sail through the outside world with reckless abandon, setting her own course (or so she thought) and asserting herself by breaking laws as she pleased, Arlene can barely manage a trip to the grocery store. Withdrawn and suspicious, Arlene can seem a mere shadow of her former vibrant, violent self.

A good way to get to the heart of the drama, in fact, is to pose the question of whether we are dealing with a tragedy—with a character who is heroic because she dares to do things we only fantasize about, who wins battles against all odds (Arlie is small and female but can make mincemeat out of just about any big male), but who is ultimately destroyed by forces too strong to resist. In this reading it is not fate or the gods who destroy the hero (as it is in *Oedipus the King* and in Greek tragedy generally) but the System: specifically the correctional system, which is hopelessly inadequate to deal with someone with life in her—someone like Arlie. The implicit difference here is that while the Greeks may have thought themselves utterly incapable of altering fate, we can do something about the prison system. In light of the following exchanges, for example, how much sense does it make that the prison and the penal codes are structured the way they are?

ARLENE: I took some beauty school at Pine Ridge.
MOTHER: Yeah, a beautician?
ARLENE: I don't guess so.
MOTHER: Said you was gonna work.
ARLENE: They got a law here. Ex-cons can't get no license.
MOTHER: Shoulda stayed in Alabama, then. Worked there.
ARLENE: They got a law there, too.
MOTHER: Then why'd they give you the trainin'?
ARLENE: I don't know. (p. 1201)

Another example:

ARLIE: I don't even remember what I did to git this lockup.
WARDEN: Well, I do. And if you ever do it again, or anything like it again, you'll be right back in lockup where you will stay until you forget *how* to do it.
ARLIE: What was it?
WARDEN: You just remember what I said. (p. 1217)

Such passages might make Getting Out seem as much political manifesto as depiction of a compelling character.

But one need not read Getting Out as the tragedy of an individual defeated by the corrupt but inscrutably powerful System. It may be that with the help of Ruby and Bennie, Arlene will successfully negotiate the passage from prison to the outside world. It may be that her moment of painful epiphany when she recalls "killing" Arlie will allow her to become fully mature—perhaps even to reconcile the two selves of Arlene and Arlie. The plants that Bennie brings (and, significantly, almost clumsily destroys) will, we gather, live. Like Arlene and Arlie they are "scraggly-lookin' things," and some of them "don't take the sun" (p. 1232). But they will live.

Questions for Discussion

1. Why does Arlene have such a hard time making simple decisions (such as where to hang the picture) when she first gets out of prison?

2. How does Arlie's father's sexually abusing her complicate our response to her dilemma? What is her mother's role in the abuse?

3. The only authority figure in the prison whom Arlie comes to trust, the only one who makes a real difference for her, is the chaplain. Is it right of the chaplain to encourage Arlene to "kill" Arlie? What does Arlene lose, and what does she gain, by doing so? Does the chaplain abandon Arlie? Is the cheaply framed picture of Jesus he sends her an adequate replacement?

4. Why is the "killing" of Arlie later described by Arlene rather than directly staged?

HENRIK IBSEN

Hedda Gabler

Planning Ideas

- To help students appreciate the difference between the stereotype and the fully developed character, I spend the last few minutes of the session before the first one on **Hedda Gabler** with the class divided into four groups. Each generates a list of as many attributes as possible for the one of the following types: the Absent-Minded Professor, the Lady's Man, the Ice Queen, and the Lecher. Each group is assigned one character to report on after reading the drama. Group 1, "How is Tesman more than an Absent-Minded Professor?"; 2, "How is Loevborg more than a Lady's Man?"; 3, "How is Hedda more than an Ice Queen?"; and 4, "How is Brack more than a Lecher?"

- Ibsen uses set design, movement, and gesture in highly symbolic ways to define and reinforce the impressions of Hedda's character and situation that we derive from the dialogue. I like to tackle the function of set design first. I divide the class into four groups and, prior to class, assign the members of each group to prepare a written analysis of setting and stage direction for one of the four acts. I also ask them to provide a simple sketch of the set Ibsen describes at the beginning of the play, altered appropriately for the act they've been assigned to discuss. Because the setting of **Hedda Gabler** remains virtually the same throughout the four acts, you don't have to ask the class to cope with several different set descriptions and sketches.

I've sometimes found students don't want to take the time to visualize settings properly when they're reading drama, but the setting of **Hedda Gabler** demonstrates for most of them that understanding setting and the characters' movements within it can provide a key to unlocking mysteries of character and theme.

When I make this assignment, if I have not already done so in earlier classes, I give a brief explanation of staging terms such as center stage, stage right, upstage, etc. I remind students to pay close attention to the use of props, lighting, color, and Ibsen's instructions about the appearance and movements of the characters. They should also note the degree to which the setting changes from the beginning of one act to its end. I suggest, too, that they review the act immediately prior to theirs (unless, of course, they are assigned to analyze the first act) to see how the setting and the characters' positions in it may have altered from one act to the next. From a description of these elements, they should derive an explanation of their significance—especially in relation to Hedda. You might explain the procedure by drawing attention to the details outlined in the commentary below.

Commentary

When the curtain rises on Act I, flowers are everywhere—in vases, bowls, lying on furniture. We soon discover that Aunt Juju is responsible for the profusion, although Mrs. Elvsted has sent one of the bouquets. At the beginning of Act II, Mrs. Elvsted's flowers appear in a vase downstage, close to the audience, but many of the other flowers are gone. (It may be well to ask why Mrs. Elvsted's flowers should be so prominently displayed.) The room seems less colorful, less full of life. It is clear that Hedda, with her concern for taste, propriety, and control, has banished the flowers from the rooms. You may want to ask your students what this suggests about her.

Between the close of Act I and the opening of Act II Hedda's piano has also been removed from the front room and placed (as we find out later) in the back room where her father's portrait hangs. An "elegant" writing table, a bookcase, and a small table have been added to the furnishings—also, we are certain, on Hedda's orders. You might ask students what the significance of the movement of furniture might be, judging from the information we receive in Act I. It isn't clear whether these additions have been purchased or simply moved from other parts of the house, but we know from Act I that the Tesmans can't afford new furniture, and we suspect Hedda has bought it anyway.

At the beginning of Act II the French windows are again open. (Hedda had drawn the drapes in Act I to shut out the bright morning sun streaming in through the windows.) However, Hedda's posture near the open windows loading a revolver makes them less inviting than they were in the first act(!). As the various student groups report on their scenes, a pattern should begin to emerge. The French windows, the back room, the stove, and General Gabler's portrait will be mentioned more than once. You may want to establish headings on the blackboard for the most important of these scenic elements and chart what parts they play in each act of the work. This will help students to realize how closely setting is tied to characterization and meaning.

During class discussion about setting and stage movement, you might encourage each group to plot Hedda's movements in relation to the other characters. Brack enters through the back door, for which Hedda criticizes him, yet she is willing to entertain him alone and to be physically near him. Why is he allowed this freedom and proximity? Hedda also allows Loevborg to be near her—in fact she places herself near him—but she avoids physical contact with Aunt Juju and George (at least while on stage). What are we to make of this? And what are we to make of Hedda's actions toward Mrs. Elvsted—the hair-stroking, the frenzied embrace? What difference might it make in the play had Hedda's father been a living presence rather than a portrait? How might his presence change our perception of Hedda?

I try to bring out, sometimes by assigning one act at a time, that we keep framing and reforming our opinions and feelings about Hedda, following a pattern of assessment and reassessment. Another way to talk about *Hedda Gabler* is to examine this pattern, as I have suggested in the text. I sometimes start by asking the class what we find out about Hedda before she appears on stage. Then I ask to what degree the impression they receive by second-hand report—through Aunt Juju, Bertha, and George—is confirmed or altered by Hedda's entrance. For example, Aunt Juju recalls that Hedda was always surrounded by admirers and calls her "The beautiful Hedda Gabler!" However, when Hedda enters, she appears elegant and tastefully attired but cold, self-contained, and merely attractive, not beautiful. I like to ask the class why Aunt Juju might call Hedda beautiful if she really isn't. More than one reason, and more than one acceptable reason, usually emerges.

As the class works through the play, their catalogue of impressions might end up something like this: When we first hear about Hedda, we expect someone lovely but difficult. When Hedda appears on stage, the latter impression is borne out; the former is not. Hedda seems haughty and bruises Aunt Juju's feelings by mistaking her new hat—bought "for Hedda's sake"—for the maid's. Later we discover that Hedda knew the hat was Aunt Juju's and insulted the generous older woman on purpose. At this point we probably think Hedda is a pretty nasty piece of work, but when we discover her attraction to Loevborg and her idealistic dreams, we may excuse her to ourselves, imagining that her lost romance with Loevborg is at the source of her frustration and despair. Our sympathy may shift briefly in Hedda's direction. Then Hedda challenges Loevborg to drink, despite his problems with alcohol, and we wonder if she is malevolently destructive. As it turns out, Hedda is hoping to wrest Loevborg from Mrs. Elvsted's influence and vicariously live out her own aspirations of nobility through him. While Hedda never has our full sympathy, Ibsen presents her in such a way that we never feel comfortable condemning her entirely. You may want to ask your students what they would direct an actor playing Hedda to emphasize so as to create the most sympathetic portrait possible. How might an actor convey that Hedda is a victim of society? a tragic heroine? The class might want to consider whether they believe the play can work if the audience has absolutely no sympathy for Hedda.

Questions for Discussion

Plot

1. The scenes between Hedda and Loevborg, then Hedda, Mrs. Elvsted, and Loevborg in Act II are central to the themes of cowardice and courage. Define the quality of Hedda's cowardice and Mrs. Elvsted's courage and how they find expression in Loevborg.

2. Why is Loevborg upset when Hedda reveals Mrs. Elvsted's concerns for him in the city?

3. Compare and contrast Hedda's envy of Mrs. Elvsted and George's envy of Loevborg. How do they conflate in the identification of the manuscript as Loevborg's and Thea's "child"?

4. Why does Hedda insist that Loevborg end his life "beautifully"?

5. Act IV opens on a note of formal mourning. In the course of the act which characters die, and what responses do their deaths elicit from the others?

6. Hedda protests Brack's hold over her because she is "not free." What freedom does Hedda require, and how does she employ it?

7. Brack's last line is an echo of Hedda's when she tells Mrs. Elvsted that "People don't do such things" regarding Loevborg's mystery woman who shot at him. How is the echo meaningful?

8. Is Hedda's suicide an act of cowardice or courage? What is your reaction to it?

Character

1. Hedda admits to Judge Brack that she purposely mistook Miss Tesman's hat for Bertha's. What in Hedda's character accounts for this cruelty? Why does Hedda behave in such an aloof manner to her new relative?

2. In her refusal to call Miss Tesman "Auntie Juju," Hedda is maintaining strict formality much as one would in addressing a friend or relation by "vous" instead of "tu" in French. Examine other occasions when the use of informal names is important, as when Hedda mistakenly remembers Thea's name as Tora, becomes upset when Loevborg calls her Hedda, and finally addresses George by his Christian name.

3. The first act ends with the apparent revelation that Hedda is the woman from Loevborg's past. What does this tell us about Hedda that we did not already know? What new expectation does it arouse?

4. What purpose does the opening scene of Act II serve besides making Judge Brack's intentions perfectly obvious? What new information do we learn? What does it tell us about Hedda's character? Why does the scene open with a pistol shot?

5. Hedda complains to Judge Brack of her honeymoon, on which she went six months "without even meeting a single person who was one of us, and to whom I could talk about the kind of things we talk about." What kind of things do they talk about? Distinguish the layers of Hedda's boredom with the world.

6. Why did Hedda draw out Loevborg and act as his "confessor" when they were young? Why does Loevborg mistake the action for love?

7. Discuss Judge Brack's character and his role in the action of the play. What segment of society does he represent? What segments do Hedda, George, and Loevborg represent? What qualities or abilities does the judge possess that allow him to create the "triangle"?

The Stage

1. The portrait of Hedda's father, General Gabler, often dominates the set in productions of *Hedda Gabler*. Why is the portrait given such a central position in the set, and how is the general's "presence" important to the play's action?

2. Miss Tesman drops some broad hints about Hedda's pregnancy early in the play. How obvious are they in the text, and how obvious should they be in production?

Writing Assignments for Chapter 1

1. In *Getting Out*, Arlie and Arlene have a peculiar relationship with food. Read the drama again, taking note of every reference to food, and use details in the text to develop a theory about why Arlie and Arlene feel the way they do about eating. Questions to keep in mind: Does the mature Arlene develop a different view of food from Arlie's? Does a simple theory like, "Prisons serve lousy food" explain the facts? Is there any evidence that Arlie (or Arlene) is worried about gaining weight? Why the problem with *eating* rather than something else?

2. Act III of *Hedda Gabler* concludes with the burning of Loevborg's manuscript, and with that action earlier references to "burning" resonate with new meaning. Write an essay that traces the development of this image by examining as many references to burning as possible. Pay particular attention to the moments when Hedda says that Loevborg will return with a "crown of vine-leaves in his hair. Burning and unshamed" and when George is shocked by Hedda's apparent ardor, surprised that "you're burning with love for me, Hedda."

3. Read the fascinating article by Elinor Fuchs entitled "Mythic Structure in *Hedda Gabler:* The Mask Behind the Face," in the journal *Comparative Drama*, vol. 19 (Fall 1985), pp. 209–21. Then reread the drama, paying particular attention to passages that bear on the relation between the characters and their mythological counterparts. Write a four-page essay that summarizes Fuchs's argument on the first two pages and, on the last two, uses textual evidence that Fuchs does not mention. Point out how this evidence either supports or refutes Fuchs's theory.

2 STRUCTURE

HAMLET: Do you see yonder cloud that's almost in shape of a camel?
POLONIUS: By the mass, and 'tis like a camel, indeed.
HAMLET: Methinks it is like a weasel.
POLONIUS: It is backed like a weasel.
HAMLET: Or like a whale?
POLONIUS: Very like a whale.

Some of our students, I am afraid, feel as if we are playing Hamlet to their Polonius when we offer a reading or interpretation of a piece of literature — particularly when the work is as complex, awe-inspiring, and, for some, hard to follow and comprehend as *Hamlet*. One way of making sense of the great sweep of its structure is to see it as mirroring the turbulence surrounding Europe's transition from a medieval to a modern sensibility. In this reading Old Hamlet embodies the passing medieval order. Or perhaps *embodies* is too strong a word: the old king is a mere ghost, straining to maintain authority as he makes his son's feudal obligation plain. Young Hamlet quickly promises to exact his revenge, but the old order's reliance on paternal authority and the sacredness of one's vows has lost its hold on the prince. Young Hamlet is, after all, a sort of protoscientist: he will attempt to observe data objectively, test the evidence, and draw his own conclusions. But the world in which he finds himself will not allow him to do so.

The Little Foxes is similarly structured according to a logic of divided loyalties. A rough analogue to the patriarchal, agrarian system of medieval Europe is the Old South of Hellman's play. As in Shakespeare's day, the passing of the old, communal order meant the emergence of a more individualist culture: a development that in both plays proves a mixed blessing at best.

WILLIAM SHAKESPEARE

Hamlet

Planning Ideas

- In view of **Hamlet**'s complexity, it may be useful to put your students, individually or jointly, in the position not of Polonius but of Hamlet and ask them, at the beginning of the hour, to write out in twenty-five to a hundred words a summary of the play. In *Writing about Literature* we have offered three such summaries of **Hamlet**:

1) A young man, seeking to avenge the murder of his father by his uncle, kills his uncle, but he himself and others die in the process.
2) In Denmark, many centuries ago, a young prince avenged the murder of his father, the king, by his uncle, who had usurped the throne, but the prince himself was killed, as were others, and a well-led foreign army had no trouble successfully invading the decayed and troubled state.
3) From the ghost of his murdered father a young prince learns that his uncle, who had married the prince's mother, much to the young man's shame and disgust, is the father's murderer, and he plots revenge, feigning madness, acting erratically—even to the point of insulting the woman he loves—and, though gaining his revenge, causes the suicide of his beloved and the deaths of others and, finally, of himself.

The first emphasizes the revenge motif, the second adds a political dimension, and the third introduces the possible Oedipal overtones. If you are lucky, your twelve, twenty, or thirty-five students will offer camel, weasel, whale, and a whole ark of readings, paired or not. They may cover most of the orthodox and unorthodox ways of looking at the play or at the hero—as an intellectual, a man incapable of decisive action, a man troubled by obesity, a homosexual, or a man too much in love with his mother. There are bound to be a number of different readings, or summaries with differing emphases. It might be profitable to have one read out and ask how many others are similar and group similar ones together, perhaps even asking the students involved to come up with a joint summary. Then you might ask for a summary that seems radically different, have it read and see if that reading has adherents, etc. If there is surprising homogeneity from the beginning, there will still be enough to generate useful class discussion in trying to determine the best wording or adding the most essential matters left out.

• If you cannot get enough fruitful controversy going with student summaries, you may want to offer a provocative reading of your own, such as the following: "Hamlet is a shrewd, ambitious politician whose actions are morally reprehensible, and Claudius is not much more than another politician who has eliminated his opponent and is in turn eliminated." Since virtually all readers and viewers find Hamlet a compelling character (what makes this moping, melancholic figure so attractive, by the way?), the notion that Hamlet is *merely* a shrewd, immoral politician is bound to generate disagreement. As the twenty-five thousand (no kidding) studies of **Hamlet** indicate, in fact, it is reductive to call the title character *merely* anything. With that caveat in mind, I'll explore in more detail below some of the play's political implications.

Commentary

Shakespeare is here concerned with questions of succession to power and the virtues appropriate to private and public persons. Because Hamlet is a prince, he has no real choice about his career, about when he is to become king, about whom he is to marry; Shakespeare and his audience shared these and other notions about the meaning of being a prince. We see Hamlet at a difficult juncture in his life. He has been brought up to rule, and we suspect with Fortinbras that he could be very effective. Yet at the height of his maturity (he is thirty), he has been denied his rightful place. Even before he sees the ghost of his father, Hamlet is behaving in a peculiar manner. He dresses in black and goes about the court with his eyes on the ground, deliberately calling attention to himself and his plight.

In the Shakespearean tragic world, order is the supreme value, and those who sin against it will ultimately be punished. Claudius is the king, Hamlet the subject, and therefore Hamlet's ambition becomes morally ambiguous. He wants to fulfill what he sees as his God-given destiny to become king of Denmark, but to do so he must commit the most disorderly act he can think of, to kill a king. He does not even have the excuse of Bolingbroke in *Richard II* that the king is doing a bad job. Claudius seems to be an effective ruler, however much Hamlet despises him. Hamlet can justify action against him only if he can prove that the king came to the throne in a criminal way. The ghost appears to offer definitive evidence, but Hamlet is aware that the devil can ensnare an unwary victim with such "proof." And even if the ghost is telling the truth, the crucial question remains: Does Hamlet have the right to take the law into his own hands and punish the usurper, or should he wait for the power that guides the universe to restore order in its own way? Can order be restored by disorderly acts?

Hamlet is a superlative actor, as I believe Shakespeare thinks that every successful public figure must be. The image that the public has of him is as important to him as it is to Claudius, who is afraid to act against him directly because of his popularity. As Hamlet admits to his mother, the ostentatious acts of public mourning are "actions that a man might play." With evidence provided by the ghost as his justification, he then proceeds to act out for the people his perception of the situation. Using the analogy of the king as the head of the body that is the state, he makes his madness into the figure of an illegitimate kingship. The disorder in his head represents the disorder in the kingdom. The plan is politically skillful, but Claudius, the play's other consummate politician-actor, sees through it at once.

The appearance of the actors provides Hamlet with a chance for the even more theatrical coup of the play-within-the-play. He proceeds from metaphor to stage representation, but he chooses to make the murderer the nephew of the king as a warning to Claudius. Again Claudius understands and takes the only action he sees as possible, to arrange the death of Hamlet. The situation reverses itself, and Hamlet sees immediately what Claudius has in mind. Throughout the play there is a struggle between two evenly matched politicians—a technique that adds to the power of the play.

In addition to the question of succession, the play engages the problem of the relation between private and public virtues. This is done through a series of foils to Hamlet and through the description of his relation to Ophelia. The primary foil is Fortinbras, who like Hamlet is a prince, the son of a dead king. The contrast between him and Hamlet is a problem even to Hamlet himself, and it is Fortinbras who is ultimately able to restore the order and assume the kingship in a proper manner. Fortinbras is more fortunate than Hamlet in two ways: he can curb his ambition, and he is in the right place at the right time. Therefore he succeeds where Hamlet fails. The part of Fortinbras is frequently cut in performances of the play, but doing so undermines some of what the play says. At the other extreme from Fortinbras are Rosencrantz and Guildenstern, the epitome of the ordinary subjects:

GUILDENSTERN: On Fortune's cap we are not the very button.
HAMLET: Nor the soles of her shoes?
ROSENCRANTZ: Neither, my lord.

They call attention to Hamlet's inability to accept the role of subject. Between these two extremes is Laertes, the person in the play most like Hamlet. They are the same age, both of noble birth. Both have a preference for living away from home, and both are expert fencers. Both are called upon to avenge their fathers' deaths, and both love Ophelia. They finally confront each other at Ophelia's grave. Laertes seems very much what Hamlet would have been if he had not been a prince. Finally there is Horatio, the good private man. Hamlet understands his virtue, but knows that it is not for him.

Hamlet's relation to Ophelia also underlines the contrast between private and public virtue. If Hamlet had been a private individual, the play seems to suggest that he and Ophelia would have married. Yet Hamlet chooses to use her for political ends just as if she meant nothing to him. His cruel treatment of her in Act III, Scene 1 (not to mention his public abuse of her in the play-within-a-play scene) is shocking, and effective as a sign of madness because it is such an incongruous way for a well-bred prince to treat a virgin of the court, and particularly for this prince to treat this virgin. As in the scene with his mother, Hamlet paints himself as unbelievably callous. It is arguable that only a man who puts political necessity above everything else would do such things. But see Discussion Question 8 under *Character* below.

Questions for Discussion

Plot

1. Although the eldest son of the king was customarily chosen to succeed his father, the monarchy of Denmark is depicted in the play as elective. Why

was Hamlet passed over in favor of his uncle in the election that preceded the opening of the play?

2. What are the circumstances of Horatio's return to Elsinore from Wittenberg? How does the timing of his arrival contribute to the exposition?

3. Describe Hamlet's behavior, his appearance and actions, before he learns even of the appearance of his father's Ghost. To what action does it prompt Claudius, of which we learn in Act II, Scene 2? Why does the King permit Laertes to return to Paris and at the same time refuse Hamlet's request to return to Wittenberg?

4. Is Hamlet surprised by the revelations of the Ghost?

5. When Rosencrantz and Guildenstern appear, Hamlet correctly interprets the King's strategy in sending for them. Does he see through other moves made by Claudius? What does this suggest about the relation between the two antagonists?

6. Why are the players introduced? Why is the King in the play-within-a-play murdered by his nephew?

7. The climax of the play occurs when the King stops the play-within-a-play. What has Hamlet learned and how does it affect his course of action? How is Claudius affected by events of the scene?

8. What prior actions bring about the death of Polonius? the madness and death of Ophelia? What later actions result from the death of Polonius?

9. What is the purpose in terms of dramatic structure for the scene between Hamlet and Horatio at the beginning of Act V, Scene 2?

10. What dramatic functions are served by having both Horatio and Fortinbras alive and on stage at the end of the play?

Character

1. What does Laertes' warning to Ophelia suggest about the character of Hamlet?

2. Hamlet tells his mother in Act I, Scene 2, that his manner of dress and his deportment are "actions that a man might play." In which scenes does Hamlet seem to be "acting," playing a public role?

3. What issues are presented in Hamlet's soliloquies that can be presented otherwise only with difficulty? Do any of the other characters have soliloquies?

4. Hamlet uses a trick of speech of repeating a word or phrase several times. Do any other characters have individual speech mannerisms? What purpose might such mannerisms serve?

5. From time to time Hamlet makes unfavorable remarks about the King's behavior and appearance. Do the other characters make such remarks? To what extent should Hamlet's remarks influence the choice of an actor to play Claudius?

6. Compare the situation of Hamlet and young Fortinbras at each of the times Fortinbras is mentioned or appears. The character of Fortinbras is frequently omitted in performance. Why is it easy to cut the role? What does such a cut do to the play?

7. As his death approaches, Hamlet asks Horatio, first, to see that his actions and death are properly reported and, second, to use Hamlet's name and posthumous influence to bring about the election of Fortinbras as king. How is the order of the two requests significant?

8. Is it necessarily true that "only a man who puts political necessity above everything else" (see the Commentary above) would behave the way Hamlet does, especially toward women? Are there other explanations? Is there any explanation that seems complete, or does each leave something out?

The Stage

1. The Shakespearean stage featured a large central acting area, around three sides of which members of the audience sat or stood. In addition there were, very probably, an elevated area above the main stage, a recessed area upstage, and one or more trap doors. If you were staging *Hamlet* on such a stage, how would you treat the various scenes? What use would you make of the subsidiary acting areas?

2. As a member of the company which performed his plays, Shakespeare seems to have written a part for a particular actor on occasion. What part in *Hamlet* might have been written for a specialist in sententious old men? for a specialist in effeminate young men? for another kind of specialist? Are there scenes in which the actor's part seems to have been lengthened or emphasized in order to take advantage of his specialty?

3. In several speeches Hamlet talks about the theatrical practices of the period and the purposes of the drama. To what extent, if any, can we assume that Hamlet's comments represent Shakespeare's own ideas? What are some of the particular abuses that Hamlet cites? Have they disappeared from theatrical practice?

4. It was not until after Shakespeare's day that women acted on the public stage in England. In acting companies like his (The Lord Chamberlain's Men,

and after 1603 The King's Men) boys who had not reached puberty played the women's parts. Does *Hamlet* refer to this? How would such a practice affect the writing of a play? of this particular play?

5. When the play ends, what should be the position of Hamlet's body relative to the other actors? How should it compare with his relative position at his first appearance? How would your staging affect the audience's experience of the play?

Symbol and Myth

1. A central image in the play is the comparison between the body and the state, the "body politic." Such an image pattern assumes an analogy between two levels of reality, the body and the state. One occurrence of the image is in the Ghost's account to Hamlet of his death by having poison poured in his ear and of the report of his death as an abuse of the ear of Denmark. Can you find others? In terms of the image of the body politic, why does Hamlet choose to feign madness?

2. There are a number of references in the play to warfare and weapons and to hunting, fishing, and trapping. Do these constitute meaningful image patterns that contribute to the internal complexity of the work? Are there other such groups of references?

The Author's Works

In a number of his plays Shakespeare seems to be commenting on the relation between virtues appropriate to public life and those appropriate to private life. In some cases—for example, Brutus in *Julius Caesar*—they seem so distinct as to be irreconcilable. Laertes touches on this issue in his advice to Ophelia. Are there other places where it is treated? What does the play say about the distinction?

LILLIAN HELLMAN

The Little Foxes

Planning Ideas

- A good lead-in to this play is **A Streetcar Named Desire** (p. 1979). Even if you're not having your students read Williams's play, Elia Kazan's fine film version offers an effective point of comparison between Blanche DuBois in **Streetcar** and Birdie in **The Little Foxes.**
- Have a group of students do some research on Lillian Hellman. What were her political convictions? She wrote this play in 1939. Does the play reflect in any way the social or political circumstances of that time?

Commentary

While much less complex than *Hamlet, The Little Foxes* is in some ways structurally and thematically similar. As mentioned above, the Old South / New South dichotomy in Hellman's play roughly mirrors the Medieval / Modern tension informing Shakespeare's; both reflect the passing of an agrarian, paternalist society and the uneasy emergence of a more individualist culture. Moreover, in both cases a protagonist—the title character in *Hamlet* and Regina in *The Little Foxes*—has been denied something that is arguably his or hers by right (in Hamlet's case the kingship and in Regina's—whose name, interstingly, means *queen*—a share in the family fortune). Both protagonists assert will and imagination to do battle with powerful antagonists. In doing so, Regina and Hamlet both do things that are at best morally dubious and at worst despicable.

All this is not to say that *The Little Foxes* is consciously modeled on *Hamlet* but only to point out that when considering matters of structure, no playwright can escape the shadow of Shakespeare—not that many of them want to. And Shakespeare himself, of course, was thoroughly indebted to various strains of dramatic tradition, including Classical, Medieval, Continental, and Elizabethan.

Questions for Discussion

1. Many different alliances are formed among the characters in this play. One central alliance is that between Birdie, a mistreated, childish woman, Addie, a black woman, Horace, an invalid, and Alexandra, a young woman. What do these characters have in common? Why is their support of each other threatening to Oscar, Ben, and Regina? What constitutes the bonds among

these last three characters? Is it family loyalty? greed? What kinds of loyalty do they have for each other?

2. How do parents treat their children in the play? Can we see the reproduction of women like Birdie and men like Oscar and Ben in the characters of Alexandra and Leo? How would you direct Alexandra's character? Does she show any independence? Why is Leo so ineffectual? Contrast Birdie with Regina. Both women are the products of Southern culture. How do the men in the play treat the women? What is Birdie's relationship to the past? What myths and dreams does she rely on? In what ways does the play examine the past lives of the family members?

3. What economic and social changes were taking place in the American South in 1900? How does the play reflect these changes? What aspects of the prewar South do the various characters want to preserve? Which are they anxious to discard?

Writing Assignments for Chapter 2

1. Some writing about tragedy talks about the concept of *hamartia*, the notion that the central character's fate is brought about by a tragic flaw or failing of character. Hamlet's speech beginning "So oft it chanceth in particular men" suggests something similar. Does Hamlet have such a tragic flaw? If so, name it and write a paper supporting your contention.

2. Another idea common in writing about tragedy is that the hero is guilty of *hubris*, an overstepping of the bounds of his destiny and the destiny of humanity. This suggests some universal moral principles beyond the control of human beings. Write an essay that discusses the play's handling of such principles.

3. In 1600 (the approximate date of *Hamlet*) Queen Elizabeth I was 67 and had no direct heirs. England had been subjected to wars and rebellions over the succession to the throne for the preceding two centuries. Write an essay that shows how these historical circumstances are reflected in *Hamlet*.

4. Write a four-page essay comparing the role of the past in *The Little Foxes* to that in *Fences* or *Blood Relations*.

3 THE WHOLE TEXT

BERNARD SHAW

Pygmalion

Part of the reason Bernard Shaw's *Pygmalion* provides an ideal chance to discuss "the whole text" is that the play presents such an artful blending of received tradition, character exposition, plot development, and social commentary. Since it begins with a myth and provides a compellingly ironic modern theatrical version of that myth, which in turn has been made into a popular movie (not to mention the musical-comedy spinoff *My Fair Lady*), and since our text includes not only the scenes exclusive to the movie but also the narrative epilogue, sorting through all the generic layers demonstrates not only what is peculiar to the stage but also how drama can shade into myth, into cinema, and into narrative prose. *Pygmalion* is fun to teach in part because of the playwright's delight in overturning typical dramatic expectations—and even in his flouting the modern dictum roared out by the MGM lion that art should never be didactic: *ars gratis artis.* No lion can outroar Shaw; the play is resolutely didactic (as with characteristic Higginsian immodesty Shaw claims in the preface that all "great art" must be). Since what the play teaches—even when we can confidently pin the message down—is at times agreeable and at times troublesome to most students' 1990s sensibilities, the enlightening business of confronting the cultural relativity of our own assumptions is bound to come into play.

Planning Ideas

- Before assigning the play, have all the students read a good translation (such as the Loeb edition) of Ovid's brief Latin account of the Greek myth of Pygmalion in his *Metamorphoses,* and divide the class into groups to report on Renaissance retellings of Ovid's version. Two groups will simply compare the Loeb translation to sixteenth- or seventeenth-century ones (Arthur Golding's *Metamorphoses* [1567] or George Sandys's *Ovid's Metamorphoses* [1626]); the others will compare the Loeb translation to a Renaissance commentary on the story (the one from William Caxton's *Ovid, His Book of Metamorphose* [1480], or *Tottle's Miscellany* [1557], or John Marston's *The Metamorphosis of Pygmalion's Image* [1598], or Carel van Mander's *Painter's Manual* [1604], or the one following Sandys's translation). In each case the idea is to see what is changed or emphasized in the Renaissance version, to comment on how the emphases reflect the culture in which they were written, and to speculate on how the Pygmalion myth might be told today. After discussing the play return to the exercise, concentrating on how Shaw's version differs from any of the others. The goal is to give students some sense of five layers of artistic tradition: that of an Ancient Greek myth, a Latin interpretation of that myth, a Renaissance interpretation, an early twentieth-century one, and a late twentieth-century one.

- Have students watch the 1941 film version starring Wendy Hiller and Leslie Howard (whom students might know as Ashley in *Gone With the Wind*). Have each student write a one-paragraph response explaining one thing he or she would have done differently if acting in or directing the play. An alternative is to show in class the scenes that are exclusive to the movie, the ones marked off in our text with asterisks, and to discuss what the scenes add to or detract from the artistic integrity of the stage version.

- After the students have read the drama itself but not the narrative epilogue, spend some time in class speculating about what happens next. Then, as a lead-in to the first Writing Suggestion in the textbook, have the class read and discuss Shaw's epilogue. In this case the question of whether to trust the tale or the teller is a fascinating one.

- To give the class a better sense of phonetics, pair students, each student with someone from a different geographic background, and have each transcribe at least a hundred-word paragraph of the other's speech. It works to use the phonetic alphabet at the bottoms of dictionary pages, but if one of Shaw's pet projects is to be fully appreciated, it is even more fruitful for students to develop their own phonetic spellings: for example, AH-ee for a Midwestern I, and just AH for a Southern one. An alternative is to have the class phonetically transcribe the lyrics of a popular song (country / western and rap work well.)

- To fill in a few of the details of the Victorian / Edwardian scene, have students provide brief reports on the following: Pre-Raphaelitism; William Morris; Edward Burne-Jones (these first three all associated with Mrs. Higgins); the fin-de-siècle Decadent Movement; Oscar Wilde (especially his witty aphorisms; see *The Importance of Being Earnest*); the Bloomsbury Group. And while footnotes are not necessary to appreciate the play, here are a few terms with which Shaw expected his audience to be familiar but which may no longer be—or which have changed their meaning: in Shaw's England a *slut* was a filthy (and perhaps impudent) girl—not necessarily a sexually promiscuous one; a *dustman* was a garbage man; a *navvy* did heavy manual labor, especially digging; *bloody* was a much more scurrilous curse word than it is today (hence the severity of Mrs. Eynsford Hill's response to Clara's outburst); *shew* meant (and was pronounced) the same as *show*; when Higgins says, "It dont matter, anyhow," he is not being ungrammatical, purposely or otherwise; the usage was acceptable. And it is of course *Scylla and Charybdis* that Doolittle butchers as "the Skilly of the workhouse and the Char Bydis of the middle class."

Commentary

Shaw claims in the preface that his *Pygmalion* is "intensely and deliberately didactic." And so it is—but not always as transparently so as he implies. The clear target of the play is the class system, and the clearest statement of the ideal comes from Higgins: "The great secret, Eliza, is not having bad manners or good manners or any other particular sort of manners, but having the same manner for all human souls: in short, behaving as if you were in Heaven, where there are no third-class carriages, and one soul is as good as another." Fair enough, most American students are likely to think. But ask them to think about whether Higgins really lives up to the ideal he claims for himself. Does he really treat Eliza as well as he treats, say, Pickering? his mother? While he can be refreshingly blunt with anyone, Higgins would hardly hurl at the Colonel the kind of abuse to which he subjects Eliza. And can you imagine hearing him call Mrs. Higgins a "presumptuous insect"? The fact is that Higgins treats Eliza as an animal or an object most of the time, and his treatment of her is a function of her socio-economic background. He *says* to her, "Remember that you are a human being with a soul and the divine gift of articulate speech," but he himself seldom remembers the fact. (Ask the class whether the speech serves Eliza or Higgins himself.) There may not be a touch of irony in Higgins's reply to Eliza's insistence that she is a "good girl": "Very well, then, what on earth is all this fuss about? The girl doesn't belong to anybody—is no use to anybody but me." Not only does he assume that a girl can be a belonging; he implies that her proper destiny is to be used.

The women, though, are on to him. Mrs. Pearce, Mrs. Higgins, and Eliza herself all object to his treatment of her; all three actually *behave* as though a Cockney flower girl should be accorded the dignity proper to all human souls. When Mrs. Higgins suggests that Doolittle financially support his daughter (he has recently been "delivered . . . into the hands of middle class morality" by the Wannafeller Moral Reform World League), Higgins flies into a rage—not that Eliza can be bought, but that he has already bought her: "She doesnt belong to him. I paid him five pounds for her. . . . either youre an honest man or a rogue." Doolittle's reply should be disarming: "A little of both, Henry, like the rest of us: a little of both." But Higgins is too self-righteous to acknowledge his own fallibility. He again insists that he bought Eliza, fair and square, and upon learning that she is upstairs says that he will "fetch" her down.

Even Pickering shares something of Higgins's obtuseness, his refusal to think of Eliza as fully human. While Pickering is aware that "the girl has some feelings," he is just as surprised as Higgins to learn that Eliza is upset at being used as a guinea pig and then, after the experiment, simply discarded. When he hears that she has thrown Higgins's slippers at him, Pickering is without clue as to the reason: "But why? What did we do to her?" He does end up treating Eliza kindly, but even this genial character helps the play dramatize the depth of the divisions among the classes and between the sexes.

In part through a witty exchange centering on the five-pound blackmail, "middle class morality" comes in for some rough treatment in this play. When Higgins offers ten pounds instead of the five requested, Doolittle turns down the greater sum on the ground that "Ten pounds is a lot of money: it makes a man feel prudent like; and then good-bye to happiness." With witty inversion worthy of Oscar Wilde, Shaw has Doolittle assure Pickering that the five pounds will be put to good use: "Dont you be afraid that I'll save it and spare it and live idle on it. There wont be a penny of it left by Monday. . . . Just one good spree for myself and the missus, giving pleasure to ourselves and employment to others, and satisfaction to you to think it's not been throwed away. You couldnt spend it better." Doolittle also turns down Higgins's half-serious offer to remake him into a successful politician or preacher, saying that politics, religion, social reform, and "all the other amusements" are not for him.

Pygmalion takes occasional swipes at the upper class as well as the middle—most obviously in the central plot device of Eliza's successfully passing herself off as a duchess. At the Embassy party Higgins's ex-client Nepommuck proudly asserts his royal lineage and claims that Eliza too must be of royal Hungarian descent. When Higgins asks how he knows, Nepommuck replies, "Instinct, maestro, instinct. Only the Magyar races can produce that air of divine right, those resolute eyes. She is a princess." The fun comes in knowing what to make not only of Nepommuck but also of the aristocratic Host and Hostess, who immediately swallow the whole story.

The play's attack on class is relentless, but upon reaching the somewhat troubling conclusion, students are likely to be more interested in matters of structure than of theme. Why does Shaw not provide the match between Higgins and Eliza that he has set us up to expect? After all, we expect verbal banter between two such healthy, attractive adults to signal sexual attraction just beneath the surface of the dialogue—as it does in the case of, say, Beatrice and Benedick in Shakespeare's Much Ado about Nothing. And Shaw provides signals in the text that this is exactly the game he is playing: after the Embassy party Higgins says to Eliza, "Most men are the marrying sort (poor devils!); and you're not bad-looking: it's quite a pleasure to look at you sometimes. . . ." Given the conventions of the Comedy of Manners, in which witty verbal exchanges go hand-in-hand with sexual exploits, and given what we know about Higgins, it doesn't take a psychoanalyst to deduce that Higgins is masking his sexual attraction for Eliza with the disclaimer that the "marrying sort" are "poor devils" and the backhanded compliment that Eliza is "not bad-looking." This, with the admission that "sometimes" Eliza is "quite a pleasure to look at," seems to tip Higgins's hand. We know what he does not want to admit to her and perhaps not even to himself: he is in love with her. Why else would the thought of Freddy drive him into such derision? And why would Eliza fall so precipitously into Freddy's arms unless she were pushed there by her true love's rebuffs? Doesn't the play **demand** that Higgins and Eliza get together in the end?

But Act V ends with the somewhat hollow sound of Higgins's laughter as he contemplates Eliza's marriage to Freddy. A little light may be shed on the situation by biographical detail. It seems that Shaw had a crush on an actress who had become Mrs. Patrick Campbell by the time she starred as Eliza in the first production of *Pygmalion.* The two had had a somewhat tempestuous relationship, as do Higgins and Eliza, and she had led him on for a while. In the end, though, she had married a much younger man. The playwright's depiction of Freddy as a bumbling weakling, coupled with Higgins's derisive laughter at the end of the play, may therefore be read as Shaw's revenge on his rival. If Shaw's epilogue is right, though—if the pairing of Higgins and Eliza should appeal only to those whose imaginations are "enfeebled by their lazy dependence on the ready-mades and reach-me-downs of the ragshop in which Romance keeps its stock of 'happy endings' to misfit all stories," then the details from the playwright's life may be moot. Regardless of any personal motive on Shaw's part, one could argue, the playwright is in control of his material. We may *want* to see Higgins and Eliza paired up, but the artistic integrity of the play demands otherwise.

Since part of the play's artistry involves reversals of expectation, Shaw's flouting the requirements of Romance and the Comedy of Manners may be part and parcel of his artistic project. If the genre insists that witty wordplay is really foreplay, then Shaw will craft a new genre. If, in our post-Freudian age, we are likely to read *all* human intercourse as ultimately sexual (can we even hear the word *intercourse* and not think *sex?*), then Shaw will teach us otherwise. If, as heirs to the sexual permissiveness of the 1960s and 1970s, which has been somewhat tempered of late (or has it?) by the spread of AIDS, we are likely to conclude that two healthy, consenting adults jolly well ought to hop into the sack (perhaps taking proper precautions), then Shaw will tell us that our destiny is something higher than that. In short, we may not like the ending, but that is precisely the point: the playwright does not want us to.

Yet for many readers Shaw's epilogue seems disingenuous; given the psychological complexity of both Higgins and Eliza, there seems to be something perverse in Shaw's insistence that Higgins means exactly what he says: that he is a confirmed old bachelor who has no time for romance. And it seems naïve to take at face value Higgins's statement to his mother, "Oh, I cant be bothered with young women. My idea of a lovable woman is somebody as like you as possible." Is there *nothing* Oedipal going on here? True, Higgins may be trying to butter up his mother; he has, after all, come to ask a favor. But Shaw's epilogue takes the statement seriously—as though any sensible man in Higgins's position, and with a mother like his, would find young, attractive women simply bothersome.

One possibility for helping make sense of the play remains to be mentioned: that in Shaw's view *Pygmalion* centers not on the love interest (or the absence thereof) but on phonetics. True, the rather arcane discipline of phonetics has implications about class division: part of the point of the play is that how we talk determines the way we are treated. And of course how we talk is largely determined by social class. But for a great many readers in the 1990s, Higgins's passion for phoetics seems an interesting aspect of his odd, passionate personality: an incidental element in the play rather than its focus. Shaw may be serious, though, when he says in the preface that the play's "subject" is phonetics. After all, his passion for the science was as strong as Higgins's. In the early years of the twentieth century, to those who shared this passion (and there were more than a few) it really seemed possible that an army of trained phoneticians could virtually wipe out social injustice: that normalized speech (supported by phonetically correct spelling) would play no small part in ushering in a utopian age. Hence Shaw's boast in the preface that although phonetics "is esteemed so dry," *Pygmalion* "has been an extremely successful play, both on stage and screen, all over Europe and North America as well as at home." Surely, though, in his more lucid moments a playwright as astute as Shaw knew that what people were flocking to see was not a play about phonetics but one about two fascinating characters whose lives intersect in a way that makes for good theater.

Questions for Discussion

1. Can you make sense of Shaw's usage of apostrophes? Why do some contractions get them while others do not? Higgins says, for example, "Youre her father, arnt you? You dont suppose anyone else wants her, do you? I'm glad to see you have some spark of family feeling left. She's upstairs." The reason is clear enough in a case like *its* versus *it's*; one is a possessive pronoun and the other a contraction for *it is*. The apostrophe needs to be there for clarity. But why *I'm* and *She's*? (Hint: leaving the apostrophe out of a contraction like *don't*, as Shaw does, can't lead to a misreading. *I'd*, though, gets an apostrophe in Shaw's system. What is the difference between *don't* and *I'd*?)

2. Certainly it strains credulity that Higgins and Pickering run into each other at the portico of St. Paul's Church just as the former is about to leave for India to meet the latter, who in turn has come to London to meet the former. Would Shaw know that believing such a chance encounter is a stretch? If so, what is he up to here?

3. When Doolitle's presence is announced, Higgins says, "Send the blackguard up." Pickering replies, "He may not be a blackguard. . . ." Higgins answers, "Nonsense. Of course he's a blackguard." Why does Higgins assume so? Is he right?

4. What is Shaw up to in having Doolittle call politics, religion, and social reform "amusements"?

5. When Higgins wants to make sure Doolittle will not return after the initial five-pound payment, he orders Doolittle not to stay away but to return often: "Stop. Youll come regularly to see your daughter. It's your duty, you know. My brother is a clergyman; and he could help you in your talks with her." Why does Higgins say what he says? Do you suppose he really has a brother in the clergy?

6. Are Shaw's stage directions more for the reader or the actor? For exam-

ple, can an actor make as much as a reader out the statement, *"Eliza's beauty becomes murderous"*? What about the fact that Mrs. Higgins is *"long past taking the trouble to dress out of the fashion"*?

7. Higgins says to his mother, "I know I have no small talk; but people dont mind." A little later, when the Eynsford Hills have stopped by, Clara says, "I havnt any small talk. If people would only be frank and say what they really think!" Higgins replies, "Lord forbid!" Why does Higgins say this? Is he being inconsistent with his own beliefs? What is the force of the italicized *I* in Clara's line?

Writing Assignments for Chapter 3

1. In Act II Higgins says to Eliza, "Well, dont you want to be clean and sweet and decent, like a lady? You know you cant be a nice girl inside if youre a dirty slut outside." Is Higgins right? Can Eliza not be a "nice girl inside" without his help? Is she better off in the end having met Higgins than she otherwise would have been? (Note the exchange in Act IV when Eliza says that before she met Higgins, "I sold flowers. I didn't sell myself. Now youve made a lady of me I'm not fit to sell anything else. I wish youd left me where you found me.") How does the idea of clean or dirty insides and outsides relate to the larger concerns of *Pygmalion*? Write a four-page essay that addresses these questions.

2. When Pickering asks Doolittle, "Have you no morals, man?" Doolittle replies, "Cant afford them, Governor." Write an essay of three to five pages that explains how the play comments on this exchange.

3. Near the end of the play Higgins delivers a speech that makes Eliza call him a "cruel tyrant." Higgins says, "If youre going to be a lady, youll have to give up feeling neglected if the men you know dont spend half their time snivelling over you and the other half giving you black eyes. . . ." Reread the whole exchange, and take either Higgins's side or Eliza's. Using the tone and diction that your character would employ after having calmed down, write a two-page letter to the other character explaining your position more fully.

∇ ∇ ∇

Exploring Contexts

4 THE AUTHOR'S WORK AS CONTEXT: ANTON CHEKHOV

In some ways the two Chekhov plays in this chapter could hardly be more different—*The Bear* representing the exuberant young playwright's foray into no-holds-barred farce, and *The Cherry Orchard* displaying the mature playwright's full complexity. In other ways, though, one can see Chekhov's characteristic concern with the vanity of human pretense carrying through from one play to the other. Both dramas feature a confrontation between a boorish man (some translators title the shorter play *The Boor* or *The Brute*) and an aristocratic woman whose powerful sexuality lies just beneath the surface. Exchanges of money figure prominently in both plays. Both satirize servants as well as their social betters.

Chekhov clearly meant *The Bear* to be a farce, but it may come as a surprise that he referred to *The Cherry Orchard* as a farce as well (and sometimes simply as a comedy). But Constantin Stanislavsky, Chekhov's great director at the Moscow Art Theatre, wept when he read the play. Insisting that *The Cherry Orchard* was essentially tragic, Stanislavsky staged it accordingly. In fact the play resists simple categorization. While no character comes off as particularly admirable, several have the truly compelling moments of epiphany we usually associate with tragedy. Side by side with these moments, though, are dashes of the broad humor that informs *The Bear*.

ANTON CHEKHOV

The Bear

Planning Ideas

- *The Bear* presents good opportunities to discuss various aspects of theatrical production in a relatively short and simplified form. Assigning a brief written analysis of character may be useful for setting up a discussion that moves to visual, aural, and staging effects. Chekhov's description of both Mrs. Popov and Smirnov is very brief; have your students describe each character more fully, detailing the way both would present themselves at first appearance. Some questions of definition: How would you have Mrs. Popov display her ritualistic fondness for grief? What clothes, gestures, or facial expressions might provide a contrast to her gloomy words? How subtle does the contrast need to be to make the play work theatrically?
- Assign several groups of students to discuss how they would direct the part of the play in which Mrs. Popov and Mr. Smirnov have their first encounter, especially the short passage of dialogue from Mrs. Popov's question, "Can I help it if I've no money today?" to her exit. Does one character speak more loudly than the other? Should both shout? Whisper? Hiss? In a speech of about twelve lines, Smirnov reacts to Mrs. Popov's refusal to give him the money he needs. How should the actor playing Smirnov deliver this speech? Should he speak his lines calmly, but with a hint of suppressed frustration? Force his words through gritted teeth? Scream? Should the tone and volume of his words remain constant or change? If the latter, which specific points in the speech mark changes of approach, even subtle ones? As each group reports their directorial instructions for the meeting between Mrs. Popov and Smirnov, I like to encourage debate over the appropriateness of their decisions and ask them what actor and actress they would like to see cast in their production.
- Dividing the class into groups assigned the same task is one way to proceed, but *The Bear* also lends itself to another sort of division: have one group responsible for stage props, another for costumes, a third for blocking and stage movement, a fourth for the gestures and intonation of actors, and have them work on a short scene together. The discussion can't go far before the students see how intertwined the questions are and how someone will have to provide clear direction based on a certain interpretation of the play.

Commentary

The Bear is hardly what we would call a realistic play. A man pops up without prior warning and demands payment of a debt in cash on the spot. The woman from whom he requests payment has gone into absurdly deep mourning after the death of her cruel and faithless husband. She treats the stranger's desperate plea for payment with infuriating nonchalance. Challenged to a duel, the woman must request that her challenger, the stranger, teach her how to fire a pistol. The two characters hate each other almost on sight but end up in a clutch a few hundred lines later. Much of the play's comedy derives from the absurdity of the characters' responses and actions. You may want to ask your students to suggest other, additional sources of comedy. Answers might include dramatic irony (given the conventions of comic drama, we know Mrs. Popov and Smirnov will get together long before they do), manipulation of sexual stereotypes, the use of stock characters (the timid but interfering servant, the warring lovers-to-be), and physical humor (Smirnov's inadvertent destruction of the furniture; the primping motif).

Comedy—a farce like *The Bear* no less than more subtle comic theater—depends on timing, gesture, and careful modulation of tone and atmosphere. Many actors and directors say comedy is more difficult to produce than tragedy because these variables are so difficult to master. To get students thinking about how to stage this comedy successfully, I like to ask them about the comic elements in the play. When we read *The Bear* initially, do we realize it is going to be a comedy from the very first line? How far into the play must we read before we know we're in comic territory? You may want to ask how the first scene might be staged to create a humorous effect from the very beginning (as the curtain rises and before Luke speaks). How might the room be lit? Should it be bright, or should it be so dark and shuttered that the footman stumbles over Mrs. Popov's footstool? Chekhov gives no instructions about background music. Should there be music? If we decide there should be, what sort of music would enhance the comic effect of the scene? Someone may suggest, and rightly, that there are advantages to delaying the comic effects—that there might be good reasons to hold back on these effects early in the play, then build to a crescendo at the end. You might want to have the class debate the advantages and disadvantages of a relatively subdued opening. If a student does not bring it up, you might ask what kind of audience your performance is intended for and introduce here the concept of performing comedies in different ways—with broad humor or subtle or both or neither—for different audiences, and perhaps introduce questions on the function of audience and (for the dramatic text) the analogy with reader-response.

Any audience will quickly realize the comic possibilities of the meeting between Mrs. Popov and Smirnov—she, young, genteel, attractive, and melodramatically determined to live out her life as though dead—he, crude, passionate, and bursting with life force. She is disillusioned with men; he is disillusioned with women. Since the plot of the play is almost entirely predictable, you may want to ask your students how it maintains our interest. Why do we want to read it through to the end? We all love a happy ending, and traditional comedy offers to fulfill our desire that things end well, but what are the play's other inducements?

Questions for Discussion

1. When Mrs. Popov describes her late husband, what details provide clues that she will find Smirnov attractive? And in Smirnov's long misogynous speech, the one in which he declares, "I can't be fooled any more, I've had enough," how do we know that he's really fooling himself?

2. If you were directing the play, how would you stage the exchange in which Smirnov teaches Mrs. Popov how to use the gun?

3. Chekhov once said that if a playwright introduced a pistol at some point in a play, it had to go off before the final curtain. Why isn't that the case in *The Bear?*

ANTON CHEKHOV

The Cherry Orchard

Planning Ideas

- Before reading the play, distribute a handout with isolated lines that could be read in a variety of ways, depending on the context. Examples: Trofimov's "A woman in the train called me that seedy-looking gent"; Lopakhin's "Let's have everything the way *I* want it." (In the latter case, note the force of the italics for the word *I*.) Have the class demonstrate various ways of delivering the line, explaining in each case what context might justify such delivery. Then, after reading the play, ask how the same lines should be spoken. Discuss the question of how the actor ought to decide on the best reading in each instance.

- When Chekhov's *The Seagull* was first staged, the audience, used to melodrama and bombastic acting, hardly knew what to make of the play's subtle treatment of the complexities of ordinary life. So they laughed at what they thought was abysmally bad theater. It wasn't until Stanislavsky staged a production that the audience appreciated the play's nuanced seriousness. Have groups of students choose a brief scene from **The Cherry Orchard** that should be played seriously but that would invite laughter if misunderstood. Have each group stage the scene appropriately, and then discuss the techniques employed to make the staging work.

- Have students provide brief presentations on various cultural movements influencing Russian life in the nineteenth and early twentieth centuries. Examples: Czarism; the emancipation of the serfs; Marxism; Darwinism; the Decadent Movement; Bolshevism.

Commentary

Twice in *The Cherry Orchard* something happens that almost pulls the action out of the realm of naturalistic theater altogether: a distant sound like that of a string breaking seems to fill the whole sky. The first time, when Mrs. Ranevsky asks, "What was that?" Lopakhin answers, "I don't know. A cable must have broken somewhere away in the mines. But it must be a long, long way off." The exchange is instructive: even though Mrs. Ranevsky is the one whose fate has been decided, her response is open-ended. She asks a question. Lopakhin at first admits his ignorance but then is quick to offer a rational explanation. It's as though Lopakhin is uneasy with this kind of mystery.

Even if we stick with Lopakhin's explanation, the sound is haunting. Nor is the mystery of its origin diminished by the fact that it seems "a long, long way off." Certainly by the time we hear it again, at the very end of the play, it seems far more than something happening in a distant mine. Probably it would be a mistake to go the way of Lopahkin, to pin down the mystery to something specific. The sound may be suggestive of the end of something we usually associate with an almost musical beauty, just as it may suggest the release of tension after a long strain. To be more specific than that, though, would be to make the same kind of mistake as pigeonholing a play like this one in a particular genre.

Just as the snapping string is enormously evocative, Chekhov's language exhibits a wonderful economy, containing volumes in a few phrases. This is true not just of the characters' lines but even of the stage directions. Take the very first comment on the setting: "*A room which is still known as 'the nursery.'*" Here Chekhov conveys a sense of tradition: presumably for a long time the room has been called "the nursery," and it is not just Lyuba or Anya or Leonid who calls it that; it simply *is still known* by that name. The *still*, though, also implies that the name is now somehow inappropriate. Are there no more babies? Has the room changed its function but kept its name? Is there something infantile about the unwillingess to admit that it is no longer a nursery, some hopeless desire to return to the fertility and security that the name evokes? Or take a line like Mrs. Ranevsky's "Nothing's changed" (p. 1576). She seems delighted that the nursery and the orchard are just as they were. But by this point we know that such things soon *will* change, regardless of her desires. The question is whether *she* will change—whether she will learn to accept the inevitable fate of the estate, and whether she will learn to recognize her version of the past—not to mention the present—as an idyllic dream.

Even in the family's straitened circumstances, Mrs. Ranevsky cannot abandon the habit of doling out money to strangers. She is fully aware that her habit is hastening the family's destruction, but she cannot seem to stop: "My poor Varya tries to save by feeding us all on milk and soup and the old servants in the kitchen get nothing but peas to eat, while I go round simply squandering money, I can't think why" (p. 1582). Why is it that she can't break the habit? Perhaps she provides a clue when she remarks to Lopakhin, "I keep expecting something awful to happen, as if the house was going to collapse around our ears. . . . I suppose we've committed so many sins . . ." (p. 1582). She says *we*, but she means *I*; it is really her own sins that bother her, as she says in her next line. But even there she refers to the destructive relationship with her lover in Paris as "bad luck." She knows that she has done things wrong, but she fails to take full responsibility for making things right. Could her continued extravagance be a way of attempting to compensate for those wrongs? Are her financial and her moral prodigality somehow related? Does she hope, rather desperately, that maintaining the appearance of *noblesse oblige* will make her morally noble?

Such a line of thought would help explain her absolute refusal to do the one thing that might make the family financially solvent: cut down the orchard to make way for summer cottages. As though refusing that option were entirely noble, she says, "Cottages, summer visitors. Forgive me, but all that's so frightfully vulgar." We may agree (as, very likely, did Chekhov). But Mrs. Ranevsky seems to think that her refusal is noble in every sense of the word—that her proud assertion of social nobility can somehow escape the charge of irresponsibility. Or consider her gratuitously biting response to Lopakhin's innocent comment that he has recently seen a funny play: "I don't suppose it was a bit funny. You people shouldn't go and see plays, you should try watching your own performance instead. What drab lives you all lead and what a lot of rubbish you talk!" (p. 1584). If such an outburst from such a generous soul seems surprising, it may seem so because she protests too much.

But Mrs. Ranevsky is not the only one who is overly sensitive about social position. When Dunyasha says that she feels faint, Lopakhin replies, "You dress like a lady and do your hair like one too. We can't have that. Remember your place" (p. 1568). There is no small irony that this comes from a *nouveau riche*, a peasant.

It is Lopakhin who comes up with the most practical, but also the ugliest, plan for saving the family estate. What he calls "a spot of tidying and clearing up" involves destroying all the old buildings, including the ancestral home, as well as the cherry orchard. Not that Lopakhin is completely blind to the estate's beauty—only for him its beauty is so wrapped up in his own financial liberation that he is blind to the fact that his financial plans will destroy its beauty: "If my father and grandfather could only rise from their graves and see what happened, see how their Yermolay—Yermolay who was always being beaten, who could hardly write his name and ran round barefoot in winter—how this same Yermolay bought this estate, the most beautiful place in the world. I've bought the estate where my father and grandfather were slaves, where they weren't even allowed inside the kitchen" (p. 1598). Can one read the drama without sharing a sense of Yermolay's triumph?

Ever the practical man, it is Lopakhin who tends to glance at his watch, who knows that the train pulls out in precisely forty-seven minutes. He has his flights of romantic fancy, but ultimately his triumph is one of crass practicality over beauty. The mark of his crassness is not so much calling Ophelia Amelia when he misquotes *Hamlet* as his failure even to think of waiting until the train has pulled out before beginning to cut down the orchard. He agrees to delay the destruction for a few minutes, but he does not really see why. His comment is, "Those people are the limit."

Why, given Lopakhin's practicality, does he not make the eminently practical move of marrying Varya, of whom he is quite fond? One possibility is that he is smitten by Mrs. Ranevsky, to whom he says, "You just believe in me as you used to, that's all I ask, and look at me in the old way, with those wonderful, irresistible eyes. Merciful heavens! My father was a serf, belonged to your father and your grandfather before him. But you—you've done so much for me in the past that I've forgotten all that and love you as a brother. Or even more" (p. 1573). But surely a man as shrewd as Lopakhin doesn't seriously entertain the prospect of a union with Mrs. Ranevsky. Her adopted daughter Varya, however, is another matter. Lopakhin doesn't seem to think of the choice as between the two women but between Varya and no one at all. He himself is mystified by his inability to act. But he fails to make the proposal. Is a lingering class consciousness in play here? Does he subconsciously consider himself unworthy not only of Mrs. Ranevsky's social status but even of Varya's? In any case, his hesitation despite his intention to act mirrors Mrs. Ranevsky's inability to refrain from giving money away despite her knowledge of the consequences.

Varya herself fails to make the connection between stated intent and actual behavior. Given her role as a woman in Czarist Russia, she may have no option of initiating a marriage proposal. But she conceivably could act on her repeatedly stated desire to join a convent—especially in light of Lopakhin's failure to suggest marriage. When she tells Anya about her fondest wish, she says, "I'd go off to a convent, then on to Kiev and Moscow, wandering from one holy place to another. I'd just wander on and on. What bliss!" (p. 1571). Even without knowing Varya very well at this point, we know better; anyone who indulges the notion that a monastic vocation is pure bliss is in the realm of fantasy, not thoughtfully planned action.

If Varya occasionally finds refuge in an imaginary world, others have even more active (and more frivolous) fantasy lives. Gayev is mentally playing billiards when he isn't offering an impassioned rhapsody to Nature or a bookcase; Yepikhodov indulges in histrionics about shooting himself.

Perhaps the most throughgoing fantasy is Trofimov's. In light of what we now know about twentieth-century Russia and the Soviet Union, Trofimov's ideals take on a force that Chekhov himself could hardly have imagined.

Trofimov is not only fond of saying, "Mankind marches on"; he also says, "I'm in the vanguard" (p. 1601). And, apparently true to his advocacy of change, he himself has changed so much that at first Mrs. Ranevsky doesn't even recognize him. But the change is superficial; he is still a student, still a tireless talker. Trofimov imagines himself a champion of work in an age of the aristocracy's smug exploitation of workers, but as both Mrs. Ranevsky and Lopakhin point out, he himself talks rather than works. He enjoys playing the role of the "seedy-looking gent" or the "desperately poor" student, but his identification with the truly poor is artificial (pp. 1577, 1589). As Mrs. Ranevsky tells him, he hasn't really suffered and so cannot possibly comprehend the human sorrow that transcends class distinctions. Nor does he understand love. More than once he says of his relationship with Anya, "We are above love". What does she think of that?

At one point Anya suggests that Trofimov has destroyed for her the beauty of the orchard: "What have you done to me, Peter? Why is it I'm not so fond of the cherry orchard as I used to be? I used to think there was no better place on earth than our orchard" (p. 1588). Trofimov's reply is no mere restatement of his antiromantic sentiments; he delivers what is perhaps the play's most moving speech: "All Russia is our orchard. The earth is so wide, so beautiful, so full of wonderful places. [*Pause.*] Just think, Anya. Your grandfather, your great-grandfather and all your ancestors owned serfs, they owned human souls. Don't you see that from every cherry tree in the orchard, from every leaf and every trunk, men and women are gazing at you? Don't you hear their voices? Owning living souls, that's what has changed you all so completely, those who went before, and those alive today, so that your mother, you yourself, your uncle — you don't realize that you're actually living on credit. You're living on other people, the very people you won't even let inside your own front door."

Trofimov's image of the ghosts of former slaves looking out from the cherry orchard and demanding retribution stands in contrast to Firs's insistence that things were better in the old order. That the more conservative sentiment comes from a servant rather than a member of the upper class lends it some plausibility, as does Firs's first-hand recollection of the serfs' reaction to their emancipation: "As I recall, everyone was very pleased, but what they were pleased about they'd no idea themselves" (p. 1585). No doubt Firs is right that a good deal was lost, a good many things were forgotten, and plenty of new problems were created by the abolition of serfdom. But it is Lopakhin, the successful son of a serf, who wryly puts Fir's wistful nostalgia in perspective: "Oh, it was a good life all right. At least there were plenty of floggings."

In the end Firs is still in the house, more or less holding his own at the age of eighty-seven. But just as *The Cherry Orchard* refuses to glorify the changes sweeping across the country, the play offers no glorification of the faithful servant who endures in the midst of change; all his loyalty, as he himself remarks, amounts to nothing. He calls himself a nincompoop.

Questions for Discussion

1. Early in the play Anya says of her mother, "How well I understand her, if only she knew" (p. 1572). Given the immediate context of the line, how is it ironic?

2. Should Firs's line "Now I can die happy" be played for laughs?

3. When Lopakhin offers to get the family a loan so that they can build the summer cottages, he says, "Give it some serious thought." Varya angrily replies, "Oh, do for heaven's sake go." In light of the fact that Lopakhin is trying to be helpful, why is Varya so angry?

4. Reread the exchange beginning with Gayev's "I am silent. I am silent.

There is something rather important, though . . ." (p. 1579). Varya responds, and after more explanation from Gayev, Anya does. Then Firs enters and addresses Gayev. In each case, how does the speaker's remark reveal his or her character? Which speaker makes the most sense? Which seems most deluded?

5. Gayev appears to be more willing than his sister to face the painful facts when he remarks, ". . . now the orchard's to be sold to pay our debts, unlikely as it may sound" (p. 1577). What details about Gayev's depiction let us know that he is in fact *not* good at facing facts?

6. Just after Yepikhodov calmly remarks that he thinks he might shoot himself, Charlotte says, "I'm lonely, oh so lonely. I'm on my own in the world, and—and who I am and what I'm for is a mystery." Are these the stereotyped "stock" characters one would expect to find in a farce, or are there real human beings who say such things?

7. What does Gayev mean when he says, "I'm a man of the eighties" (p. 1579)?

8. Lopakhin offers Trofimov money, saying, ". . . I'd like to lend it you because I can afford to. So why turn it down? I'm a peasant, I put it to you straight." Trofimov replies, "Your father was a peasant and mine worked in a chemist's shop, all of which proves precisely nothing" (p. 1600). What is Trofimov's point here? Why does he turn down the money? Does the play as a whole bear out the idea that parentage means "precisely nothing"?

Writing Assignments for Chapter 4

1. Imagine you were playing the part of Smirnov in *The Bear*. You would need to develop a plausible motive not only for each line but for each action. For example, consider your motive for walking right up to Mrs. Popov just after her lines, "Oh, go away then. I'm so furious! Don't you come near me, I tell you." Would the move be instinctive on your part? Impetuous? Defiant? Would you be consciously reading her repressed invitation? Attempting to gain control of the situation? Subconsciously inviting her rebuke? Some combination of such factors? Write a page-long explanation of why you would make the move. Use other lines in the play to argue that your decision is psychologically consistent with Smirnov's character.

2. At times Chekhov's method of filling in background information seems stiff and artificial. In part to explain why Mrs. Ranevsky has been in Paris, for example, Chekhov has Anya say, "It's six years since Father died. And a month after that our brother Grisha was drowned in the river. He was a lovely little

boy, only seven years old. It was too much for Mother, she went away, just dropped everything and went" (p. 1572). The speech might seem for the reader's benefit only—gratuitous for the characters in the play since they would already know about everything Anya mentions. Later in the play Mrs. Ranevsky covers some of the same ground: "My little boy was drowned and I went abroad, went right away, never meaning to return or see the river again . . ." (p. 1593). Write a three-page essay that focuses on such "set pieces" (Charlotte has more than one) explaining why they are more than artistically awkward ways of filling the reader in on background information.

3. On the evening of the estate's auction Mrs. Ranevsky remarks, "What a time to have the band here and what a time to give a party! Oh well, never mind" (p. 1590). Write a one- or two-page essay explaining why throwing a party at such a time is or is not an appropriate thing to do.

4. When Trofimov says, "Mankind is marching towards a higher truth, towards the greatest possible happiness on earth, and I'm in the vanguard," Lopakhin replies, "Will you get there?" Trofimov answers, "I shall. [*Pause.*] I'll either get there or show others the way" (p. 1601). At this point comes Chekhov's stage direction, *"There is the sound of an axe striking a tree in the distance."* Focusing on this moment as well as others, write an essay of three or four pages explaining how the timing of Chekhov's stage directions comments on the surrounding dialogue.

5. Suppose a politically active friend wrote you a letter saying, "I've just found the clearest statement of revolutionary [or conservative; you pick] ideals in all of literature: it is Chekhov's *The Cherry Orchard.*" Write a reply to your friend in which you build a case against the argument that the play is entirely revolutionary (or entirely conservative). Of course, your position will be stronger if you cite specific passages.

5 LITERARY CONTEXT: TRAGEDY AND COMEDY

Each of the two plays in this chapter admirably reflects its genre. *Oedipus the King*, model for the Aristotelian definition of tragedy that was to remain the formal ideal for centuries, depicts the hero / king's preordained violation of a universal law, his vain struggle against his destiny, and his acquisition of knowledge so painful that the appropriate mark of his enlightenment is the loss of his eyes. *The Importance of Being Earnest*, in contrast, defines its characters in terms of social roles, twits convention with some of the most sparkling humor in English literature, and in the end provides a wonderfully contrived resolution that reinforces the comic expectation of a happy ending replete with marriages.

SOPHOCLES

Oedipus the King

Planning Ideas

- A few days before starting on **Oedipus the King,** divide the class into five groups, and have the members of each read a Greek tragedy other than **Oedipus the King.** Group 1 might read Sophocles' **Antigone,** Group 2 Aeschylus's *Agamemnon,* Group 3 Aeschylus's *Prometheus Bound,* Group 4 Euripides' *The Bacchae,* and Group 5 Euripides' *The Trojan Women.* At the beginning of the discussion on **Oedipus,** each member of each group does a one-minute presentation on some aspect of the similarities or the differences between **Oedipus** and the other tragedy. (This assignment can be done in conjunction with Writing Assignment 4 below.)
- In view of the fact that virtually everyone in Sophocles' audience would have known the story of Oedipus, you might use this play to broach the topic of why one should bother to see or read a play the ending of which one already knows. You might relate an anecdote about one of Flannery O'Connor's first public readings of *A Good Man is Hard to Find,* a story about a Southern family out for a drive in the country. O'Connor told her audience that the story ended with an escaped convict's shooting the entire family. With the ending revealed, she proceeded to read the story. Why would O'Connor do such a thing? What point was she trying to make with her audience?

Commentary

Our students are faced with an uncertain world, and we see them groping toward contemporary oracles. Time and again they are forced to choose between equally unpalatable alternatives, without being able to find comfort in the knowledge that everything is foreordained, whether by the stars, or by a Calvinist God, or by the *moira* (fate) that rules the life of Oedipus.

In a different way, Oedipus was faced with such a situation when he visited the oracle at Delphi before the play begins. Informed that his fate was to kill his father and marry his mother, he saw two alternatives—to return home and realize his *moira* or to refuse to accept his destiny. When he decided on the latter, he refused to accept the limitations of his mortality, a refusal called *hubris* by Aristotle in his influential definition of tragedy. What happens to Oedipus as a result of his choice is an education in human limitation.

Nothing in the play is more theatrical and more significant than the contrast between Oedipus as he first appears and Oedipus as he appears at the end of the play. The first scene has a ceremonial or hieratic quality. The Chorus of Theban Elders is lamenting the plague when Oedipus appears and asks what is going on. He knows the answer; he has already sent Creon to Delphi for help. The question is part of a ceremony in which the King (or Tyrant, as the Greeks called him, using the word differently than we do) allows his subjects to make requests of him and promises to help them. He sees himself as a king, a god on earth. He has conquered the Sphinx; surely he can conquer the plague.

What Oedipus does not realize is that beneath his royal robes there is only "a poor, bare, forked animal," as Lear discovered. The Greek audience was constantly reminded of this because Oedipus's name, which means "swollen-footed," reminds us that when he was a baby, his father drove pins through his ankles and arranged for him to be left to die of exposure. We do not know how the Greeks represented his wound on stage, but there must have been some reminder of his physical infirmity.

Forgetful of his infirmity, the reminder of his mortality, Oedipus must learn again that he is human. Coming to Thebes as a young man, he saved the city by killing the Sphinx. He was acclaimed as king and married Jocasta, an older woman, but a queen and still presumably beautiful and sexually responsive. Over the years his reign has been happy and his marriage fruitful. He is the man who has everything, but he has come to believe that his success and happiness are the result of his own choices. The fact that the Elders want him to save the city from the plague suggests that they believe he can do so, and Oedipus also believes that he can.

The body of the play recounts the steps by which Oedipus comes to realize, as the Chorus points out at the end, that we can "Count no mortal happy till / he has passed the final limit of his life secure from pain." At first, proud and forgetful of his humanity, Oedipus initiates his own downfall with his promise to the people that he will not rest until he has brought the truth to light. At this point Creon has returned with the message of the oracle that the murderer of

Laius must be punished. If Oedipus had asked the right questions, he might have discovered the truth at this point, but the dramatic movement depends on the tension between discovery and the failure to react properly to that discovery. The dramatic effect is further intensified by the use of dramatic irony, as in Oedipus's speech in which he swears, essentially, to drive himself out of Thebes without understanding the true meaning of what he is saying. The dramatic irony is intensified when Oedipus says that he must punish the murderer of Laius lest the murderer of one king should move against a second. He does not understand that his oath insures that Oedipus, the murderer of Laius, must punish himself for that act.

The second discovery is made by Teiresias, and it is not ambiguous. Teiresias tells Oedipus that he (Oedipus) is the murderer, but again Oedipus refuses to understand. He sees Teiresias's statement as part of a conspiracy led by Creon. We see in this attack something of the insecurity that Oedipus feels in relation to his wife and her brother, who are, after all, older, more experienced, and natives of Thebes. The resulting quarrel between Oedipus and Creon brings Jocasta to the stage.

Jocasta is an interesting character: she does not believe in oracles because, as she tells us, an oracle said that Laius would be murdered by his own son. Oedipus does not make the connection with what the oracle has told him. He resists discovery again, instead focusing on the question of whether Laius was murdered by a "robber" or "robbers" at the place where three roads met.

The next discovery is that of the First Messenger, who comes to tell Oedipus that his father is dead, but instead tells him that his parentage is unknown. Jocasta understands and leaves the stage to kill herself, but Oedipus yet again resists discovery. He fears that Jocasta feels shame for his humble birth. Jocasta has tried to prevent Oedipus from searching for the truth, but he moves forward to the inevitable revelation. In the moment before the final discovery Oedipus finally understands.

SHEPHERD: I'm right at the edge, the horrible truth—I've got to say it!
OEDIPUS: And I'm at the edge of hearing horrors, yes, but I must hear!

After the ultimate revelation the play moves rapidly to its conclusion. Jocasta has killed herself, Oedipus has put out his own eyes, and Creon is left to rule, however unwillingly.

At the end of the play Oedipus appears again, deposed, self-blinded, self-exiled from the native city in which he had felt himself a stranger. At the beginning of the play Oedipus was different from other people because he was happy, successful, and powerful. Now he is different because of his overweening pride and the crimes that he has committed because of it. Yet Oedipus is a tragic figure because he has learned to hate his crimes but not to hate himself. He might have chosen to kill himself, following Jocasta's example, but the fact that he does not expresses his basic dignity, his acceptance of himself, and his humanity.

Questions for Discussion

Plot

1. Does Oedipus already know what the Priest "tells" him in the opening exchange with the Priest? If he does, why is the scene included? How might it be staged to make it more plausible?

2. How does Oedipus react to the message that Creon brings from the oracle at Delphi? Does he have any other motive for his decision to seek Laius's murderers than his desire to rid the city of plague? Why had there been no earlier search for the murderer of Laius?

3. Why do the members of the Chorus, in their first ode, say, "I am stretched on the rack of doubt, and terror and trembling hold / my heart" when, in fact, the response of the oracle implies a solution to their problems?

4. What dramatic device is used in Oedipus's oath to avenge the murderer of Laius? How does the choice of the words used reinforce the dramatic effect? The story of Oedipus would have been familiar to the Athenian audience. How might this knowledge have affected their reaction to Oedipus's oath?

5. What is Teiresias's initial response to the summons and questions of response? What does he finally tell Oedipus? Why does Oedipus not believe him?

6. Why does Oedipus suspect Creon of plotting to gain the throne of Thebes? How is this suspicion related to Oedipus's later assumption that Jocasta is upset about the possibility that Oedipus may be of low birth?

7. Why does Jocasta tell Oedipus what she knows about the death of Laius? How does Oedipus react to the various details of her account? Does he ignore any important ones?

8. Why does Oedipus begin his account of his adventure at the place where three roads meet with an account of what happened to him in Corinth and at the oracle in Delphi? How does Jocasta react? Does she suspect anything out of the ordinary?

9. What is the reaction of the Chorus to this scene between Oedipus and Jocasta? Why does the ode end with the Chorus figuratively turning its back on oracles?

10. What news does Messenger 1 bring? What revelation is brought about by it? How do Oedipus, Jocasta, and the Chorus react?

11. Why is one shepherd both the man who escaped from the murder of Laius and the one who was to have exposed the infant Oedipus to death? Does

Oedipus ever clear up the question of the number of "robbers" involved in Laius's death?

12. Referring to his self-blinding, Oedipus says, "It was Apollo, friends, Apollo, / that brought this bitter bitterness, my sorrows to completion. / But the hand that struck me / was none but my own." How does this statement also refer to the entire tragedy of *Oedipus?*

Character

1. What elements of Oedipus's character caused him to go to Delphi after Polybus and Merope had denied the story that he was not their son? Do similar impulses inform his other actions?

2. What parts of Oedipus's downfall come from his own character? Which ones come from the circumstances of his life? Is there evidence in what we know of Laius and Jocasta that Oedipus's guilt might be in part inherited?

The Stage

1. Since the opening scene is a public ceremony of sorts, how should Oedipus be dressed? Would his appearance in full royal regalia be appropriate? How would such an appearance add to the impact of the final scene?

2. This play was written to be performed by only three actors. Which roles would have been performed by each of the three, assuming that no two actors played the same role?

3. How does the actual time of performance relate to the amount of time required by the events of the play? How is the passage of time indicated?

Genre

1. The terms *hubris* and *hamartia* are frequently used in discussions of tragedy. How are they relevant to the story of Oedipus?

2. How does the account of Oedipus's search for the murderer of Laius resemble a detective story? What makes it different?

OSCAR WILDE

The Importance of Being Earnest

Planning Ideas

- While this play is positively crackling with wit, there are those who miss a great deal of it. What is wanted can be extraordinarily difficult to teach: a sense of what is funny. Although I was at first suspicious of any kind of exercise that tried to explain jokes (nothing is less funny than such explanations), I have found that some students respond well to a sort of "find the humor" exercise. The idea is to offer certain of Wilde's favorite techniques, with examples, arranged in categories on a handout. The students then find other examples of the same types. Examples:

a. Non sequitur

> ALGERNON: Please don't touch the cucumber sandwiches. They are ordered especially for Aunt Augusta. [*Takes one and eats it.*]
> JACK: Well, you have been eating them all the time.
> ALGERNON: That is quite a different matter. She is my aunt.

b. Unexpected word

> ALGERNON: I hear her hair has turned quite gold from grief.

c. Parallelism

> LADY BRACKNELL: To lose one parent, Mr. Worthing, may be regarded as a misfortune; to lose both looks like carelessness.

d. Pun

> JACK: It is very vulgar to talk like a dentist when one isn't a dentist. It makes a false impression.
> ALGERNON: Well, that is exactly what dentists always do.

- Staged readings of scenes from this play can be quite effective; most students manage the requisite timing surprisingly well.

Commentary

At the heart of the play is the basic comedic plot: a young man and a young woman wish to marry. Some difficulty is interposed that renders the union seemingly impossible, but then the difficulty is removed and all live happily ever after. The plot here is double, for there are two young men and two young women: the romance of the second pair is triggered by the complications of the romance of the first pair and resolved by the resolution of those complications. This is the heart of comedy, for the typical comedic plot is concerned with someone who is denied his or her rightful place in society, but who ultimately overcomes the denial. In comedy—as opposed to such forms as farce—marriage is viewed in its social aspect rather than its sexual one.

The concern is with the wedding rather than the wedding night, and therefore the surface unconcern with sexuality works. Many other comedies overlap into the area of sexuality but not *Earnest*; it stays strictly within the proper domain of comedy. Jack and Algernon are eminently suitable to be husbands except that Jack has no parents and Algernon no money, and those two characteristics are important to marriage in its social aspect. As healthy young women, Gwendolyn and Cecily are admirably suited for marriage and motherhood, and we feel that it is well that difficulties are so expeditiously resolved.

While it is a perfect comedy, *Earnest* also exemplifies the narrower genre called the *comedy of manners*. The comedy of manners differs from other comedies in its emphasis on life among the wealthy, with people who "toil not, neither do they spin." Their concerns are those of high society rather than of society in the general sense. Algernon, for example, is deeply concerned with such burning issues as who his dinner partner will be or what music is to be performed at a party. The values of such people may seem superficial to many people, including today's students, but if nothing else, these serve to make the play even more amusing. That Wilde himself understood this is clear in the brilliantly funny interrogation of Jack by Lady Bracknell. Throughout we are confronted with a comic inversion of values. When he hesitantly admits to Lady Bracknell that he smokes, she is delighted because she thinks a man should have some occupation.

Lady Bracknell, as a senior matron, is one of the controlling forces of society, who can change either the fashion or the side, or both, if necessary. Her values are totally consistent and totally inverted from our perspective, and their inversion gives them much of their humor.

The play is also a brilliant example of the artful use of comic stereotypes. Jack and Gwendolyn are representative of such "witty lovers" as Beatrice and Benedick in *Much Ado about Nothing* and Mirabell and Millamant in *The Way of the World*. Algernon and Cecily are "sentimental lovers." Miss Prism is an old maid, anxious to marry Canon Chasuble, a slightly dim clergyman, and Lady Bracknell is the managing matron. Yet though all are "stereotypes," Wilde succeeds in giving each of them more than enough individuality to maintain our interest in them. For example, Algernon is portrayed throughout the play as being excessively interested in food, not a usual trait in a sentimental lover.

The glory of the play is as much in its language as its structure and characterization, for Wilde was a master wit. Some of the devices he uses are worth examination, as discussed in the Planning Ideas, above. One is the *non sequitur*, as in Algernon's remark to Lane: "Speaking of the science of Life, have you got the cucumber sandwiches cut for Aunt Augusta?" That the connection between the science of Life (whatever that is) and cucumber sandwiches is at best tenuous is the source of the humor here as in other places. A second technique is the use of the unexpected word. When Lane mentions his marriage, Algernon is shocked because "Really, if the lower orders don't set us a good example, what on earth is the use of them?" The question would not be funny if he had said "upper" instead of "lower," but the unexpected word provides the humor. Another form of humor is the use of rhetorical balance and parallelism, as in Jack's remark that "When one is in town one amuses oneself. When one is in the country one amuses other people." Puns may be the lowest form of humor (and then again they may not), but Wilde uses them brilliantly, as in the title of the play, which leads to the final line. Another form of humor is the establishment of apparently logical categories that have no real meaning, as when Algernon explains why he does not intend to have dinner with his aunt. "To begin with, I dined there on Monday. . . . In the second place, whenever I do dine there I am always treated as a member of the family. . . . In the third place, I know perfectly well whom she will place me next to." A final form of humor is the use of speeches that clearly contradict facts, as when Gwendolyn, replying to her mother's command to go into the next room with her, answers, "Certainly mamma," and remains behind. As explained in the first of the Planning Ideas, these examples can be multiplied many times from other sections of the play.

Questions for Discussion

Plot

1. What is the purpose of the opening exchange between Algernon and Lane?

2. What do we learn about the opening situation of the play from the conversation between Algernon and Jack? How does Wilde use the cigarette case for expository and comic purposes?

3. What does Algernon offer Jack in exchange for a free dinner? How does he fulfill his share of the agreement? What plot complication results from it?

4. How does Lady Bracknell react to the news of Gwendolyn's engagement to Jack? What does her maternal interrogation of Jack tell us about her values and those of her society?

5. How does Wilde make use of the fact that Jack was found in a handbag? What further information do we get from Miss Prism early in Act II that contributes to the solution of the play's problems?

6. Why does Algernon suggest that Jack's brother died of chill rather than of apoplexy? What use is made of this later in the play?

7. How does Algernon discover the address of Jack's country place? How has Jack attempted earlier to keep it secret?

8. What bargain does Jack offer to Lady Bracknell? How does she react? What might have happened if the problem had not been resolved?

9. Describe the steps by which the problems are resolved by the appearance of Miss Prism, including any new misunderstanding that may have arisen.

10. Are we prepared for the embrace of Miss Prism and Canon Chasuble? If not, why do we accept it?

11. What is the meaning of the final line of the play?

Character

1. Certain of the characters in this play have names that suggest something about their characters. Of which ones is this true, and what do we learn about each from the name?

2. Why does Gwendolyn insist that Jack make a formal proposal of marriage?

3. In the opening scene of Act II what conclusions does the audience reach about the attitudes and relative intelligence of Miss Prism and Cecily?

4. Why is Miss Prism shown misunderstanding the meaning of the allusion to Egeria?

5. Describe the relation between the attitudes of Gwendolyn and Cecily and what they actually say in the opening scene of Act III.

Patterned Language

1. The last part of Act II, the scenes between Gwendolyn and Cecily, then between them and the two young men, and finally between the two young men, are full of examples of syntactic and rhetorical balance and parallelism. Describe the effect of this device.

2. Compare Lady Bracknell's examination of Cecily in Act III with her interrogation of Jack in Act I. What accounts for the similarities and differences?

3. A good bit of the humor in this play, and a good bit of the meaning, depends on the contrast between appearance and reality. For example, in the first exchange of the play Algernon asks Lane if he has heard what Algernon was playing on the piano. What are we to make of Lane's reply that "I didn't think it polite to listen, sir"? Can you find other examples of this phenomenon? What do they tell us about the meaning of the play?

Symbol and Myth

1. There are numerous references to food and drink; find examples of them and comment on their meaning in the play.

2. How does Wilde make use of diaries as a structural and comic device in the play?

Writing Assignments for Chapter 5

1. What view of the gods and their decrees is presented in *Oedipus the King*? Does the fact that the oracle has said that Oedipus will kill his father and marry his mother absolve him of guilt in doing so? If not, why not?

2. There are a number of references in *Oedipus the King* to blindness and sight and to light and darkness. Find some of them and write an essay examining the role of this group of images in the play. Consider questions like these: With what *kinds* of enlightenment and darkness is the play concerned? What is it significant that Apollo, the sun god, is also a god of prophecy? Why is Teiresias, a prophet inspired by Apollo, presented as blind? What is the relation between his blindness and that of Oedipus?

3. Write an essay that centers on the function of the Chorus in *Oedipus the King*. Consider questions like the following: Why does the Chorus consist of the elders of Thebes? Does the Chorus consistently express a point of view different from that of any of the major characters? If so, why does the play *need* to have such a point of view expressed? Why by a group rather than an individual? What part does the Chorus play in the action? How is the content of the choral odes related to the action around each ode?

4. It is sometimes said that in comparison with his younger contemporary Euripides, Sophocles in his best-known plays seems generally to favor the status quo and the powers-that-be. Choose one of the following options:

A) Read a play by Euripides (*The Bacchae* and *The Trojan Women* are good choices), and compare and contrast it with *Oedipus the King* in terms of political conservatism and subversiveness.

B) Using only the text of *Oedipus the King*, write an essay that demonstrates how it either conservatively controls a potentially subversive response by the audience (such as anger at the gods for their cruelty and perhaps anger about authority in general) or subtly invites such a subversive response.

5. Write a short essay on *The Importance of Being Earnest* that either supports or refutes the following thesis: "Wilde wrote the play strictly as entertainment; any attempt to find a moral is misguided." (You could use a great many of the play's lines in building either case. A couple of examples: Does the behavior of Miss Prism and Canon Chasuble suggest anything about the values of conventional moralists? Do the Canon's remarks about his sermon on "the meaning of the manna in the wilderness" have a serious implication about institutional religion?)

6. After reading *The Importance of Being Earnest*, do some research on Oscar Wilde's life and literary career. Then read the play again, and write an essay on how your research changed your reading. How does the play seem different after you have learned about the playwright's troubles with the social strictures of Victorian England?

6 CULTURE AS CONTEXT: SOCIAL AND HISTORICAL SETTING

I tell my students there are two ways of spending a few weeks in a foreign country. One way is to seek out the familiar: to find people who speak English, to spend time, as much as possible, in the way one would spend it at home, to eat familiar foods (there's a MacDonald's everywhere), generally to try to make the place seem less strange. The other way is immerse oneself in the foreign culture: to try to converse in the native language, to participate in activities that seem unfamiliar, to try the local cuisine, to experience, as much as possible, the culture from the inside. Most students agree that the second way is better.

Of course I'm developing an analogy about reading plays that center on social groups or historical periods different from our own. While we can never completely negate the complex cultural assumptions that have shaped us and have made us see the world the way we do—just as we will never be natives of the foreign country—we can to a certain degree immerse ourselves in the world of the characters in the play. We'll never be Lizzie Borden or Troy Maxson. But we can, if we exercise some curiosity and some sympathetic imagination, live with them for a while—not as critics whose job it is to measure their lives against ours, but as fellow travelers in a journey that is all the more valuable for its oddness.

SHARON POLLOCK

Blood Relations

Planning Ideas

- Before assigning **Blood Relations,** * have students do some work in the library and come to class with a one-paragraph summary of the events surrounding the Lizzie Borden case. After discussing the play, have each student write another one-paragraph summary, this time of the play's handling of the central event. Comparing the two paragraphs should make it clear that history comes to us in various versions. The exercise can easily be developed into the playwriting project described in the first of the Writing Assignments below.
- The twist at the end is good places to begin a discussion of **Blood Rela-**

tions. The point to help students see is that the playwright, and the play as a piece of imaginative re-creation, seeks to do something more than build a case for or against Lizzie as murderer.

- Another way of getting at the issue of imaginative re-creation is to focus on the play-within-the-play. Pollock skilfully employs this "metadramatic" device, as does Shakespeare in **Hamlet** [see Writing Assignment 1 below]. To illustrate the idea of metadrama (theatrical techniques that deliberately call attention to the play's status as something contrived, as fiction) one needs only to refer to a TV show like David Letterman's. Part of "getting" Letterman is accepting his repeated revelations of the artificiality of television imagery. The technique makes the viewers feel like insiders in the art's production. Does the play-within-the-play (in either **Blood Relations** or **Hamlet**) work at all similarly?

- It is difficult to imagine the effect of having the same actors play different roles when you are reading this play as a script. Calling attention to and discussing this aspect of the play will help, but the best way to see what the playwright had in mind is to stage a part of the play in which the actors switch from one character to another. This play does not lend itself well to the acting out of scenes, and the stage directions make it explicit that the action should flow uninterrupted. If there is time, then, stage all of either the first or second act, paying particular attention to the problem of distinguishing between two characters played by a single actor.

Commentary

This play not only re-creates a specific historical situation, it presents several models for reconstructing the past. The interaction between the Actress and Lizzie, for example, calls up from Lizzie's own mind images that she herself has forgotten. The process uncovers memories and feelings that have been long buried. For the Actress, who was not present in the house ten years before, the role of Miss Lizzie is an exercise in losing oneself in a character. She is able to speak in Miss Lizzie's voice and participate in the drama without a script, because she understands the woman whose part she is acting. This might be why she has no name other than "The Actress." The courtroom trial offers another model. It represents the use of formal interrogation under a pretense of objectivity. Juxtaposed with the dramatic re-creation of events, the defense that wins acquittal for Lizzie seems strangely unsatisfactory. Finally, the children's song that runs through the play represents the collective memory of the community. Lizzie's mythic place in its past, despite her acquittal, remains one of horror and mystery.

In these various ways, Pollock explores the complexities of memory, point of view, objectivity, and judgment in order to challenge the notion that we can somehow discover the "truth" about the past. Emma's obsession with whether Lizzie did or did not "do it" seems absurd, a representation of those who want to know only the facts. The play refuses to answer the question of whether Lizzie committed the murders. All evidence leads us to believe that she did, but of course the point is that that isn't the point. What the play explores is the question of just what the artist can make of historical facts.

Questions for Discussion

1. By constructing a play-within-the-play, Pollock can include dimensions of Lizzie's life that simply re-creating the trial would not allow; for example, Lizzie's feelings of strangeness, her attachment to the farm and to animals, her lack of desire to marry, her longing for her father's affections, and her philosophical justifications for murder. Pollock combines all of these aspects of Lizzie's character to give us a portrait of her psychology. Is it a consistent portrait? Why does Lizzie suggest acting out the parts in the first place? How would you describe Miss Lizzie as she emerges from the play-within-the-play? How does her behavior in 1902 contribute to the way we see her in 1892? Why is it important that Lizzie not play herself in the internal drama? What does she learn about herself through this enactment?

2. Pollock uses some literary devices to foreshadow the final scene and to create an ominous mood of violence. What role does the image of the carousel play? The story of the drowned puppy? The killing of the birds? How do you imagine these scenes on stage? Would you emphasize any particular aspect of Lizzie's character above the others if you were directing this play? How?

3. How much pressure does Lizzie feel to marry? How does Lizzie's friendship with Dr. Patrick figure in the drama? What is the logic of having him play the Defense? How is Lizzie treated in her family? Why does the family deceive her about selling the farm?

AUGUST WILSON

Fences

Planning Ideas

- Since everyone in the class has dreams of a life somehow larger and more fulfilling, it is helpful to have students come to the first session on **Fences** with a one-page description of the fences that stand between their own dreams and everyday life. Are the fences matters of race? Gender? Education? Social background? Age? Demographics? Innate ability? Physical health? Habits? Responsibility to others? Customs? Laws? Beliefs? Some students may be unwilling to discuss openly their fondest dreams but perfectly willing to discuss the barriers that keep those dreams from being realized.

- Some discussion of visualness seems necessary for this play, and for me the most convenient way of leading into it is to turn to the issue of the fence. The question, which you can pose just as profitably at the end as at the beginning of your discussion, is how to stage the fence, using it as a silent commentary on the action taking place all around it but without making explicit reference to it. In its unfinished state in plain sight through most of the play, the fence is a visual reminder of intentional and unintentional barriers—as well as of incompleteness and lack of control. Have your students look up "fence" in a good dictionary. How many of the meanings found there might apply to the play? What is the significance of Troy's unrealized plan to mend the fence with Cory? For what reason does the fence eventually get fixed?

Commentary

Fences is at least partly about what happens when a man of heroic stature finds himself without any avenue for heroic exploits. *Oedipus the King* can be the tragedy that it is because the title character is born a prince in a culture that rewards the actions of a royal hero. But Troy Maxson, the son of a brutal farmer, finds himself as a very young man in a strange city, one that will not welcome blacks as it does Europeans. Just as Troy is literally homeless, he is also without any mythological home—any broadly shared system of values that would give him a sense of his place in the world. His superb talent for hitting a baseball would make him a hero if he were white. But mainstream America knows almost nothing about the Negro Leagues. So Troy creates his own mythology. His only mode of apprehending the world is competitive: he has fought his father and has been jailed for fighting and killing the man who shot him. But because racism makes it impossible to turn his competitive spirit into the fruits of the American Dream—the dominant culture's mythology—Troy bitterly fashions his own myth and his own rigid moral code. For him the test of any course of action is whether it feels right in his heart. But his heart is made of iron.

Troy is not only physically powerful; he is also a formidable wordsmith. He decks out his exploits in epic proportions. His account of wrestling with Death for three days and three nights, for example, owes something to the Bible, something to folklore, but most of all to his own invention. As Rose points out, there is a perfectly ordinary explanation for what happened: Troy was not locked in mortal combat in some mythic arena but "right down there in Mercy Hospital. You remember he had pneumonia? Laying there with a fever talking plumb out of his head" (p. 1758). But Troy knows it would be a mistake to construe his hard-won triumph over Death as merely the delusions of a fevered brain. Even though he embellishes the story differently every time he tells it, I think he is entirely sincere when he says, "I ain't making up nothing. I'm telling you the facts of what happened."

Gabriel too sees himself as taking part in cosmic history. At once less pretentious than Troy and more so, he firmly believes that he is Saint Peter's trumpeter, that it will be his job to signal the opening of heaven's gates on Judgment Day. His bizarre, ritualistic song and dance at the very end of the play, when his trumpet fails to sound, is described in the stage directions as *"eerie and life-giving. A dance of atavistic signature and ritual."* Mentally impaired though he is, Gabriel manages to summon up some of the ritual of past generations, forging a living link with his ancestors and imparting life to his extended family.

But by that time Troy is dead. While alive he bought his house on Gabriel's disability check and then signed the papers for his brother's confinement in an institution; his example led to his son Lyons's stint in jail; he ruined his other son Cory's chance for a football scholarship and then drove him out of the house; he brought home to his good-hearted wife the child of his mistress, who died giving birth to that child. Yet there are abundant signs of life as the other characters gather for Troy's funeral. One line of thought is that this life flourishes in spite of Troy's private, exclusive mythology rather than because of it. In this reading, more accurate than Rose's faint praise at the time ("I don't know if he was right or wrong, but I know he meant to do more good than he meant to do harm") is her earlier accusation: "You take and don't even know nobody's giving!" (p. 1787). Another line of thought is that Troy does indeed give—but in a strange way. The argument here is that Rose would not have her beloved Raynell and that Cory would not have his promising future had Troy treated them in a more humane way. Regardless of which approach we take, it is clear that August Wilson has allowed us to be wayfarers for a while in a strange and fascinating land.

Questions for Discussion

1. What are Troy's values? How do they conflict with those of his children? his wife? What would you count among his successes? his failures?

2. The play is enriched by the presence of stories and songs. What do the stories—Troy's wrestling with Death, his meeting with devil—contribute to the play's themes? What do they contribute to the experience of watching the play? How does Gabriel's vision of St. Peter function in the play? How would you stage the final two scenes—Raynell's song and Gabriel's ceremonial trumpet blowing?

3. When Lyons finally repays some of the money he owes his father, Troy will not accept the payment. What is Troy's motive for this refusal?

4. Why doesn't Cory go to his father's funeral? Is he right to refuse?

5. How do Rose's dreams, though always overshadowed by those of Troy and the other men in the family, emerge to give us a sense of her life and frustrations? What is her relationship to the myths that the men around her have

created for and about themselves? How does she figure in the conflict of generations between Troy and his sons? How do women figure in the central issues of that conflict: professional athletics, self-sufficiency, education? Why did Rose marry Troy? What does she expect from him? What does the birth of Raynell do to her relationship with him? What does raising his daughter mean for her?

Writing Assignments for Chapter 6

1. Having completed the two-paragraph exercise described in the first of the Planning Ideas for *Blood Relations* above, compose a short dramatic scene that centers on your characters' subjective recollections of some historical event.

2. Some playwrights are fond of various "metadramatic" devices—techniques that deliberately call attention to fact that the play is a play. One such device is the play-within-the-play, which often serves not only to comment on the main action but also to invite speculation about the playgoer's relation to the fiction on the stage. Write an essay that discusses the effectiveness of the play-within-the-play in *Blood Relations* by comparing it to the "Mousetrap" scene in *Hamlet* (Act III, Scene 2).

3. Compare the social and family pressures exerted on women as represented in *Blood Relations* to those represented in *The Little Foxes*, set in 1900 in the American South.

4. A research paper topic that should appeal to fairly advanced students, particularly those interested in military history, involves relating the implications of the relations between art and history in *Blood Relations* to two very different accounts of decisive battles: Michael Shaara's *The Killer Angels* (a popular, romanticized version of the Battle of Gettysburg) and John Keegan's *The Face of Battle* (a complex, soldier's-eye view of the battles of Agincourt, Waterloo, and the Somme).

5. Taking into account the differences in the experiences of a working class black family and that of a middle class white family in the 1950s, compare Troy with Willie Loman from *Death of a Salesman*. What are their attitudes toward their responsibilities, wives, sons, jobs, other women, authority, the past? Compare the myths and values that sustain them. What do these two plays seem to be saying about the American Dream? Compare Linda's speech in the "Requiem" at the end of *Salesman* to Rose's final speech. Compare the mood Miller wants to create at Willie's funeral with that Wilson creates in Gabe's trumpet scene. Look for other structural parallels between these plays.

Do you find any evidence that Wilson had *Salesman* in mind when he wrote *Fences?*

6. Near the end of *Fences,* Rose says to Cory, "You Troy Maxson all over again." Cory replies, "I don't want to be Troy Maxson. I want to be me." Rose answers, "You can't be nobody but who you are, Cory." In a three- or four-page essay that sets this exchange in the context of the rest of the play, explain what Rose means.

Evaluating Drama

The two plays in this chapter are such undeniable masterpieces that they can make the question of evaluation difficult; it's easier to be specific about what's wrong with a play than what's right with one. For college-age readers the problem of evaluating *Death of a Salesman* is compounded by the play's central focus on a middle-aged man who has been steadily worn down by years of disillusion. The diminution of an aging salesman is not the topic nearest the minds and hearts of most twenty-year-olds. (*Salesman* is almost never performed by college theater groups, and it shouldn't be.)

A *Midsummer Night's Dream*, in contrast, can be a big hit on college campuses, but much of the play's success depends on humor—which is to say on timing and great lines. Because a "sense" of humor is a difficult thing to teach, *Dream* too can be a hard case for classroom evaluation. Perhaps the ideal situation would be to contrast *Salesman* and *Dream* with less masterful dramas by the same playwrights (such as Miller's *The Man Who Had All the Luck* and Shakespeare's *Titus Andronicus*). Few of us have the luxury of spending class time on second-rate plays, but the comparison makes a good writing topic (see Writing Assignment 4 below).

ARTHUR MILLER

Death of a Salesman

Planning Ideas

- Before assigning the play tell students to be on the lookout for repeated phrases (examples: "well liked," "the woods are burning," "I'm going to lose weight"). There are others. After reading the play spend some time discussing the purpose of such repetitions.
- A good way to approach the difference between reading the play and experiencing it in the theater is to focus on the stage directions. When we read the play we learn of Happy, for example, that "Sexuality is like a visible color on him, or a scent that many women have discovered." How do you

get that across in performance? (Spray the theater with musk?) Is there a universal color, scent, acting style, or even appearance that would do? Sexuality or "sex appeal" may not mean the same thing to everyone. Most of us, no doubt, can understand why Arthur Miller was attracted sexually to Marilyn Monroe, whom he married, but can we all understand what Monroe saw in Miller?

- Having introduced students to "tragedy" earlier, you might now introduce the term "pathos" and allow the discussion to pursue the question of whether **Salesman*** is pathetic or tragic. Linda's evaluation of Willy and his situation is quoted in the chapter: "He's not the finest character that even lived. But he's a human being, and a terrible thing is happening to him. So attention must be paid . . ."; this is perhaps the basis on which one might want to argue about the possibility of a "tragedy of the common man," and of course the discussion would double back to the use of common rather than elevated language. Most definitions of tragedy also involve the protagonist's recognition of himself and his situation, so that Biff's claim in the Requiem that Willy "never knew who he was" would have to be evaluated in terms of the text. Finally, the Greek gods may be here replaced by "society." To what extent is Willy the victim of his society, that is, more specifically, of capitalism?

Commentary

From the earliest scene in *Salesman*, it appears almost inevitable that Willy will eventually kill himself. References to suicide are scattered ominously throughout the play and more liberally in the latter half before Willy actually takes his life. The play's title, together with the fact that he does eventually commit suicide, generates a sense of tragic destiny. Does Willy have any choice in the matter? What role do the members of his family play in that choice—or lack thereof?

Like much previous drama, from *Oedipus* to *Hamlet* to *Hedda Gabler* and on and on and on, *Salesman* significantly, though not necessarily centrally, concerns parent(s) and child(ren). It should not take much to get your students to talk about parents, their weaknesses, imperfections, responsibilities, but you may want to hang out some bait, like the question about why Biff steals, or why Happy just can't help seducing executives' girl friends. Willy claims Biff ruined his own life to spite his father; Biff claims Willy filled him with hot air. Who is right? How much responsibility lies where? You may, indeed, want to begin with the family character and conflict (even bringing in Uncle Ben, perhaps), and only later, when righteousness and deflected guilt are exhausted, descend to the more particular, pedantic, and poetic element of language.

The set design, lighting, and music are all key elements in the production of *Salesman*, and you may want to lead your students through a discussion of how these can contribute to the movement, effect, and even meaning of the play. Jo Mielziner, who designed the scenes, writes informatively of the problems, intent, and solutions in *Designing for the Theatre* (New York: Atheneum, 1965), and you may want either to tell your students about the initial production or to ask that one or more students read and report on the issues discussed in that book.

More readily available for full class discussion is the device of the flashback, not only the meaning but the structure. All stories have a past, but in most plays the "necessary" past is supplied by exposition. You may want to ask you students how Miller might have used exposition to tell his story, perhaps asking them to reduce one or another of the flashback scenes to exposition of various kinds (not just the narration of a past scene such as Willy's description of Biff on the football field). This exercise can be expanded into an interesting writing assignment; see the third of the Writing Assignments below.

Questions for Discussion

1. The play is set in post-World War II New York City, while the flashbacks take place in 1928. Why should Willy choose precisely the year 1928 to recall?

2. Biff seems driven to steal. Why? What personal or family reasons are there? What, if any, societal reasons?

3. Willy seems constantly badgered by machines (his cars, the washer, the refrigerator, the wire recorder, etc.), yet Charley remarks that Willy was "a happy man with a batch of cement," and Willy himself desperately wants to grow things and laments that "I don't have a thing in the ground." What positive and negative values are suggested by these details? How do they relate to the vocation of "selling"?

4. The drama never mentions what Willy sells. Why not?

5. Several characters in the play are searching for the "American Dream." What is Willy's definition of this dream? Happy's? Biff's? Linda's? Charley's? Howard's? What characters appear to share the same vision?

6. Some critics have suggested that the idea that a boy would react so strongly as Biff did to his father's infidelity seems dated in the 1990s. You might ask your students if they agree with this. To what degree have we grown used to infidelity in our culture? To what degree do they think changing mores would affect their own reaction to discovering a parent had been unfaithful?

7. In Act I Willy describes himself as "fat," "foolish to look at," and a man who "talks too much," which does not fit his own philosophy of success. How does he reconcile the two? What, if anything, does he do to make aims and reality coincide? How does the contradiction reflect on his words? his beliefs?

8. Why are Willy's interview suggestions to Biff so contradictory? Does Willy follow his own advice in his interview with Howard Wagner?

9. Do the names Miller chooses for his characters have allegorical implications? If so, why would the playwright include allegory in this apparently realistic play?

10. The Requiem makes no mention of the twenty thousand dollars in insurance money. What do you think would have happened to it?

11. Miller tips us off with the title that Willie will die in the end. Why reveal the ending before the play has begun?

WILLIAM SHAKESPEARE

A Midsummer Night's Dream

Planning Ideas

- This play includes a number of scenes that play extremely well when acted out, especially the scenes involving the rustics. The Pyramus and Thisby play-within-the-play in particular almost always works—even better if performed with makeshift props and costumes rather than elaborate ones.
- Students reading **Dream** are more easily confused by who is in love with whom than they would be if they watched it. It helps to sort things out ahead of time as follows: at first both men love the same woman, then each loves the wrong woman, then both love the other woman, and finally each loves the right one.
- Have the class untangle in a prose paraphrase the "tangled chain" of Peter Quince's Prologue beginning at V.1.126. A volunteer can then deliver the speech as Quince might.

Commentary

At the end of A *Midsummer Night's Dream*, Demetrius loves Helena because he is still under the influence of the love potion; he hasn't had the antidote sprinkled into his eyes. The fact that his condition isn't very troubling to us is instructive. In a play that depicts erotic love as foolishness (significantly, *fond* meant *foolish* in Shakespeare's day), it doesn't really matter whether the condition of being in love is induced by a chemical from a plant or one from the lover's own glands. Either way, it's a kind of temporary insanity. The convention of ending the comedy with a marriage celebration (in this case a triple marriage) assures us that the young lovers' infatuation will develop into mature love. But of course comedies *end* with weddings because a good, stable marriage doesn't make for good theater; erotic lovers' ups and downs do.

Dreams, of course, blur the line between reality and fantasy. Although imaginary, they are based on ordinary actions in real life—and seem real enough while they are going on. If the lovers find dream and reality "strange and undistinguishable," so do the rustics. Nothing could be more real to them than what to us is pure fantasy: the prospect of their performing great theater in the court of Theseus. The rustics are hopeless dreamers, but they do end up providing very pleasurable theater at court.

In the end, of course, we enjoy the Pyramus and Thisby play every bit as much as do the courtiers. The whole of A *Midsummer Night's Dream*, in fact, is immensely enjoyable in part because of the dreamlike rapidity with which we are whisked from the company of courtiers to that of rustics and fairies. The implicit largeness of the world in which these groups can interact in a small space is something of a marvel. Puck's epilogue makes it clear that the whole play is to be thought of as a dream. Surprisingly enough, the effect is not to remind us that we are really ordinary human beings who have been watching other ordinary human beings stand on a stage and say things. It is to remind us that we have lived for a while in the imagination of one of the very best ever to give to airy nothing a local habitation and a name.

Questions for Discussion

1. Despite the fact that A *Midsummer Night's Dream* is classified as a comedy, there is a great deal of anxiety and danger in it: Egeus threatens his daughter Hermia with death, love is withdrawn from Hermia suddenly, and for no reason, insults and mockery are perceived by Helena. What makes the play funny? What aspects or parts of the play strike you as comical, and why? Can peril be an ingredient of humor? Does some of the humor stem from the audience's recognition of irrationality in their own lives—such as the capriciousness of love?

2. Are the rustics (Quince, Snug, Bottom, Flute, Snout, and Starveling) in the play for any reason other than comic relief? How might the Pyramus and Thisby play be related to the main action of *Dream?*

3. What different views or aspects of love are represented by Oberon and Titania? By Theseus and Hippolyta? What characterizes the male and female roles in those couples? How do those roles compare with those of the four young lovers?

4. Discuss the proposition that female society is made an issue in this play. Is there evidence to suggest that Hippolyta's past, Titania's relation to the changeling, or Helena and Hermia's friendship shapes the direction of the play? Or are such things only obstacles to be overcome by the males?

5. Why do we read of Theseus's ideas about the imagination at the beginning of Act V? Why does he associate it with love? What might that indicate

about his attitude toward the antics of Shakespeare's comedy? Is Theseus's conception of the imagination one the play itself accepts? Is it a comment on the position of the powerful?

6. Why does the audience keep interrupting the play-within-a-play of Act V? Are they entirely contemptuous of what they are watching?

7. Is Shakespeare talking about his own play or drama in general by ending with the play-within-a-play and Puck's closing address to the audience?

Writing Assignments for Evaluating Drama

1. It is hard to imagine two works more different from each other than *Death of a Salesman* and "A Rose for Emily," but a comparison of the two either as "elegies" or as stories suggesting the clash of cultures or generations makes a good paper topic. An alternative is to compare *Salesman* with "The Rocking-Horse Winner" in an essay centering on the role of money in the two works.

2. Write two or three pages of dialogue between Linda and Willy in which she confronts him about his suicidal tendencies and attempts to convince him that killing himself would be a mistake. Of course, the dialogue should be consistent with the facts and evidence of the play.

3. Choose a play you have already read, such as *Oedipus* or *Hedda Gabler* or *Streetcar*, and write a Salesman-like flashback. Then, in a one-page evaluative analysis, explain how adding your scene would change what Sophocles or Ibsen or Williams wrote.

4. Evaluate Miller's *Death of a Salesman* or Shakespeare's *A Midsummer Night's Dream* by comparing it with a drama by the same playwright generally considered inferior—such as Miller's *The Man Who Had All the Luck* or Shakespeare's *Titus Andronicus*.

5. Choose a relatively minor character, such as Egeus or Philostrate, and explain in a four-page essay what this character adds to *A Midsummer Night's Dream*. Be careful not to focus on the level of plot; it is obvious that without Egeus's prohibition of a match between Hermia and Lysander, for example, the adventures in the woods would never take place. Focus instead on how Egeus or Philostrate reinforces the play's thematic concerns.

Reading More Drama

TENNESSEE WILLIAMS

A Streetcar Named Desire

Streetcar is a useful play for reviewing large contextual issues, whether historical, social, or philosophical. Besides being a characteristic Tennessee Williams play, it is also a characteristic Southern play, a characteristic American play, and a characteristic modern play. You will know that, but your students are not likely to have read widely enough to know it or even to know what features might define these categories. But you have some other plays to draw on now, and a brief glance at questions of topicality will give you a chance to review some features of plays already studied, especially those by Chekhov, Ibsen, Hellman, and Miller.

Planning Ideas, Commentary, and Questions for Discussion

- Ask your students what features, characters, scenes, or stage directions here remind them of plays they've read earlier. Get them to explain exactly what the similarities (and differences) consist in.
- Here is another specific way to get the class to consider questions of setting, character, language, and symbol as well as social and cultural questions. Ask the class to describe the place that, although not shown in the play, is central to its conception: Belle Reve. (This exercise would also make, properly limited, a good paper topic.) List everything we actually know about Belle Reve. What do we assume, beyond what we're told, about its appearance, size, and value? How important is it that the audience makes specific assumptions about Belle Reve? What emotional associations does it have for Blanche? for Stella? What values for each? In what ways do the two

feel differently about it? about their earlier lives? What aspects of the character of each are involved with their experiences of Belle Reve? with their memories of it? with their sense of what it stands for personally? with what it stands for symbolically? What does Belle Reve stand for to Stanley? How important are the particulars of Belle Reve's history? Why does the play not go into more detail about the plantation? How fully does Belle Reve represent "old Southern values"? What does the history of Belle Reve tell us about conflicts within the tradition? about interruption of the tradition? Who are the heroes in the myth of Belle Reve? the villains? In what specific ways might a Southern audience be likely to understand the symbolism of Belle Reve more fully than another audience? How does the name of the plantation (literally "beautiful dream," of course,) comment on what happens in the play?

- Like Belle Reve, New Orleans is portrayed in ways that are somewhat stereotypical: there is ever-present music, an easy (although superficial) mixing of blacks and whites, a strong consciousness of different ethnic traditions, a preoccupation with food and drink, a lot of emphasis on play, gambling, leisure. Does this kind of "typicality" weaken the play? What advantages does such satisfaction of expectations have? What other stereotypes does Williams use in the play? with what effects? How do these stereotypes affect the themes of the play?

- Another, complementary way of approaching some of the staging issues is through close analysis of Williams's stage directions. Williams pays much more attention than most playwrights to details of production—from the appearance and clothes of actors to specific stage directions—and he gives full and precise accounts of how he expects the play to be staged. If you have spent time in class earlier having your students analyze in detail the staging of a scene from another play, have them compare the stage directions in that play with those of Williams. *The Bear* works particularly well as a contrast because Chekhov's directions are relatively brief and only suggestive. Even if you haven't spent class time on staging in *The Bear*, you can easily look back to it and invite the students to compare the two strategies. Help them notice, too, how Williams's staging—like Ibsen's— suggests visually some of the larger themes of the play. Have them walk through, for example, the end of Scene 11 in which Williams's directions, as well as the dialogue, suggest the uncertainties of Blanche and Stella while emphasizing the simpler determination of the men. Ask them to interpret the effect of having the men walk between the women, spatially dividing them. Get them to speculate at length, after they have seen classmates walk through the scene, about the effect on the audience. Have them relate the visual effects specified here to specific passages of dialogue in the play; that is, make them back up their interpretation of character and themes with specific evidence in the text. What advantages and disadvantages are there when a playwright is so visually specific about his intentions?

- Now that Tennessee Williams's *Collected Stories* have been published

(New York: New Directions, 1985), some of your best students might wish to take on the difficult (but rewarding) task of comparing some of the stories to other Williams plays. The reading of the stories can, of course, extend the points made in the chapter (and in class) on authorial context, for the stories present many of the same themes, concerns, and character-types as **Streetcar** and the excerpts in the text. Williams is not as skilled a writer of stories as he is a playwright, but his often more tentative art in the stories is sometimes an advantage in looking at the relationship between his life and work. Several of the stories are sort of "trial" versions of the plays and offer especially promising paper topics for students capable of independent work and longer writing assignments. The different demands and effects of narrative and dramatic art can become quite evident in close comparisons. If you can offer your students the time to do the extra reading and writing, try having them make one the following comparisons:

1. "Portrait of a Girl in Glass" with *The Glass Menagerie*
2. "Three Players" with *Cat on a Hot Tin Roof* (the story version lacks some of the play's central characters, Big Daddy, for example)
3. "Night of the Iguana" with *Night of the Iguana*
4. "The Yellow Bird" with *Summer and Smoke*

CARYL CHURCHILL

Top Girls

During the 1970s Churchill wrote in collaboration with several London the-ater companies. Typically a group (such as Joint Stock or Monstrous Regiment) that had agreed to develop and stage one of Churchill's new plays would begin working with one of her ideas, improvising and developing the script during the rehearsal process. Churchill would attend these sessions, gradually crafting the play through this collaborative process. A good many scholars now think that much of the best Elizabethan drama, including Shakespeare's plays, evolved in this way. Just as the characters in a play like *Hamlet* may be very much a func-tion of the particular acting strengths of the Lord Chamberlain's Men, Churchill's plays are tailored to the strengths of particular groups. Since finan-cial constraints kept the number of actors small in some of the theater compa-nies with which Churchill worked, she relied on the age-old system of doubling and tripling of roles—a system in force as early as the time of Sophocles.

In writing plays with lots of characters but only a few actors, and in refusing to try to hide the fact that the actor is taking on more than one role, Churchill is able to focus more on patterns of thought than on individual performance or character. A second patterning strategy also informs a play like *Top Girls*, in which very frequently two characters are speaking at once. To get the full effect, the drama's reader takes in all the words but must imagine what the overlapping speeches sound like on the stage. The play's audience, in contrast, experiences the overlapping immediately but may have difficulty hearing all the lines. Even if individual lines are lost, though, the patterns of thought stand out.

Planning Ideas

- The first thing to do with **Top Girls** is sort out Churchill's system of overlapping dialogue. The best way is to assign roles and read several representative passages in class, working at each passage until the timing is right. The class can then discuss the effect of hearing characters talk over and past each other. Why would a playwright bother to write words that the audience may well not hear? Or can the audience process both speakers' words simultaneously?
- It's good to show a slide or pass around a reproduction of Brueghel's *Dulle Griet* and compare the "rhetoric" of the painting to that of the play. (The painting features a sort of parody of the Harrowing of Hell; the scene is not Christ leading the blessed souls out of confinement but a peasant housewife who is such a fierce nag that she can storm hell, giving the devils their due.) How is Churchill's depiction of Dull Gret different from Brueghel's?
- In Act II, Scene 3, Marlene says that she will treat Howard, who was in the running for the job Marlene got, no differently from any other colleague. Mrs. Kidd says to Marlene, "I think it is different, because he's a man." Your students are bound to have strong feelings about the question of gender roles in the workplace. Since most are likely to favor equal pay for equal work, regardless of gender, it is useful to divide the class arbitrarily for a short debate. One side argues Mrs. Kidd's point: a man like Howard, one with a family to support, should be given preference for a job like Managing Director over a single woman like Marlene. The other side takes Marlene's view. Encourage both sides to use the play to point out what is weak in the other side's position. Then, if time allows, you can switch the sides. The idea is to get the class to experience the ambivalence about gender roles that fuels this play.

Commentary

What emerges clearly and insistently from the restaurant scene, despite the characters' tendency to talk past rather than listen to one another, is that they have all felt the constraints of being a woman in a man's world. The occasion is a victory celebration: Marlene seems to have won a decisive battle in the gender wars, beating out her male opponent for the position of Managing Director of the Top Girls Employment Agency. All of us, male and female, can appreciate her struggle to get such a promotion, just as we can admire Isabella Bird's bold, pioneering spirit, Lady Nijo's courage, and Pope Joan's audacity.

But the play does not stay with these colorful characters from the past; it follows Marlene's story. And in her case it eventually becomes apparent that her victory has been gained at a terrible cost. Even in the first scene there are hints that all is not well. Why is it that Marlene suddenly asks, "Oh, God, why are we all so miserable?" Is it true that everyone at the table is miserable? If so, have men made them that way? Or is there something in the very nature of the struggle toward self-sufficiency that invites misery?

The line immediately before Marlene's is Isabella's: "I wore myself out with good causes." Marlene has already said not only that she doesn't go to church but that she doesn't do good works. No doubt her manner of delivery at this point is light and nonchalant; she's not making a heartfelt confession but being chattily honest about her habits. (Just after her line "I haven't been to church in years" comes "I like Christmas carols"; her "But I don't do good works either" is immediately preceded by "Make that two steaks and a lot of potatoes. Rare.") In this moment Marlene assumes a value so broadly shared in the late twentieth century that our students are hardly likely to find fault with it: she is honest about what she believes. Moreover, she says a few lines later, "We don't all have to believe the same." Who in the 1990s would disagree?

But by the end of the play Churchill forces us to confront the fact that this honest, ostensibly tolerant character has abandoned her only child and has been too self-absorbed to acknowledge the child's existence (Christmases and birthdays go by so fast, after all). What is the value of honesty if the behavior one admits to is deplorable? Does Marlene really champion tolerance and pluralism? She hardly seems tolerant of her sister's beliefs, and it is her sister who has sacrificed tremendously in bringing up Marlene's child.

Nor does Joyce come across as very heroic—at least not at first. She verbally abuses Angie. Is it any wonder that Angie is slow, lazy, and frightened when her adoptive mother habitually calls her things like "a big lump" and says, "You make me sick"? When Marlene asks Angie, "What do you want to do?" it is Joyce, not Angie, who answers: "She hasn't an idea in her head what she wants to do. Lucky to get anything." A little later Marlene tells Joyce, "You run her down too much. She'll be all right." But, since Act III takes place a year earlier than Act II, we already know that Marlene will say a year later, "She's not going to make it."

Part of the problem is the brutal economic system that allows one to "make it" only by sacrificing human decency. It is this system that has excluded women as recently as Louise's early adulthood (she's the middle-aged one who isn't appreciated at work because she's so efficient—and who says, "I don't care greatly for working with women.") Now the system allows women to compete, sort of. Women are allowed in the work force but are still suspect. As Nell warns Shona, "They think we're too nice. They think we listen to the buyer's doubts. They think we consider his needs and his feelings." Shona gives what is, I suppose, the right answer: "I never consider people's feelings."

This comment inspires Nell's proud assertion, "I'm not very nice." Does her success in business redeem her inhumanity? Does her cheerfulness? Does her honesty? She seems to assume so, just as easily as Marlene admits that she doesn't do good works. But pulling against that glib assumption is another force—call it subconscious guilt or the need to confess. Why should someone in Nell's position be telling a client (and especially one like Shona) about her own selfishness? For that matter, why does Win need to tell a client, "I drink"? Why does she need to tell her colleagues about her weekend affair with a married man? Why does she tell her life story to Angie (of all people), who falls asleep in the middle of it?

The characters in this play are struggling, sometimes on a subconscious level, against the myth of self-sufficiency that the economic system embraces. But if that system offers no real freedom, neither is there any retreating to Griselda's ethos or to Lady Nijo's. The days of overt patriarchal control may be over, and good riddance—we don't want Marlene to give her job to Howard just because he is a man—but does that emancipation make anyone truly free? There is still control, but now it is subtler: Marlene's female clients are advised to remove their wedding rings before interviews. In this play, as in many of Churchill's, the women remain trapped. Frightening.

Questions for Discussion

1. What is the effect of Churchill's collecting in a restaurant women from various historical periods and cultures? Of all the choices available to Churchill, why do you suppose she chose *these* women?

2. What is the effect of depicting in Act II action that takes place a year later than the action of Act III?

3. At the dinner party Marlene remarks, "I don't wear trousers in the office. I could but I don't." What is the subtext of her comment?

4. At various points the play touches on organized religion—whether Pope Joan's medieval Catholicism or Lady Nijo's monastic Buddhism. Do the comments form a pattern?

5. Why does Kit fantasize about standing at ground zero when an atomic bomb is dropped? What do her fears have to say about growing up in the late twentieth century?

6. Angie says in Act II, Scene 2, "I think my mother's really my aunt." What do you think of her speculation at the time? Does the comment reflect on her differently when you discover she is right?

7. When Louise describes younger, more aggressive women (women like Marlene), she says, "They take themselves for granted." What does Louise mean?

8. What does Marlene's suggestion that Howard deal with his sleeplessness by taking sleeping pills tell us about her?

9. In the heat of her quarrel with Joyce, Marlene offers to take over as

Angie's mother: ". . . I'll take her, wake her up and pack now." What do you suppose would happen if Joyce took Marlene up on the offer?

Writing Assignments for Reading More Drama

1. See the descriptions of the paper on Belle Reve and of the story / drama comparison in the second of the Planning Ideas for *Streetcar*, above.

2. Read another of Churchill's plays, and write an essay of four to six pages comparing it with *Top Girls*. *Vinegar Tom* and *Cloud Nine* are good choices; like *Top Girls*, both deal with women's dilemmas, employing creative methods of examining these dilemmas through history.

3. All the characters in *Top Girls* except Marlene are played by actors who also play other characters. Is there any relation between this arrangement and the fact that it is Marlene who is the most vocal advocate of freedom? (As she puts it, ". . . I want to be free in a free world.") Is she "her own person" and so free in a free world, or is she somehow even less free than the others at the dinner party? Address these questions in a three-page essay on the subject of freedom in *Top Girls*.